Dear Hugh,
    with loving we
        from
    Fay Halmes.
            Xmas 1960.

Curtain-up on South Africa

CURTAIN-UP
ON SOUTH AFRICA

PRESENTING A NATIONAL DRAMA

by

GARRY ALLIGHAN

PURNELL AND SONS (S.A.) (PTY.) LTD.
CAPE TOWN : JOHANNESBURG

MADE AND PRINTED IN GREAT BRITAIN BY PURNELL AND SONS, LTD.,
PAULTON (SOMERSET) AND LONDON

Programme

Photographs

Curtain-up on South Africa

The Proscenium

The Proscenium

LICHÉS may be regarded in some quarters as the last refuge of the mentally destitute, but many of them can be traced back to Shakespeare whose priceless epigrams have now become common coin in the currency of expression. When he wrote "All the world's a stage, and all the men and women merely players", he invented a cliché which, although now overworked to near-death, is immortal because imperishably accurate. On that stage, throughout history, mankind has been playing all the roles—from walking-on parts to "star" —in hundreds of national dramas. And one of the most engrossing is the Drama of South Africa.

EVERY drama on every stage of every theatre requires contrasting characterisations and intriguing situations. Every drama must have its appropriate setting and every scene its contrived staging. Every dramatic performance has to conform to the constructional sequence that Greek tragedy and Shakespearian art have made traditional. All these factors are present in the romantic drama of South Africa, the script of which possesses all the emotional ingredients and "situations" that the most exacting playwright could demand. It is a "from-rags-to-riches" drama, a drama of love and hate,

3

of violence and virtue, of frontier war and pastoral peace, of cruel suppression and sensational emancipation, of striving and succeeding. On that drama, staged over an area of half a million square miles and a time-distance of three centuries; with a cast of characters drawn from ten generations of people of all colours and of a dozen races—on that drama, the curtain is rung up.

No action is more overdue than to raise the curtain on South Africa so that, at last, its true character is revealed— the whole truth; the bitter and the palatable, the dark tones and the bright, the deplorable and the creditable. Overdue not merely because South Africa is "the unknown country", but because the direction that world affairs are taking makes it, inevitably, the crucial country. It is that segment of a continent which, because five great powers are in a competition for control, is the final component that will weight the balance of powers. To the north of South Africa, the rest of "the Dark Continent" is rapidly becoming a dark continent—the irresistible upsurge of Black nationalism will turn Africa into a dark-skinned empire whose constituent elements reveal the possession of varying degrees of self-governing competence.

Special and fateful importance attaches to South Africa, hinging on the question: Can it retain its Western character when all around it is developing an indigenous nationalism? Will it become the southern anode to the northern cathode? Is the whole continent to be black or piebald? Holding, as it does, the answers to those fateful questions affecting human destiny, there can only be found cause for amazement, heavily tinctured with dismay, in the fact that South Africa remains "the unknown country", a country of which the rest of the world appears to have a conception compounded only of misconceptions. And that, at a time when the candle of Western civilisation in the African continent is burning unnervingly near to its socket; when new dominations menace the fine upholstery of our days.

Just as most Americans know Africa only as the jungled rendezvous of Livingstone and Stanley, so, to many British people, South Africa is merely the locale—best forgotten—of a war from which not even the glamorised versions in school history-books have completely deleted the shame. To most people overseas South Africa is a country whose city streets are the sauntering lanes for lions and a crucible of racial conflicts whose witches' brew threatens to boil over. Those are the most generally held conceptions—more than twelve years spent in all parts of that country have revealed them to me as utter misconceptions.

Outside the Johannesburg Zoo, where people watch them at play, I have yet to see a lion in South Africa; and a Native uprising against the White people would, if it ever occurred, be so rare as to chase a successful American launching of a satellite off the front news-pages.

South African officialdom and semi-officialdom are to blame for one of these misconceptions. For the past quarter-century official South Africa acted as if it imagined that the country could only be of interest to the rest of the world as a tourist stop-over place. And so, what official South Africa thought would intrigue visitors was played up. Wild beasts and wilder natives formed the motif of tourism's publicity. Most of the picture postcards that are on sale, and therefore mailed to overseas recipients, are of "typically" African animals and "typically" African scenes—ferociously-dressed natives a-whirl in aboriginal war-dances, beautifully-proportioned negresses with tip-tilted breasts, straight backs and supple thighs. Most of the "typically" African novelties purchaseable in the "curio" shops as gifts for dispatch overseas consist of ebony figures of elephants and ivorined wild buck and leopard-skin bags and "native bead" bracelets. Even the handsome murals that frieze the walls of South Africa House in London present nothing but scenes of wild animals and Zulu village-life. The official accent is on "wildness" and an uncultivated existence as being the predominant characteristics of the country. And they have helped create the overseas misconception.

It is almost as if tourists have been enticed by false representations. Those who snatch a few weeks from their overseas city-life to see "typical" African wild-life in South Africa will probably only see a replica of their own normal existence. Where its cities are concerned, South Africa is as modern and modernly-organised as any Western country. The only jungle-life in South Africa can be seen on the floor of the Johannesburg Stock Exchange.

THAT disposes of one popular misconception; the other is far more serious and equally fallacious. It is not my business to unearth reasons but to report facts—the word can never be greater than the fact. Not all the words that have been spoken, written or printed about "Whites threatened by Black uprising in South Africa" can supersede the hard fact that never since self-government was acquired has there been one uprising of the Black people against the White people. Even the very serious events that took place in the Vereeniging district this very week of writing, when 58 Bantu were shot, was not an anti-White riot; 25,000 Bantu besieged 100 policemen in the police station to defy the Pass laws and, when faced with that huge mob of screaming Black people, the police opened fire out of what might be regarded as rather natural fear for their own lives.

There have been a few spasmodic and small-scale riots of Blacks against White laws but they have not been directed against the Whites as a race; they have been expressions of defiance of the laws. This idea that the Black people are in underground warfare against the White people—of people, as such, against people—is not only a misconception; it is a falsity. If it is argued that the laws are bad—as are laws, also, said to be in other countries—they should be altered; they may not be broken. They are the laws of the land, made by democratic processes.

There is a great and traditional respect among the Bantu for the White people; there is an occasional protest—sometimes violent—against laws which the legislators have passed. The fact that the legislators are white is irrelevant—those protests against laws that some sections of the Bantu found irksome would have been made even if the laws had been promulgated by Bantu legislators.

In their ignorance of South Africa, and of the facts, many people in Britain and America have denounced that country because some natives rioted in Durban, others in Johannesburg, others in Windhoek, others in Paarl, the delightful Cape town. In each case, those were not violent uprisings against the White people—as they were misrepresented to be —they were protests against the implementation of laws, passed democratically, promulgated officially and implemented so indiscriminately that the overwhelming majority of Natives accepted and obeyed them.

To sympathise with the few rioting Natives is to support

lawlessness. If the steelworkers of America or the miners of Britain disliked some law of their lands and staged violent riots in opposition to them, the American and British press would not thank South Africa if it urged the rioters on in their law-defiance. Nor would the rest of the world stigmatise America and Britain as "police states" if the Governments of those two countries called on their policemen to do their duty—enforce the law.

It has been part of my job to seek out the facts of Native outbreaks. Investigation proved that they fall into two cate-gories—riots against the law, and faction fights. Numerically speaking, the latter have been the greater by far. Not only are the Bantu split up into several ethnic tribes; tribes are also factionalised and even within the factions there are anti-pathetic groupings and clans. Worse still; among the clans there are thug-elements whose criminal acts against their own people are no different in principle, only in degree, from America's gangsterism and Britain's cosh-boy outbreaks. Faction-fights of Natives against Natives—blown up in the overseas press as "uprisings" and "riots" with the inference that they were directed against the White population—are of frequent occurrence. There was a period when I had to report at least one faction-fight every Sunday—sometimes I had to rush from one outskirt of Johannesburg to another the same afternoon.

Of these faction-fights, this fact must be clearly recognised: they do not involve any of the White population and are not aimed at them in any way. They are purely inter-tribe feuds. In fact, there would be far more of them were it not for the White peoples' regulations, enlightenment and control. They are not even the result of White legislation, nor connected in the slightest with White affairs. They are caused by Native practices, customs or antipathies. Some begin as a family quarrel over the lobola—wedding price—to be paid by the family of the man to the father of the Bantu girl he proposes to make his wife; or one of his wives. Some are manifestations of centuries-old feuds between tribe and tribe.

No faction-fight is, to non-Native eyes, a pleasant sight. Spores of ancient fevers, which have lain dormant in the blood, suddenly erupt from an equatorial jungle of passions. One faction of dark-skinned men advance on another, chanting war-cries, as meaningless as a bull-frogs' chorus, that have been propagated through a complex system of historic echoes. Inflamed by the quiddities and wiley-beguilies of the witch-doctors, armed with assegais and knobkerries, they attack each other with almost Islamic fanaticism and certainly with the fury of their ancient savagery, their minds reverting to the bleak, anonymous dark of the jungle.

Although such fights break out with unexpected suddenness, they are the over-boil of tribal cauldrons that may have simmered for years. At one hour, the Natives may have been conforming to their new de-tribalised way of life—sleepily amiable, doing nothing with engrossed thoroughness; or they may have been ringing a bevy of Native girls dancing, clap-clap-clapping the shoulder shimmies, the pelvic flips, the hip-swings, while the arched bodies of the girls posed concave questions to which the bent-double clappers gave convex answers. And then, the normalcy of their lives bursts as if, after the long crouch, the pounce. The scene abruptly changes into horribilia—and next day, the world's press headlines: "Savage blood-riots by Natives in Johannesburg's shacktown". Readers are not told the facts—they are left to assume that it is a Black uprising. Against the Whites?

It is impossible to have eleven million Bantu, of different

tribes, varying ethnic origins and deep-rooted tribal customs
living a heterogeneous life without such reversions to inherited passions. What is amazing is that White laws and
White-provided education have had such an effect on the
Bantu population that such faction-fights are becoming rare—
so much, in fact, that the world's press, in their ignorance of
South African ignorance, blow up into sensational proportions
any solitary instance of what was once a normal occurrence
in Bantu life.

British and American life have or have had similar manifestations—the histories of Britain and America are similar to
that of South Africa in the possession of black spots which not
time but perhaps eternity can expunge. South Africa has been
a nation for fifty years—it would afford the people of Britain
and America a more realistic standard by which to judge South
Africa if that developing country were measured by the events
that form the pattern of Britain's and America's first fifty
years. Britain's feudalism might be compared with the feudalism of South Africa in the pre-Union era and the social
conditions contemporaneous with Britain's industrial revolution might be compared to those accompanying South
Africa's more recent industrial revolution—both to Britain's
disfavour. The squalor and tumble-downery of Britain's
slums, as long as 1,000 years after the first English king was
crowned, were infinitely worse than the native "shack-
towns" only fifty years after South Africa, in becoming a
nation, became responsible.

A much better—because fairer to all concerned—basis for
assessment is a comparison between South Africa and America
because their history and development are marked by amazingly
identical similarities. Both countries were discovered by
European adventurers—Columbus and Diaz—in the same

decade: Diaz made discovery of South Africa five years before Columbus bestowed his benefaction on the world and the way in which the early European settlers of North America treated the natives of that newly-discovered land—the "red" Indians —if compared with the way the first European settlers of South Africa treated the Hottentots and the Bushmen aborigines, does not place South Africa in second place for the humanities.

A few years before the Dutch settled on Manhattan Island, the Dutch arrived at the Cape—and, for constructive pioneering, the South African settlers, again, do not take second place. How those two groups of Dutch settlers obtained their respective settlements does not bestow, on the South African exploit, comparative discredit—van Riebeeck found the Cape a desolate, uninhabited, uncultivated land and purchased his occupancy by giving it husbandry, inhabitants, and cultivation; Peter Minuit tricked the Indian inhabitants of Manhattan out of their land with a handful of trinkets worth sixty guilders. Incidentally both van Riebeeck and Minuit built a five-pointed fort on their newly acquired possessions and gave the same name to the first street they made—Heerengracht.

In both countries gold was discovered in the same generation and each country achieved nationhood by a War of Independence against Britain with whom, once that was done, each has maintained friendliest relations ever since. Another striking similarity is that when the two respective wars for independence from Britain ended and nationhood was secured, the chief military commanders of the two anti-British rebel forces were elected to the foremost national positions in the two new nations—General George Washington became the first President of the United States of America and General Louis Botha the first Prime Minister of the Union of South Africa.

There is one dissimilarity—there has never been a lynching in South Africa; that form of "colour discrimination" has never invaded this "U.S.A.".

In addition to all in the past that should give America and Britain an intimate interest in South Africa is a factor that has vital concern for them in the present and the future. South Africa holds what could be a decisive strategical position. However much South Africa may be "the unknown country" to the peoples of those two countries, their Washington and Whitehall—to say nothing of the Kremlin—must be fully alerted to that particular factor. Strategic importance is vested in South Africa by virtue of two far from inconsiderable facts: with the political developments north of the Zambesi it is almost certain that South Africa will be the last remaining White-governed country in a Black continent; and its geographical location makes it a promontory between the West and the East.

Those are stated as facts because I am not, here, concerned with political theories. Reporting facts, it becomes necessary to record that, whatever virtue there is in granting self-government to the Black races of the North, not even those emergent nations claim either the economic or technical advancement that would enable them to be completely independent of such assistance from other and longer established nations. And as they have made it clear that, in world-politics, they are "neutralist"—"uncommitted" to the West or the East—that can only mean that their "open-door" policy is available to either. If greater advantage were to be taken of that policy by the Eastern bloc, the fact that South Africa is committed to the Western bloc gives that country an enormous strategical value.

Viewed geographically, South Africa also holds a vital

12

strategical position. That is a self-evident fact which is only
stated in order to point out that however demoded infantry
and armoured forces may be in atomic warfare, naval facilities
will continue to be in urgent demand. Submarine bases,
fuelling and victualling stations and dockyard facilities for both
merchant ships and their naval escorts will contribute as much
to victory as lack of them would to defeat. Situated at the
water-shed of East and West as it is, South Africa is a potential
asset, of decisive value, to whoever are her allies.

THERE are, therefore, many reasons why South Africa should
cease to be "the unknown country" and why a completely
objective portrayal of the scene is a necessity if ignorance of
that country is to be replaced by well-balanced understanding.
Sporadic efforts have been made to hold the mirror up to
South Africa but too often a distorting mirror has been used.
Any observer, armed with a full complement of prejudices
and pre-conceived ideas, can produce a picture of South Africa
that will force the facts to fit his theories. That can be done
—and has been done—with the benefit of no more than two
weeks' stay in the country.

South Africa has become "the unknown country" of the
Western civilised world not despite but because of the enterprises in enlightenment that have been essayed. There has been
no paucity of descriptions; only objective truth has been
missing. Any fool can criticise, complain and condemn—and
most fools do. Well-intentioned clerics, suffering somewhat
from moralistic dyspepsia, and hobby-horsical politicians on
safari into axe-grinding propaganda, have come to South Africa
—some for as long as three whole weeks—and returned

overseas, impregnated with their own negatives, to show to their publics the South Africa which their distorting mirrors have reflected. Spotlighted in the amphitheatre of their emotions they have preached their sermons, written their pamphlets, orated their speeches and given their press-interviews. Their versions have differed in detail but they all had one identifying characteristic in common—their versions of the South African scene, after visiting the country, completely confirmed the views of it which they had expressed before their visits, like a post-hypnotic patient responding to a prior-injected idea.

That, in itself, evokes a somewhat sceptical thought: it must require a special kind of genius for a man to compose a mental picture of a country he knows nothing whatever about, except in self-created theory, and when he does visit that country to discover nothing but "facts" which prove the imaginings of his occult mind to have been miraculously correct. Cynics might think that such a genius must have twitched the truth around to fit the theory as if it were a two-way-stretch girdle. Smuts once referred to "altering the torso of the soul" but that was before there had been a cavalcade of overseas "experts" rushing into speech and type with their "solutions" to South Africa's problems.

Compared with such psychic genius, the lesser mind, un-blessed with the impervious armour of pre-conceived ideas that must be confirmed at all costs, composes his picture of South Africa with actual facts gathered on the spot, undistinguished by any florid and self-conscious coloration. He will not be miraculously right; merely right. It is because so many of that genius class, inspired by unserviceable thoughts floating on a stream of undisciplined emotions, have assumed the functions of describing South Africa that it remains "the unknown country".

14

In addition, it is a complex country. Its complexity is formed by its peculiar problems. Those problems have not been created in a decade; they are not a legacy from the World Wars; they are not even twentieth-century products. They have existed since the first Europeans settled in the country and every European, ever since, has faced them, grappled with them and endeavoured to find solutions for them. Three centuries of problems; three centuries of facing them and trying to solve them. And they remain unsolved; have defied 300 years of serious thought and earnest endeavour. They must, therefore, be pretty tough problems.

Not so: they are in the abecedarian class; they are mere kindergarten puzzles; just childish riddles. Any lofty theocrat, with eyes forever raised above mundane reality, can emerge from his ivory-towered cloisters, spend a month's holiday in South Africa and return to the common plain as another Moses from Sinai, with a one-syllabled "solution" neatly engraved on tablets of stone. Any youthfully-ambitious politician can assign himself to a well-publicised "fact-finding mission"—if necessary, even visit the country—and, dipping his pen into a vocabulary of sloganeer words, write a pamphlet explaining how the age-old problems can be readily solved. It is not that these men of genius are fabricating as they go along; they are merely exercising an over-cautious use of the uncomfortable properties of truth. They are courageously attempting to do what that salty cynic, Henry Adams, described as "suggesting unintelligible answers to insoluble problems".

That the people on the spot, whose ancestors were on the same spot for ten generations, finding the problems far from sustaining glib "solutions", regard the pontificating parsons and posturing politicians as somewhat impertinent, should not be unduly surprising. They lose a little relish for the Light of

Truth if it has lost many units of its customary candle-power. If the problems of South Africa were soluble so simply as the High Priests of Quackdoodledum claim, they would not be problems at all. And they are. If they were as easy as a crossword puzzle, highly intelligent men would not have failed, in 300 years, to find the key-clue.

Blissfully unaware that distinctions in fact should be expressed by distinctions in words, these problem-solvers from the outside have given the world such distorted versions of the real South Africa that it cannot avoid being "the unknown country". America would be equally unrecognisable if the only picture the world had of it was composed of lynching scenes in the Deep South, gangster outrages in the northern cities and Hollywood high-life. Much more than such foreshortened kodaksnaps are needed; much more intimate study and factual knowledge in order to reflect the whole and properly-proportioned picture.

To live and work in the country; to become part of its day-by-day life; to travel in all directions and study all the aspects of its life—in the cities, in the dorps, in the industrialised areas, in the platteland—to converse with its men and women of all races and colours and in all social categories, for nearly thirteen years, is a better way of securing the panoramic picture. Opinion can then become honed by experience and the mind swept clear of fusty cob-webbery.

And to view the scene through the somewhat cynical, certainly sceptical, eyes of a hardened newspaper reporter; one in whom the realities of life have destroyed illusions if not emotions; who has rubbed shoulders with too many celebrities in shirtsleeves and seen too often that most emperors are, under the ermine, naked; one who has had far too much experience of "apostles" with axes to grind and men of genius busy writing Apocrypha's ephemeral footnotes—such mental equipment enables a realistic and correctly-balanced view of all the constituent elements that comprise the true scene.

It is when history is looked in the face that the South African vista gets into focus, taking on new proportions with perspectives shortened and altitudes attenuated. Ignorance of history's bitter record—to say nothing of ignorance of contemporary facts—has so distorted the picture that the real South Africa must remain "the unknown country" until its every facet is presented. Prejudice may be sired by ignorance but it is abattoired by facts and, in noting the fallacies, it is possible to be guided to the truth. From that antiseptic experience has emerged this honest representation of the drama of South Africa, with all the traditional dramaturgic ingredients—the contrasting characteristics of courage and tenderness, of piety and viciousness, of violence and industry, of good and evil—on a stage of 450,000 square miles and a time span of three centuries.

The curtain goes up.

Stage Setting

Stage Setting

THIS drama has a *mise en scene* of depth, colour and variety such as no designer could hope to depict. Viewed geometrically it is triangular, and the easiest visualisation of physical South Africa is obtained by seeing it as three main points connected by two long sides, approximately 1,000 miles in length, and a short base-line 500 miles long. To follow this simplified illustrative description of a vast country —into which 5 United Kingdoms or 33 Hollands could be placed and lost—Cape Town can be assumed as the apex of the triangle. From it, a broad highway 1,000 miles long, with macadamised surface, runs to Johannesburg, in one direction, and another highway, a little longer, east and coastwise to Durban, with a 500-mile road connecting that city with Johannesburg to the north.

Like that of a theatre, the stage on which the dramatic portrayal of South Africa is being presented has two entry-points but, unlike the "L" and "R" of the theatre, South Africa is entered from the north and south. Each entrance has its own distinctive type of fascinating beauty. South entry, at Cape Town, is by sea; north entry, at Johannesburg, is by air. To step on the stage by either is to experience a memorable thrill.

After two weeks at sea, to come up on deck one early morning and see Table Mountain looming out of the dawn-mist as if impaled on infinity, shining like a frosted confection with its own special sunshine, was for me an entrancement only equalled by my first glimpse of the Canadian Rockies through the CPR train window one morning as the train approached Calgary, when I mistook the serrated ridge of snow-covered mountains in the distance for sun-goldened clouds.

Table Mountain, as ageless as Iolanthe and as changeless as an ivory figurine, dominates Cape Town in more ways than one, forcing the Mother City into an elongated shape not much more than a mile wide because, with the foothills of the mountain running down to the sea, a one-dimensional effect is compulsory—length without depth. Table Mountain, with its precipitous approaches up 3,549 feet of ancient sandstone to its monotonous flat top, has become so synchronous with the name of the city—or vice versa, to be exact—that Cape Town seems to have acquired the corrosive lustre of fame as the Table Mountain City, as if it possessed no other virtue than crouching along the bottom of a mountain. In actual fact, Table Mountain, which is Cape Town's boast and its chief identification in the minds of overseas people, is its chief handicap.

Had there been no mountain there, Cape Town could have become by now one of the biggest cities of the world—and lost its emulsive calm of serenity in the process. Instead, it is one of the smaller, except by the incorporation of suburb-towns which extend around the back of the mountain and across the isthmus to the Indian Ocean. Because of the juxtaposition of mountain and sea, land is in short supply and, therefore, costly. This precludes expansion because, quite apart from the physical difficulty of expansion, immigrant industries can find land elsewhere at cheaper rates.

Cape Town's economy, like its history, is closely related to the sea. As the first port on the trans-Atlantic route, its harbour and dockyards provide a ramified variety of commercial undertakings such as are integrated in the life of all sea-ports. It is a dockside town but not a growing one because, of late years, Port Elizabeth and Durban have entered into fierce and threatening competition, both having the advantage over Cape Town of a shorter rail distance for imports to Johannesburg, the business centre.

As an industrial area, Cape Town is most attractive to those manufactures which produce finished and processed goods from imported raw materials. This is declining. Time was when the Cape was the centre of the clothing industry whose raw product was imported, but as a South African textile industry is growing apace, able to supply the needs of the clothing factories, the latter are now a major feature of the Rand industrial complex. This shift of industrial emphasis is being accepted by the Mother City with a modesty that is almost a deformity.

Struggling valiantly to avoid taking her place in the gloriously irrevocable, Cape Town has, of recent years, made a gallant gesture of defiance at the assaults on her eminence by a feat which has no equal in South Africa and few competitors in the whole world. Many square miles of the foreshore and its encroaching water-logged flatlands have been reclaimed and given the permanence of solidity. On this great stretch of land, fine sweeping boulevards have been laid, sky-scraping blocks of offices built, huge industrial establishments erected. Cape Town's main street has been extended from where it had ended in a pier jutting into the Atlantic Ocean, and now takes the place of the displaced pier to run for miles where the ocean, a few years back, seeped over the land. It is a stupendous engineering achievement and the foreshore is becoming an irresistible magnet that is drawing the heart of the city

CURTAIN-UP ON SOUTH AFRICA

from where it has been located since van Riebeeck first established his fort—two to five miles away from where the new land stands—to where van Riebeeck sailed his ships. This amazing accomplishment, providing large industrial estates for immigrant and indigenous industries, may save Cape Town from the conclusive restriction with which the towering Table Mountain threatened it.

Parliament is quite a significant factor in Cape Town's economy because, for six months every year—the length of its sessions—it brings into Cape Town a horde of Parliamentarians and civil servants with their families. This is a feature that is peculiar to South African life. Special trains are run from Pretoria—the administrative capital, the civil-service city—bringing hundreds of officials, their wives, children, domestic pets and belongings at the beginning of each year.

They live in Cape Town for the six months that Parliament is sitting and form a compact colony of annual immigrants, making demands on housing and educational facilities—and on local commerce. They have been worth many millions of pounds to the city's revenue—an ephemeral contribution because, like all civil servants, they are committed to the soft treacherous desires for pensioned security in the civil-service city. All the strong, empirical arguments put forward for making Pretoria, now only the Whitehall of South Africa, its Westminster as well have been drowned in equally strong, if emotional, arguments from Cape Town which stands firmly on the fact that as it was the birthplace of Parliament it must remain the home of Parliament—a plea based on history but not entirely empty of commercial self-interest.

Despite all the claims to the contrary, I never found Cape Town—where I was based for six years—a beautiful city as a whole, and what physical beauty it possesses—relics of its

founding days—are being trampled under the marching feet
of progress. It is a two-street large town outside of which
there is enough beauty to satiate the insatiable. Cape Town's
asset of beauty is not invested inside Cape Town but outside
the city. In the Constantia Valley there are miles of woodland,
lush vale, forested hills and leafy lanes which, when seen
tinted to radiance under the saffron effulgence of the Cape
sun, made me think that I was back in Kent or Surrey, my
favourite English counties. Few motor drives in the world—
the Grand Corniche is one—are superior to the Marine Drive
to Hout Bay on a fine tarmac road that is a curvaceous ledge
cut into the side of the mountain—at that point gashed by
bushy ravines into the magnificently craggy "Twelve Apostles"
—overhanging the sea and the picturesque village of Landudno,
600 feet below. Hout Bay, itself, falls away below the road
in picture-window beauty—a fishing village, reminiscent of
Brixham in Devon but in an even prettier setting: the Mediter-
ranean-blue bay ringed by mountains silhouetted against
lustrous skies and quilt-patterned with cornfields, forests,
wild flowers and verdant meadowland.

To be fair to Cape Town it must be regarded not as a place
to go to but as a place to go from—a hundred delight-spots are
within a half-day's car run in all directions. As a terminal
from which to go to such centres of unspoiled beauty as Paarl
—capital of the wine-country—or Ceres or Kleinmond or
Caledon or Darling or Worcester or Malmesbury or Swellendam or the Wilderness, as the famous honeymooning spot is
grotesquely named, Cape Town is ideally situated. So also
is it as a departure-point for all kinds of angling—from inland
rivers for trout and bass to the coastal spots for off-shore and
deep-sea fishing which includes in its generous ambit the
tough-fighting tuna and marlin.

I am not writing a Conducted Tour Through a Guide Book and so do not pause to describe in any detail the fascinating attractions of the 5,000 square miles of beauty and interest of which Cape Town is the centre and departure-point. It is also central to the origins of history because it was here that White civilisation began and, for almost a century, was confined. Cape Town dominated the growth and development of South Africa for more than 200 years and, to this day, has an influence on national affairs exceeding, by far, its municipal importance. It is the capital city of the Cape Province and that means that it is the focal point of a distinct way of national life.

No understanding of South Africa will be secured if that fact is not fully appreciated because, in many significant ways, South Africa, which is a Union of four regions, consists of four countries. Known as Provinces—the Cape, Natal, the Orange Free State and the Transvaal—each possesses such distinctive characters, derived from distinctive histories and distinctive peoples, that they appear—and not too super-ficially so—to be four different countries. There is a sharp and inescapable difference between Natal and its contiguous neighbour, the Free State, in several fundamental respects. There are equally profound differences between the Cape and the adjoining Transvaal, even in the political outlooks of the same political party.

There are several logical reasons why Cape Town should manifest its own peculiar character. What is known as "the Cape tradition" is a reflection of English liberalism which immigrated with the early English immigrants, and settled with them in the place where they landed. Cape Town is at the confluence of two streams—first the Dutch-French and, later, the British settlers. Both have left their impression on the Cape way of life and thought. That is why there remain

26

so many evidences of tradition and history; to such an extent that Cape Town is as different from any of the other three provincial cities as they are from each other—if for differing reasons.

A MODERN tarmac highway links Cape Town with Johannesburg, about 1,000 miles away. The former is left via a mountain pass which is a triumphant testimony to South African civil-engineering skill—as are many thousands of other miles of South African roads. Du Toit's Pass covers the first lap in the ascent from sea level to Johannesburg's 6,000-feet height and in its construction Italian war-prisoners were astutely used—astutely because the builders of the original Roman roads have left reminders of their skill in several lands.

Paarl, at the foot of the pass, is the "pearl" that its Dutch name signifies. Resting, gem like, on the soft velvet of verdant beauty, it has retained sufficient of its 300-year origins to offer one of the best remaining evidences of South Africa's beginnings. Its oak-lined streets reflect the peace and tranquillity which Jan van Riebeeck's burghers established with their establishment of the quaint little town. Abutting the seven-mile main street are the straight soldierly rows of vines—a picture as delicate as an Aubusson carpet—which the early Huguenot settlers planted when they brought French viticulture with them.

Despite the encroachments of modern architecture, there remains a large number of old Cape-Dutch, wide-stoeped homesteads, their cool-white walls festooned with elegant gables and blue-shuttered windows leading to a crown of thatch. They fit into the historic atmosphere of the town and

27

contribute to its cloistral repose, its meditative calm. Vines trellis the fronts of those picturesque houses as they do the surrounding fields because Paarl is the "capital city" of the wine industry, the home of the "KWV", as the Co-operative Winegrowers' Association is known—for its excellent products—the world over. This, the basic activity of Paarl and the surrounding districts, drops with harmonious neatness into the calm circumference of the town's normal existence.

It is from just outside Paarl, up the Du Toit Pass, that the run to Johannesburg begins to leave the Cape proper behind. I have known businessmen to make the car-run to Johannesburg in a day. They got behind the wheel before dawn and sat there well into lighting-up time with their foot jammed down on the pedal for 1,000 miles. Only business urgency could excuse such barbarism because none of the glories of that trip can register when they are whizzed through at an average of more than sixty m.p.h. To do the trip with one stop-over—preferably at Colesberg, the exit-town from the Karoo—is reasonable but the better plan is to stop-off at Beaufort West, a delightful town which is an echo of South Africa's youth, and again at Bloemfontein, the old-world capital of the Orange Free State and the centre of South Africa's judiciary.

Through the Karoo, the road is in the ascendant, the arid or semi-arid Karoo, itself, being more than 3,000 feet above sea-level. Only about one to three rainy days a month are the Karoo's ration—in official figures: an average of less than ten inches of rain per year. A single shower sometimes accounts for half of the annual rainfall. Daytime has a very extreme fluctuation in temperature—from the excessive noon-tide heat of 110 degrees Fahrenheit to 60 degrees in the late afternoon.

To get through the Karoo as quickly as possible is the motorist's set plan—to reach Bloemfontein with relief. One day in the not-far future the Karoo will find a valuable use for itself. It is under-exploited, it includes near-virgin territory, it has a fabulous future: the lid of this immense Pandora Box has only been slightly opened but wide enough to get glimpses of the hidden treasures within.

At present, the Karoo consists of either vast stretches of scrub and bush or courageous farmlands, some of them mort-gaged to the tree-roots, on which *nil desperandum* farmers, striking a note of strenuous fortitude, sweat blood and tears to scratch crops out of the reluctant soil. Karoo agriculture is augmented, if it is at all, by animal husbandry and it is a minor miracle of nature that the beasts manage to get meals off a veld where vegetation is so rare that one patch of really green grass would stick out like a hairpin on a bachelor's pillow.

Town-life is infrequent and some of the dorps are suffi-ciently gloomy to have enticed Cerberus from the Stygian caves. The physical and natural characteristics explain why the people of the Karoo are so hardy, so pertinaceous, so obstinate and so courageous that the territory has produced some of South Africa's finest sons. To motor through the Karoo from can-see to can't-see is a tour of ever-everland— ever striving, ever hopeful. Its urban communities are isolated from each other and insulated against outside in-fluences.

A typical Karoo town measures four petrol stations long by two hotels wide. Such towns seem mainly populated by people valorously engaged with the humdrum tragedy of the struggle against monotony, the eyes of their minds fixed on no horizons beyond their shuffling feet. It would be a fan-tastic achievement for them to be otherwise. They have seen

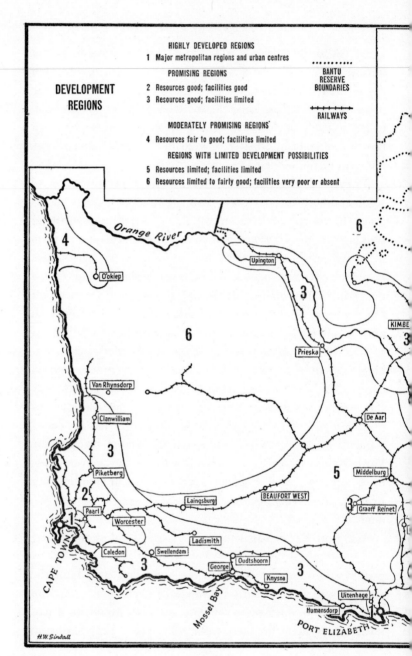

DEVELOPMENT
REGIONS

HIGHLY DEVELOPED REGIONS
1 Major metropolitan regions and urban centres

PROMISING REGIONS
2 Resources good; facilities good
3 Resources good; facilities limited

MODERATELY PROMISING REGIONS
4 Resources fair to good; facilities limited

REGIONS WITH LIMITED DEVELOPMENT POSSIBILITIES
5 Resources limited; facilities limited
6 Resources limited to fairly good; facilities very poor or absent

BANTU
RESERVE
BOUNDARIES

RAILWAYS

H.W. Sindall

BECHUANALAND

RHODESIA

Limpopo River

6

LOUIS TRICHARDT

6

3

Pieterburg

MOÇAMBIQUE

Kruger National Park

Zeerust

Nylstroom

Tzaneen

3

Mafeking

4

Rustenburg

Lichtenburg

PRETORIA

Lydenburg

Witbank

JOHANNESBURG

4

Klerksdorp

Vereeniging

Heidelberg

1

2

Nielspruit

2

Bethal

Barberton

Standerton

Ermilo

Odendaalsrus

Kroonstad

Frankfort

3

Volksrust

SWAZILAND

LOURENCO MARQUES

WELKOM

2

3

PIET RETIEF

3

BLOEMFONTEIN

Bethlehem

Newcastle

2

3

Ficksburg

Harrismith

Vryheid

3

Ladybrand

4

4

Ladysmith

BASUTOLAND

4

Eshowe

PIETER MARITZBURG

NAL NORTH

Ixopo

DURBAN

BARKLY EAST

3

2

Kokstad

4

PORT SHEPSTONE

Queenstown

Umtata

PORT ST JOHNS

INDIAN OCEAN

3

illiamstown

2

EAST LONDON

FRED

Scale of Miles

0   50   100   200

the fine black-topped highway come to their towns—and go, leaving them behind in whiskered rusticity, their ambitions corroded with the acid of the years. If a young man is ever stirred out of the delicious somnolence and makes a plan for his life he must leave because, in a Karoo town, the infinitives "to plan" and "to perform" belong to entirely different categories.

Someday in the not-far future, I repeat, all this will be changed. Nature nor man will allow this extensive territory to fail to fit into the new South African setup. This is the future development sector and, as nothing can brake the impetus under which the rest of the country is propelling itself forward, the untapped, because unrecognised, resources which the dead-pan-faced Karoo conceals in its hand will grab another royal-flush jackpot.

Passing through its dorps, in a silence dead enough to be buried, the road to "the big city" unwinds, its consuming maw taking a town like Philippolis in one swallow. Philippolis is a casket containing the ashes of South Africa's dead past. Rich in history, it gazes at the future with a look of mongolian sorrow as if modernity were a dirty word. Its solitary main street, bleached by the yellow gangrene which the seldom-refraining sun drops on it like a universal pus, is a manuscript in the archives of South Africa's fruitful past. This little town, which out of its spiritual virility has helped make South Africa virile, is a living condemnation of the madly gadarene rush and ulcer-creating tempo that "the big cities" nurture as virtues. It may look as sluggishly idle as a painted ship upon a painted ocean but it contains within itself the yeasting activity of authentic purposiveness.

From dawn to dusk, the journey continues; and a dusk in this flamboyant country is as restfully beautiful as dawn is beautifully stimulating. As the sun rampages across the sky with a runaway stain, the twilight-less night descends with abrupt but haggard beauty to be lost in Cimmerian darkness. Less than eight hours later, the bedded sun arises to brush the cloud-humps with carnival colours and sprinkle the mountains with fibres of gold that fork into self-propagating filaments before it begins its merciless pounding of men and things. Natural beauty is, like its mineral wealth, one of South Africa's treasures freely available for man's benefit.

Passing through the under-developed but highly potential towns of Trompsburg and Reddersburg the road goes straight to Bloemfontein with unerring directness. Bloemfontein is a city in which the centuries meet and where, to paraphrase Goethe, fate has changed horses often. Rubbing shoulders comfortably with ultra-modern business premises are 200-year-old, but still functional, buildings which house members of the legal fraternity who practise their profession in and around the nation's chief courts. And close by, Naval Hill can be seen, on whose grassy slopes herds of zebra lazily graze.

Bloemfontein, whose sons have written some of the most vivid chapters of South Africa's history, shows a quaint mixture of hustling commerce and the leisurely gait of the judiciary; of expanding industrialism and the serenity of university life. Its jog-trottery was jolted into a gallop when the Free State, of which it is the capital, discovered that it possessed enough unearthed gold to make the Witwatersrand look like an experiment in gold-mining. A city whose main preoccupations—when it was not gazing down the death-rimmed years into its great past—was scholastic and legal, is now adjusting its tempo to the phrenesis of a new gold-rush with calm detachment.

Being the capital of one of the four "countries" which is

South Africa's real composition, Bloemfontein bears the imprimatur of its own distinctiveness. Its city-centre is the well-organised, well-controlled and well-directed hub of its commercial and entertainment life, reeking with modernity. Here there is no sign whatever of that flatus of decay which is often the unmistakable odour of age. Its spacious stores are for ever a-jam; its cinema theatres packed; its hotel life a-throb. An imposing central Post Office has its marbled ornateness set off by the contiguous gardens, flaming with flowers and mellowed by fountains. Even in its down-town sector, Bloemfontein retains the beauty from which it derived its name.

This city has written extensively on the cryptic manuscript of South Africa's history and continues to do so. It retains decisive influence in the South Africa of today which neither the solemncholia of Cape Town nor the frantic frenzy of the Golden City can gainsay. From the sheltered byways of the past, the voice of Bloemfontein can pontificate with the profound utterances of age-steeped wisdom—and does. It is a city that it would be fatally foolish to underestimate.

This is not merely a city of the past, resigned to back-number position; but the palladium of the nation's laws and a seat of national learning. All the social agitations and political fevers that send up the temperature in Cape Town and Johannesburg, opaque Bloemfontein with well-poised indifference; as an elder, she observes the convulsions of the new cities with glacial contempt. Bloemfontein dips deep into the well of her history and finds her strength.

Johannesburg, the modern product of gold-rush malaria, is less than 300 miles away—the last lap of the 1,000-mile side of the triangular stage on which the drama of South Africa has been played; is being played. The road runs through some of

34

South Africa's finest specimens of its finest agriculture—before all else, the Orange Free State is the Union's agricultural province and it is, primarily, Afrikaner-land where the original Boer way of life and thinking are most manifest. On either side of this broad highway, multi-morgened farmland rolls away into infinity—corn-fields and vast mealie plantations, because this is at the extremity of the "mealie triangle", an area of many thousands of square miles which produces mealies (maize) worth anything around forty million pounds a year: a quarter of the Union's total value of agricultural produce. This rich loamy land is as good as a gold-field—time was when it was South Africa's only gold-field.

It is far from being a populous area. Farms are anything but postage-stamp sized—many of the farms of Britain would be small-holdings by comparison. Some of the Free State farms that this highway dissects may be as much as 10,000 morgen—a morgen is just under 2.2 acres—compared with 400 acres which would, in Britain, be a large farm. And so the population has to be very sparse per square mile. In the 150-mile run from Bloemfontein to Kroonstad the road passes through only three towns—Brandfort, Winburg and Ventersburg—and these would rank, in Britain, as not much more than villages.

Each is far more busy than its size would suggest because each is the only urbanised centre for miles around. Saturday afternoon and night in either is a time of excitement, activity and hilarity as the menfolk, their wives and families drive in to replenish their stores and refresh their spirits. The psychological temper of such towns corresponds with the economy of the surrounding agriculture which rises and falls with drought and rain as the flux and reflux of equinoctial tides. It is highest when the crops are safely gathered in, when doubt and drought are irrelevant; different from Britain where rural spirit flaunts itself when spring marches in like an army with banners.

At other times, the small towns are very small-townish, wrapped snugly in a cocoon of convenient quietude, the people content to devour the apple of life a nibble at a time with complete absorption in such nebulous assumptions as the infertility of this year's batch of red-billed finches which make constant war on the grain-fields and are killed off at a cost of £66 per morgen or £211 per million bird-corpses. The people's dread of drought and pests in such districts has been burned into their thinking by the acid of adversity which not even the alchemy of sunshine nor the abrasive of time can erase.

Serving the agricultural area as a kind of "capital" is the bustling town of Kroonstad which has a mid-West appearance built round an Afrikaner character. Kroonstad races along under the whiplash of bustling vitality which finds its outlet in civic excellence—it is an exceptionally well-conducted town. Mainly from staunch Afrikaner stock, the people express that fine tolerance and acceptance of the English-speaking overlay in the spirit that gave South Africa her great past, the absence of which could, alone, rob her of her greater future.

Kroonstad has undergone ruthless change during the past decade so that the economy of the town has had to practise— and has successfully practised—brilliant skill in grazing the very edge of disaster. Ten years ago gold was discovered on the town's doorstep. Kroonstad went into top gear. Less than fifty miles away, it was rumoured, a bonanza was to be unearthed and the town saw itself as Johannesburg the Second —hectically active and monumentally wealthy. Land values soared; shopkeepers consulted extension plans; the Town Council studied the rateable valuation through rose-coloured magnifying glasses. A picture-window had been opened on to a new life, lustrous and luxurious—and then the window was slammed, the mocking reverberations mounting to a thunderous crash of hopes which has continued to make the night of disappointment murmurous with bitter echoes. There was gold on the doorstep; it never crossed the threshold. Instead, it activated a breath-taking achievement which, as if with the aid of an Aladdin's Lamp, created four brand-new towns only a step away from Kroonstad's front door.

ONLY ten years ago (this is written in 1960) what is now these four towns was bare and barren and burned-up open veld. In less than a decade, a miracle of growth and development has made that wilderness literally blossom as the rose. And not only with the bright-hued flower of dividend-paying gold but, also, with a million trees and uncountable millions of blooms in private gardens and public parks. On an area of more than 200 square miles, which, ten years ago, was a treeless, dusty, scrub-covered desert, stand four compact, modern towns, hysteric with new life, laid out to conform with the latest principles of town-planning, housing a total population of nearly 170,000 people, with all the implications of permanence. Two hundred square miles of the primeval jerked almost in the wink of an eye out of its million-year sleep into the heart of the atomic age—land that might have gone on sleeping for another million years. It is an epic of the indomitability of industry.

Welkom, as the largest of the four, provides the silhouette of the rapidly-unfolding future. Where it now stands there was no human habitation whatever a decade ago. It is now the second largest town in the Orange Free State, second only to Bloemfontein, the capital, whose origin is 100 years old and which Welkom will firmly displace from first position for size before another ten years have passed. Welkom is a model town in every conceivable respect, including the fact that it is owned by its inhabitants. Without any cynically minute perscrutation of the interplay of act and motive, it can be reported that Welkom was created by a mining-company subsidiary on a non-profit basis, and which, after spending nearly five million pounds on the task, handed a finished town over to a citizens' Board of Management, an elected local authority. Anyone who would question the generosity of that action would doubt the eternal course of the planets.

When the late Sir Ernest Oppenheimer announced, in May 1947, that his Anglo-American Corporation proposed to sink the first shaft at Welkom, with reasonable prospects of striking a basal reef, and rumours heavily loaded with overtones of excitement ran wild, Kroonstad grinned with excusable delight, seeing itself as a boom town. It even dreamed of ousting Bloemfontein as the Free State's biggest city. It never occurred to any in Kroonstad that, before the end of "the frenzied fifties", there would be four new towns within fifty miles of it, two of them so much larger that they pushed Kroonstad down from second to fourth place in the Free State's municipal list.

Welkom and Virginia, with Odendaalsrus and Allanridge, are symbols of the potentialities for expansion and development which South Africa possesses to a unique degree. They are dream-towns: a man who ten years ago stood where they stand and returned, unwarned, to the area would rub his eyes convinced that he was dreaming. Even this present inadequate profile-sketch will provide some unbelievable idea of the

A view from the mountain of Paarl in its fertile valley of vineyards.

Hermanus bay with its fishing harbour and the boats just drawn up from the Indian Ocean.

Aerial view of Welkom, the "dream town" laid out where, nine years ago, was bare veld.

One of the Anglo-American mines, showing the headgear and the ore-conveyor to the screening and crushing plant.

transformation of that scene—from empty, inhospitable veld to four highly-organised towns complete from crypt to spire, with their own suburbs and Native townships and replete with all amenities.

Harnessing more energy than the Kariba Dam develops, the engineers made their first assaults on the hidden treasure below the strata of rock-formation, sand-sediment and conglomerates which unnumbered centuries had deposited; but Sir Ernest Oppenheimer, an enlightened and modern-thinking mine-magnate, insisted that the human element should be catered for in advance of the actual mining operations. His declared policy was to expand South Africa's gold-producing capacity but, in accomplishing that, to create a town for its workers; one that, he said, "must combine the attributes of a garden city with the utilitarian needs of an industrial community". Always an uncommunicative man, Sir Ernest never disclosed whether he then envisioned what Welkom became or whether to him also it was merely a "dream town".

It is likely that he did. His ideals were not floated on an unreturning stream and his actions were those of a man making his own dream come true. Town-planning experts were called in and, in 1948 before drilling had begun, blue-prints prepared depicting a thriving, well-housed community, with tarmac roads, shopping centres, churches, schools, parks, sports fields and every modern amenity of the modern town. That was the blue-print of a dream: the reality at that time was burned-up veld as far as eye could see, its only connection with civilisation being a rough and rutted dirt-track to Kroonstad.

Before ten years had passed dream and reality had exchanged places in a union of the static and dynamic. It is now almost impossible to imagine limitless desert; what requires no imagination is the sight of this mushroom-growth town. Its wide main street—Stateway—is a boulevard of double carriage-ways and central grass strips that sweeps through the heart of Welkom with an imposing Civic Centre on the right and a horseshoe-shaped shopping zone on the left. Behind the Civic Centre—such is the stuff of which the Oppenheimer dream was made—sufficient ground has been set aside to develop it to meet the needs of 50,000, instead of its present 30,000 European citizens.

All the town-planning faults of older towns have been avoided. Welkom is laid out in zones comprising commercial centres, industrial areas, residential districts and such communal amenities as schools (of which there are eleven), churches (twenty-five), technical college, parks and public gardens—the actual desert actually blossoming as the rose. No residential premises or industries are allowed in a shopping area behind which runs a road exclusively for vehicles loading and unloading supplies to the back of the shops. Residences are pleasantly located close to the parks and public gardens. Hotels (there are four) and theatres are sited away from shopping areas to avoid congestion of traffic—for there are already more than 10,000 local car registrations.

Some regard Welkom as the finest tribute to Sir Ernest Oppenheimer's memory. They are wrong. His greatest memorial—and so he would wish—is the Bantu hospital there that bears his name. It is, in many respects, unique, and, in all respects, the finest hospital serving non-Whites in the world. Cared for as the Bantu workers in the Anglo-American mines are—working and living conditions are a model for all other countries to emulate—it is at the hospital where the humanities reach the zenith. Beautiful in appearance, ultra-modern in design, it houses all that is latest and best in the sublime art of healing.

Instead of a dirt-track, Welkom has 120 miles of its own internal tarmac roads with through-roads to Bloemfontein at the south and Johannesburg to the north. An internal bus service runs between the town and its suburbs. There is a main railway line which, in addition to normal passenger trains, is used by the Orange Express—an equivalent to the famous Blue Train—and a twice-daily air service from Johannesburg and from Durban touches down on the airstrips of the goldfield's own excellent airport.

Although the industry of Welkom is goldmining, it has its own industrial centre because the demands of the mines are so extensive and varied that there are incessant requirements to be met. Welkom can supply all its own needs—from the squeal to the sausage. In addition to actual mining material, engineering works, building contractors and allied traders as well as millers, concrete-pipe manufacturers, petrol companies, soft-drink and foodstuff manufacturers are located on the first industrial area which, 1,000 acres in extent, has more than 200 built-up premises with a rateable value of £3 million.

Five suburbs are conveniently sited to the five mines so that employees can live near their work. The suburbs have park strips in which are schools, children's playgrounds and an open-air amphitheatre. There are hundreds of miners' homes in each suburb—a typical cottage consists of three bedrooms, living-room, dining-room and kitchen with fitted electric stove. Rents for these are £4 10s. 0d. per month. Even in the case of somewhat better houses for mine officials the highest rental is only £5 7s. 6d. per month.

There are sports grounds within reach of all the suburbs and the Welkom Club, standing on thirty acres of finely laid-out grounds, has rugby and hockey fields, baseball and softball pitches, squash courts, cricket fields, tennis courts, bowling greens, jukskei pitches, floodlit football fields and a swimming bath. Dances are held in the spacious ballroom regularly while concerts, lectures and theatre shows are staged there frequently.

All this and much more shows how Sir Ernest Oppenheimer's dream-town has become reality—in less than ten years. Parallel with it has been the crœsus-like product of the mines, proving that it isn't success that destroys creative energies—it's the stink of failure. And to make this industrial romance more fantastic: in the heart of the veld, Welkom can enjoy its own annual regatta. Members of the Flamingo Yachting Club sail their craft on the Theronia Pan, a lake one and a quarter miles long and three-quarters of a mile wide—formed of water pumped from the mines!

Sixteen miles from Welkom is Virginia—an even younger town. Housing commenced there in 1954 and, five years later, it had grown to be the Free State's third largest town. More than £7 million was spent in providing houses for its 39,000 population and, such is the rate of expansion, all town-planning is complete for an 80,000 population within the next three years and is designed for an ultimate population of double that figure.

Excellent tarred roads dissect the town and run through in all directions, and the street lighting of Virginia is recognised throughout South Africa as the best in that country. In most civic respects all that has been said of Welkom is applicable to Virginia although the number of its mines is smaller. Virginia is distinctive by reason of its wide roads; its main thoroughfare is one of the world's widest—350 feet across —with gardens in the centre, commercial buildings on one side and administrative offices on the other.

Educational and social facilities are at least equal, in proportion, to those of South Africa's most famous cities. There are two nursery schools, three primary schools, a high school, a convent and a technical college with 107 teachers responsible for the 2,384 pupils. There is the Virginia Golf Club, with grassy tees fringed with trees—where once was wilderness—and the Harmony Club, one of the finest in the land, with bowling green, tennis courts, a swimming pool built to Olympic standards and spaciously beautiful lounges.

Entertainment facilities are ample. The people of Virginia do not have to go to Johannesburg for films and stage shows—that would be as silly as a professional evangelist going to a rival mission to get saved. Virginia has a 700-seat theatre and a cinema—appropriately named The Phoenix as it arose from the dust—which is the first in South Africa to have a baby cry-room. It is equipped with loud-speakers so that mothers with fretful babies can sit and watch the screen through the wide windows which are plateglass and—of necessity—soundproof.

Odendaalsrus and Allanridge are smaller towns but the record and rapid growths of Welkom and Virginia make that immediate fact irrelevant. What has happened in Welkom and Virginia will be repeated in this burgeoning country. These four new towns have a total population rapidly approaching the 200,000 mark. Elsewhere in the world, it would be cause for amazement if a fully-organised and integrated community established itself in one generation—for four towns to have done that, in the centre of completely uncultivated wilderness, in less than ten years is one of the miracles of South Africa's miraculous development.

Within the 150 miles that separate the Free State goldfields from their parent city of Johannesburg there is a contiguity of the sylvan beauty of rusticity and the grim magnificence of

43

industrial achievement. These are symbolised in the picturesque riverside resort of Parys and Vereeniging with its neighbouring Vanderbijl Park steel-town. For some inexplicable reason, a surveyor named Schilbach on seeing the Vaal river meandering the Klipspruit farm, seventy-five years ago, had memories of Paris revived in his dreamy mind. He laid out a township with the intention of turning the Vaal into another Seine and calling it Parys.

It has never become a metropolis and has never achieved the slightest resemblance to the French capital. Instead it is a sleepy little town and parts of its riverside reaches most startlingly resemble Maidenhead, the Thames riverside resort. The tree-lined banks of the river, the lush gardens, manicured lawns, the willows sweeping the surface of the water with their tearful tresses, the canoes that paddle past the churning pleasure steamers, all combine to produce a remarkably English scene in this Afrikaner town.

Half an hour's motor drive and the scene abruptly changes. Here is Vanderbijl Park, as unpark-like as possible. It is a smoke-belching steel-town, named after Dr. Van der Bijl, the famous South African steel-master whose expert advice was recruited by the British Government continuously during the last world war. These huge and most modern steel works which have brought into existence the town that is named after him have helped Iscor—the Iron and Steel Corporation —to make South Africa not only nearly self-supporting in respect to steel but enabled steel to be exported to America during that country's 1959 steel strike, and threatens the invasion of other world markets in successful competition with Britain and Germany.

Not far from Vanderbijl Park is Sasolburg, another miracle of post-war development. It is the home of the world's largest oil-from-coal project, a State enterprise. With a thirty-million gallon output of petrol, Sasol is not only fuelling thousands of vehicles on South African roads but is, also, creating vast opportunities for new industries, through its numerous by-products, and increasing trade both internally and export.

Ten years ago this Orange Free State industrial centre of Sasolburg did not exist. It is a Government enterprise and during its first three operational years involved the taxpayers in considerable losses, but a £3,395,000 loss in the first year was progressively reduced until, last year, it operated at only £500,000 loss, and, from now, the past losses will be wiped out by an increasing scale of annual profit. Among its valuable by-products are fertilisers, superphosphates and sulphuric acid.

These are the very latest of South Africa's industrial achievements; as they are left behind and the drive continues along the west side of the triangle, the industry on which has been founded all others comes into view—a range of mountains of dull-yellow sand: the "dump-heaps" of the Golden City.

F ROM experience, after reaching South Africa three times by the "south entrance"—the sea-route to Cape Town—and three times by the "north entrance", I am irrevocably decided that the best first-glimpse of Johannesburg is not over the steering wheel of a car on the road-approach from Vereeniging but from a plane window. It is also the most revealing, as revealing of Johannesburg as the Table Mountain view of Cape Town is of that city.

Arriving at night, as the South African Airways plane circle-swoops around to Johannesburg the scene is dazzlingly fascinating. Below is an unimaginable, indescribable fairyland of a million lights, in palpitating dots and variegated streaks, of clashing and harmonious tints and colours. The earth is strewn with luminous confetti defying, and defeating, the twinkling coruscation of the star-sprinkled sky above, looking like a sequin-spangled gown, glittering in the clear air of sub-tropical night. It is Johannesburg.

The scene depicts the soul of the city just as the stolidity and solidity of Table Mountain, awesome and ancient, mature and deep-rooted, symbolises Cape Town's soul, mind and character. Permanence, immovability, imperturbability, the leisured reflectivity of age is seen in the mountain that broods over the "south entrance" city; the frenzied, highly-coloured brashness of youth is seen from the plane. Three hundred years are inscribed in the Cape Town scene; the sky-defiant chandelier of neon and sodium which is unveiled below the plane above Johannesburg is a city not much more than sixty years of age. All that artificial lighting which cocks a snook of youthful impertinence at the aeon-aged firmament is the index to Johannesburg, its people, its history, its life. A city of a million souls, covering nearly a hundred square miles, as modern as tomorrow—it is a highly-coloured meringue: sweetly hollow.

Johannesburg began as a mining-camp town; it is still a mining town. The naphtha flares and gaudy mirrors and brass rails are gone; now there are fluorescents, fluted marble and chromium. Where once were tents and shacks and reed structures are the enparked mansions of Dunkeld and Illovo, the select residential area of snobocracy where society is spelled with a capital £. Instead of dirt tracks, compulsorily lighted by the oil-lamps outside the noisy saloons of early Johannesburg, are limousine-crowded broadways, canyonised by skyscraping monoliths of concrete and steel. And beneath all the banal magnificence is a mining-camp town.

It is a restless, turbulent city; as restless, as turbulent as a mining town should be—as Johannesburg always has been. Born in turbulence, it has lived sixty-two years of turbulent life. Not only its past but its present is founded on gold; the streets may not be paved with the stuff but beneath them is gold. That yellow metal, in whose name all the sins of Satan have been committed, is the material of which the pulsing heart of the city is composed; it is the substance which, for sixty-two years, has been the main constituent element of what passes, with Johannesburg, for its soul.

Violence, crime, robbery, blackmail and fraud—early Johannesburg was covered with a fine patina of grand larceny. Disaster, plague, drought and war were included in the inventory of undesirables. Not, be it emphasised, that all these negatives excluded the glorious positives of human nobility and virtue, by any means. It is because these latter have been triumphant that the civilised qualities so noticeably transcend the vicious in the Johannesburg of today.

One poor itinerant house-builder snapped off a piece of rock on a farm, in 1886, and tried to raise a few shillings on it because, he avowed to the sceptics, it contained gold. When silence was wisdom, his was the voice of an ass braying in the wilderness. The news reached the ears of a diamond magnate named Robinson in Kimberley and he stage-coached the intervening 300 miles, bought the farm for £6,000 from its widow-owner and a few years later had made £18 millions from its gold. Legality was on his side, "business ethics" supported him—with that justification no one can question the morality of that enterprise even if that word was not in the vocabulary of the gold-miners of seventy-four years ago.

47

That was how Johannesburg was born; or, rather, that was its pre-natal period, because when the late Sir J. B. Robinson bought Widow Oosthuizen's farm the name which is now known the world over as the City of Gold had never been heard because never uttered. Pretoria existed nearly forty miles to the north and Potchefstroom eighty miles to the south. A few farms straggled from both towns into the direction where Widow Oosthuizen lived and had given George Walker, who earned a precarious living by doing building repairs, a job on her new farm house. Strolling around one Sunday, with nothing to do, Walker was attracted by the metallic glints in the rocky land. He broke off a piece and the following Sunday rode the eighty miles to Potchefstroom and hawked it around. Had he been able to afford to keep his mouth shut it might have been George Walker who died the multi-millionaire.

There was no need for any mouth to remain shut once J. B. Robinson started to drive down through the rocky surface in search of the golden reef because his successful exploits in diamond mining, and his association with such other Kimberley magnates as Cecil Rhodes and Abe Bailey, made anything he did in mining tell its own unmistakable story. The gold-rush set in bringing both workmen and adventurers from all parts of the country and the world—from Rumania, Bulgaria and god-knows-whereia. Miners from Barberton and Lydenburg, with diggers from Kimberley who saw the diamond treasure-trove get smaller as the "big hole" got deeper, converged on the "ridge of the white waters"—Witwatersrand or, colloquially, the Rand —and pegged their claims. On horseback, on foot, by stage-coach or wagon they came, consumed with the gold-fever, and to cool it nothing was permitted to stand in the way—some of the newcomers had no more scruples than a fish has fur.

Tents were erected and rough shacks hurriedly thrown up with the virtuosity of a St. Vitus. Within two months, a sixty-mile strip of bare veld was crammed with 3,000 frenzied miners and their families; but with no sanitation, light, roads or water. This last necessity was secured from distant springs and hawked among the tents at sixpence a bucket. It was Colorado all over again.

Pessimists declared that the feast would not last to the fish-course but that, if it did, after the banquet would come the bellyache. Defying them, the first steps to create a coherent communal life were taken. After a piece of land had been unable to find an occupant it was set aside for use as a "township". Tents and shacks were concentrated on it, but its chief defect, from a town-planning point of view, was that it was divided by the shaft of an existing gold-mine. Plots of this land were sold, the most attractive portion going for as much as £280, and the entire "township" was allocated for £13,000 —the price of what is now Johannesburg with its present £466 million rateable value. Where the intruding shaft of the gold-mine had been sunk, the Law Courts now stand.

Johannesburg's first decade of catch-as-catch-can activity set the tempo of the town's life, characterised its growth and marked the character of the present-day city. It spelled a saga of disasters, tragedies, social and public upheaval, storms, mass-starvation, water-shortage and famine—a violent, restless, turbulent period when original sin was original. During the succeeding half-century there have been similar manifestations and the "typical Joburger" is the product: loud-spoken, aggressive, raucous, violent-minded, assertive, boastful, arrogant, hard-driven by hormic impulses—the projection of the strong opinionation of the founder-father's insurgent era.

49

These attributes are, for Johannesburg, virtues. It is still a gold town. Basic to the entire economy is gold-mining. The thermometer that records the psychological health of the city rises or falls with Stock Exchange evaluation of gold shares which traces the uninterpretable graph of boom and slump. All the commercial life of the city is geared to that, and the extremes of reaction—from unbounded exaltation to a bad fit of the jitters—are merely reflections of the fluctuations of the mercury in that barometer.

This sensitivity to the gold market must, of necessity, produce a general psychology of temperamental extremes. In so doing, it creates a thrustful, energetic, enterprising and forceful people who invest those qualities in commerce, industry and civic life. Johannesburg's brashness finds constructive outlets: a modern manifestation of the city founders' reckless pioneering spirit which created the industry from which South Africa's phenomenal progress has derived.

Gold is the lynch-pin of the nation's economy as it was its salvation seventy-four years ago. At the time when George Walker was doing a building job for buxom Widow Oosthuizen on the farm "where gold began" white-bearded President Kruger did not know where the Treasury's next meal was coming from. Like a Chancellor of history, he was "seated on an empty chest by the side of a bottomless deficiency fishing for a Budget" after having received and studied Armfield's historic report on his investigations into the possibilities of gold-mining—"not a field for the prospector". Two years before Widow Oosthuizen gave George Walker a month's work, Kruger had gone to London to raise funds and the extent of his success can be measured by the fact that he was unable to pay his bill at the Albemarle Hotel—the unfortunate man had miscounted his trumps.

On that embarrassment much of South Africa's subsequent history hinged. It directly led to the gold-rush, the founding of Johannesburg, the Jameson Raid, the Boer War and the South Africa of today. In his dilemma, Kruger sought help from Baron Grant who, as a prominent figure on the London Stock Exchange, was very intimately interested in the Lydenburg goldfields which were not progressing too well—nor were the shares—because of a shortage of miners with overseas knowhow. When the penniless President appealed to the wealthy Baron, the latter agreed to help on condition that President Kruger relaxed his "Afrikaners only need apply" attitude and publicly encouraged British immigrants with assurances of goodwill and protection. Although it was like the lamb getting a whiff of mint sauce, Kruger had to agree— and the door was opened through which British immigrants came to the Transvaal, to share in the gold-rush, to help found Johannesburg and to contribute to the situation from which the Jameson Raid, leading to the Boer war, was to emerge.

Neither of the latter disasters would ever have become chapters of history had Robinson never opened the first Rand gold-mine. Nor would Johannesburg have become the city it is. Nor, for that matter, would South Africa have become a "problem" because, had gold and other minerals never been unearthed, the world would not have had the South Africa of today. South Africa means gold, Johannesburg means gold— that is why, in this report of the stage-setting to South Africa's drama, I am compelled to occupy so many pages with the subject. That is why, from the incoming plane, Johannesburg is seen as a vast, throbbing, thriving city under a canopy of multi-coloured lights—it is the City of Gold.

As a city it is far from the eminence, judged by international standards, that most of its citizens think—or, at least, top-voicedly say—it has attained. Unlike the city it roughly jostled from first place—Cape Town—it has neither roots nor traditions. It is a massive juke-box—gaudily lighted and raucous. Its most evident qualities are superficiality and youthful immaturity. It is a city without a citizenry because citizenry needs to have a many-generation genealogy. Every living person in Johannesburg is either an immigrant or the child or, at most, grandchild of an immigrant. There is not, cannot be, such a person as a fourth-generation Johannesburger.

Ancestry, blood, roots, tradition—they all count for much in the human composition of a nation or a community. Johannesburg is populated by people who cannot look back further than two generations of citizenry. They are the recent descendants of people from elsewhere. Some of them are tenth-generation South Africans—which makes them the descendants of immigrants from other lands. Many of them are the grandchildren of Kruger's contemporaries—which does not make them of Johannesburg descent. Most of them are immigrants, the children or grandchildren of immigrants who came to South Africa within the last century. All must, by that token, have very shallow roots in Johannesburg because the soil of that city is, as a city, shallow.

Viewed as a city, Johannesburg is a disappointment. It is a city without a basic character; not so much nondescript as conglomerate. Patterned precisely, geometrically, it is inchoate architecturally. Those city-founders of sixty years ago planned the layout on the new-world style of straight criss-crossing, north-south, east-west roads. It is as if a huge waffle-iron had been used in designing and a checker-board pattern produced. The result is excellent for appearance, practicability and traffic facilitation.

Excellence ends there. Streets so capably laid out are lined with architectural disorder. Massive steel and concrete sky-scrapers stand alongside one-storey shops, roofed with ancient corrugated iron, in deliciously comic incongruity. Brief rows of modern buildings are punctuated with small unfenced patches of dirtland used for public parking so that a quick glance along a main street is like looking at some hobo's teeth, gappy with decayed molars. Not far from the regality of His Majesty's Theatre, its twin sky-reaching towers thrusting massive illuminated crowns into the hands of heaven, are derelict shops and down-at-mouth little buildings that look as if a trade-union meeting had just been held in them.

Either municipal modernisation has progressed too fast and fitfully or the past has taken an unconscionably long time a-dying. It is probably the former because Johannesburg has been blessed with a continuity of enterprising and enlightened City Corporations for years—in contrast to their headquarters: the City Hall is a grimly oppressive hangover from the dear dead days beyond recall. Building never ceases. To re-visit Johannesburg after six months' absence is to make a guide-book necessary: new and strange structures adding to the eruptive skyscraper jungle make old and familiar places unrecognisable. That manifestation of non-stop change is a true reflection of the entire Johannesburg way of life.

Sidewalks of the main streets look like long horizontal escalators: jammed with eager-beaver pedestrians—brokers dashing along in a cascade of cigar-ash; typists clad in OK Bazaar frocks and spurious sophistication; businessmen, their heads full of invoices and each heart a computator; matrons wearing an air of talcum-powdered superiority and sybaritic opulence. Cars crawl past in bumper-bumper continuity while parking is such sweet sorrow. Finely furnished store-windows provide a convincing façade to even better within. Restaurants and cafés are as prolific as their dishes are enticing and satisfying. In a few words: Johannesburg is as brightly-modern as any big city in the world but possibly more infected with the malaria of competitive acquisitiveness. Its chief distinction is that its character cannot be aspersed with accusations of the crime of maturity.

Kaleidescopic in appearance, it lives its life well above tempo, nerve-wear considerably exceeding the norm, making psychiatrists work double time to break up break-downs. "It's the altitude" is the everlasting alibi for every departure from normalcy, whether it be high divorce-rate or low production quotas. That alibi is not without considerable truth—in these steamy latitudes, living at 6,000 feet above sea level, it is as if the entire population were, twenty-four hours daily, living in an aeroplane. Unlike the oxygenisation of New York air, such rarefied atmospheric pressures do not promote energy so much as the necessity to restrain energy.

Culturally speaking, Johannesburg is not unduly mentally athletic, its draughts of artistic curiosity contain more water than bonded-spirit. From my own knowledge of the two cities, it does not approach the cultural standards of Kansas City which, in many respects, including approximate age, size and origins is comparable. It requires the joint subsidies of the South African Broadcasting Corporation and the City Corporation to maintain a small-town symphony orchestra. Theatre life was strangled by the mass-cinema combine years ago and is only kept breathing by the valiant efforts of semi-professionals most of whose last performances are too near

Full-length portrait of Johannesburg—mines in the foreground, the gold-dump heaps and the city beyond.

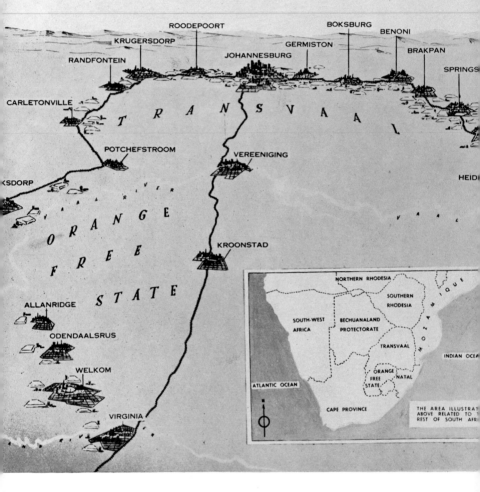

ROODEPOORT
BOKSBURG
BENONI
KRUGERSDORP
GERMISTON
BRAKPAN
JOHANNESBURG
RANDFONTEIN
SPRINGS
CARLETONVILLE
T R A N S V A A L
POTCHEFSTROOM
VEREENIGING
HEID
KSDORP
R I V E R
O R A N G E
F R E E
KROONSTAD
V A A L
S T A T E
ALLANRIDGE
ODENDAALSRUS
WELKOM
VIRGINIA

NORTHERN RHODESIA
SOUTHERN RHODESIA
SOUTH-WEST AFRICA
BECHUANALAND PROTECTORATE
TRANSVAAL
INDIAN OCEA
ATLANTIC OCEAN
ORANGE FREE STATE
NATAL
CAPE PROVINCE
THE AREA ILLUSTRAT
ABOVE RELATED TO
REST OF SOUTH AFRI

This shows the roughly circular layout of the present gold-mining reef running from the four Free State towns on the right to Heidelberg—the end of "the Johannesburg influence"— with the Golden City in the centre.

opening night to be a financial success. When "the Opera Season" makes an occasional break-through, the story is different: the theatre is sold out nightly—demand for seats is heavy from the *haut monde* of Houghton for whom the opportunity to display their closeted fur-wraps is too valuable to miss: the theatre is redolent of gardenias and moth-balls.

It is not a city that is pleasant to the eyes. Its skyline is a design of towering buildings over-towered by the gold-mine dumps that ring the city. The main streets in the heart of the city are narrow and their buildings high so that, although Johannesburg's average of sunshine is nearly nine hours a day throughout the year, only the centre of the streets is sunlit: the tall buildings throw the porticoed sidewalks into merciful shade. There is little, if any, beauty in the city-centre where a half-acre garden in front of the very fine Public Library is the only oasis in a desert area of shops, offices and ticker-taped brokers' premises. I was officially informed that there are 154 parks and open spaces in Johannesburg, but in that case providing them is less an achievement than hiding them.

Being a parasitic city—its main occupation that of the entrepreneur, not of the producer—Johannesburg is necessarily a centre of commercial and financial activity. In that respect we come to no mean city. It is the throbbing heart of South Africa's business world and it is highly improbable that more than a dozen cities in the world show a greater through-put of traded money every day of its five-day week. And money, anywhere, talks—in all languages, even if at times with a deplorable accent.

Known as "the City of Gold", and being the capital city of South Africa's gold-producing world, Johannesburg has, with wise forethought, put other nuggets in its basket. If the reef around the city ran dry of gold, while that would shake the Stock Exchange, it would not mean the end of Johannesburg because the city's industrial and commercial development is so extensive and firmly-based—and so rich in potential expansion—that the local economy could well withstand a shock that would quiver the foundations of the Stock Exchange.

That is Johannesburg's greater achievement. Founded on gold, it is not dependent on gold. In and around the city has developed a far-ranging complex of industrial and commercial enterprises which have made Johannesburg the fourth capital city of South Africa—the business capital; Cape Town is the legislative capital, Pretoria the administrative capital and Bloemfontein the judiciary capital. It is also the centre of an area with the greatest concentration of population in the entire country—more than one-third of South Africa's population live within that area.

And, therefore, despite all the evidences of superficiality and artificiality, Johannesburg is a city of substance. With each passing year it becomes the centre of gravity for an increasing sector of the national economy. It is growing rapidly, growing up rapidly and growing out of its past rapidly. Garish and crude and raucous and brash as it may be, those defects are being eliminated by a people made conscious of the challenge to maturity, the urgent necessity to "put away childish things" and, having attained adulthood, to accept the implicit responsibilities. Johannesburg gives a detached observer the positive impression that its past, which has been short but great, can be replaced with a future, greater and longer.

THERE should be a law prohibiting entry to South Africa via Johannesburg to anyone undergoing initiation to the country—newcomers can gain such a completely false idea; and even with visitors of frequency it is a very wise procedure to get away from Johannesburg and see South Africa: modest, productive, amiable; the sturdy foundation of integrity which is the hallmark of the nation.

It is a day's run to Durban if a dawn start is made. And that is not a bad time to see the gold-dumps—especially to see the last of them. As the first streaks of dawn candle the velvety blackness of the sky, and the sun reluctantly climbs out of its horizon-bed, the soft luminosity of a new day reveals those mounds of yellow sand to be golden mounts of glory, worthy of a better cause, when the road skirts the three Busy Bees— the mining towns of Boksburg, Brakpan and Benoni—at the eastern end of the gold-bearing reef. Some geologists claim that the reef is the rim of a huge subterranean basin. It is circular in layout and the workings so far form two-thirds of a circle with the "three Busy Bees" at one end and the Free State Goldfields at the other.

Whether the gap will ever be worked—whether it is the vault of treasure, buried by hoarding Nature millions of years ago—and the circle completed no one has ever been able to assure me. Stories that are legends or rumours, there are a-plenty. One is that the geologists of the Ministry of Mines have mapped out the entire range of South Africa's underground, so that the whole extent of the gold-potential is known but its mining is being carefully controlled so as not to create a gold-glut that would cause an embolism in the world price-structure. It is a thought-stimulating hypothesis that, if too much gold was unloaded on the market, it would become as valuable as peanuts and the world have to find an alternative, such as going on the soya-bean standard.

As the road unreels itself, Heidelburg is reached—a quiet

town whose narrow little streets are rubbing the sleep out of their eyes in a silence that crackles like celery when the alarm-clock call of the rising sun breaks it. Heidelburg marks the end of the Johannesburg influence. While the "three Busy Bees" and their neighbour, the highly-industrialised Germiston, have caught the razzamadazzing infection of the Golden City, with its strident gaiety and juke-box argot, Heidelburg has nailed the flag of Transvaal tranquillity to its weather-beaten, age-bitten mast and shows not the slightest intention of either lowering it or going down with it.

Another town with equal fidelity is the next—Standerton, nearly a hundred miles along the road. Standerton is not content with defying the supremacy of Joburgism—it has acquired the best of its features and integrated them, subordinately, into its own unalterable way of life. Essentials of true South Africanism remain dominant while the desirables of modernity have been absorbed. It is the natural centre of some of the nation's richest farmland and has produced some of its finest cattle, sheep and racehorses. From its fertile fields come huge quantities of maize, beans, sunflower and teff grass every year, and most of the milk that—among more popular liquids—Johannesburg drinks was, originally, Standerton meadow grass.

While retaining its rural virtues, it has been developing industrially and several factories have been established. One is a large French-owned cotton mill; another, a big textile plant; another, a huge milk-processing establishment; another, a meat cannery; another, a factory producing rayon and cotton suit-linings. All this in the last ten years so that the rateable value of property has risen from £500,000 to £6 million and the town's income trebled. Standerton adds another gay patch to the quilt of South Africa's development.

Fifty miles onwards to the next town—Volksrust, which marks the Transvaal-Free State border and best-known to touring motorists, who make the early-morning getaway from Johannesburg, as the town with a fine garage with outdoor café where no meal in all the wide, wide world is as enjoyable as ham-and-eggs, *al fresco*, in the warmth of the well-risen sun. Volksrust is predominantly Afrikaner—it is the only place in South Africa where, when I asked a shopkeeper for some goods in English, he allowed me to go out, with my money in my pocket, rather than relent and reply in the language which he knew but refused to allow on his tongue.

Breakfast enjoyed, on to Newcastle, thirty miles away. Like its English namesake, it is a coal-mining town. Ill-informed persons overseas think of gold and diamonds as the key products of South African mining, but coal is also a very extensively mined mineral. Because of the low cost of production—compared to European countries—coal is very cheap in South Africa; hence the cheap electric-power supplies which contribute so mightily to the enviable national economy. Newcastle is a considerable source of coal-supply.

Had it footwear, the car would be taking off its shoes for it is running through sacred ground—an area sanctified by the sublimation of the cold logic of duty into the quintessence of heroism with which the names of Majuba Hill, Colenso and Ladysmith will be forever identified. History unrolls like a ribbon under the car's spinning wheels. This was the battle-ground for a nation's freedom—the victory of Majuba Hill, the success at Colenso and the siege of Ladysmith are emblazoned on South Africa's imperishable battleflags.

Ladysmith could be the *Old Lady Who Shows Her Medals* if she were not too concerned about the present and the future to concentrate—as do far too many South Africans, especially politicians—on the past. A sharp right-hand turn of the road discovers Ladysmith as a hustling, bustling centre of commerce, its main street as restless and agile as the antennae of an insect. Under the impact of this scene of modernised activity and enterprise, it is difficult to appreciate the crucial Anglo-Boer war background behind its almost ostentatious air of debonair optimism. Responding to the upsurge of productive life which is the renaissance of a nation, Ladysmith is now an eloquent testimony to the complete recovery of South Africa from the sickness of war.

This condition of resurgence is, also, seen a few miles further on when the road slices into the Mooi River-Nottingham Road district, an area of agricultural modernisation. On either side, rich loamy land undulates over an immense mileage; mahogany soil and lush pasturage. Here are some of South Africa's finest experimental farms, masterpieces of agricultural artistry and not by any means worked by "stoep-farming". Here in a world untroubled and untrammelled by the tumult of population, Sir George Usher, a distinguished Englishman with an unquenchable faith in South Africa's prospering destiny, has engaged in the breeding of the highest-prized of high-prize cattle in a restless pursuit of perfection. Fifty miles of road dissect hundreds of square miles that can be regarded as a huge model farm for what, by employing the same modern methods, the whole of South African agronomy is capable of becoming.

As it nears Durban the road skirts Pinetown which, ten years ago, considered its function to be that of providing upper-bracket residences for top Durban executives. It is still that but, as there is little municipal revenue derived from being a de-luxe dormitory, an enterprising Town Council in its enjoyment of municipal eupepsia decided to swing Pinetown into the main current of South Africa's expansionism. It is now a commercial and industrial centre of wealth and activity, in tune most harmoniously with the keynote of development which is resounding throughout almost every part of the country.

This fine national road, with its fly-overs and scientifically-cambered curves and double carriageways, drops down from Pietermaritzburg to Durban through sumptuous residential areas and carnival-hued flower gardens, with the incomparable Valley of a Thousand Hills on the left, until it opens into an entrancing view of the Indian Ocean into which the city of Durban can be seen dappling its toes.

DURBAN is no more like Johannesburg than is Cape Town but has managed to absorb some of the qualities—and defects —of both into its make-up. It ranks, in terms of population, third to those two cities but its people are unlike either, as their source of subsistence differs. It is, like Cape Town, a dockside town and, like Johannesburg, a manufacturing centre. Where it is superior to industrial Johannesburg is that its ever-expanding catalogue of industries has its imported raw materials delivered to the door. Where it excels over Cape Town is that it has deliberately converted its sea-front into a huge holiday resort.

At some time in the fairly recent past the City Corporation had to make what the late John Foster Dulles would have described as an agonising re-appraisal. They had to define a settled municipal policy by answering the question: "Shall it be a holiday resort or an industrial town?" It cannot be both, said the prejudiced advocates of one or the other. "You must gear-up the city's life to cater for visitors," recommended one. "Forget visitors and industrialise the economy," countered the other. With great courage—generally admitted—and great wisdom—generally doubted—the City Fathers decided

to do both. They have achieved a notable success: a polarisation
of industrial and holiday resort amenities.

More than a million visitors from all over Southern Africa—
and even from Northern Rhodesia and Kenya—spend a few
weeks and a total of fifty million pounds in Durban each year.
While winter in Cape Town can often be an ordeal—even
then, not so blusteringly cold as its wide-spread reputation
declares it to be; a reputation that is sufficient to dampen
enthusiasm even if the weather is not—Durban has a slightly
better reputation. As the municipal authorities have pro-
longed the holiday-making amenities over the full twelve
months, while Cape Town hauls the flag down with the
Parliamentary exodus, Durban has sold itself as "the seaside
resort with an all-the-year season". Durban's enterprise and Cape
Town's defeatism make a vivid comparison. So do the results.

While the lights go out in Cape Town when its six-month
Parliamentary season ends, Durban remains one huge spirit-
lilting kaleidoscope of colour, vivacity and brightness. Its
beach road is illuminated by an enormous chandelier of inter-
twining chains of multi-coloured lights suspended from lofty
pylons of neon which march in step for miles along the
waterfront. Although its bathing beaches are small in size if
not in number, they are flanked with immense public gardens
which include wind-resistant resting alcoves, children's
pools and playgrounds, fairgrounds, tea-gardens and entertain-
ments, to say nothing of one of the finest snake-pits in the world.

Durban scores over Cape Town by making a cardinal policy
of the principle of going out of its way to cater for visitors.
Capetonians look on visitors—and act as if they do—as a
bunch of poor relatives whose inconvenient arrival must be
made the best of with resignation but the cheering knowledge
that their stay will not be for long. Visitors to Durban are

made to feel, from their very arrival, that the city's sole object
in life is to make them welcome, make their stay enjoyable and
make them realise that it has been too short. Zulu boys shriek
with apparently sincere, but probably phoney, enjoyment as
they bounce up in mid-air while taking a visitor on a ricksha-
ride. The staffs of hotels, stores and cafés wear an enamelled
expression of undiluted—but, no doubt, studiously simulated
—pleasure as they gratify even a visitor's most inconsiderate
requests. Policemen, bus conductors, and even—pause here
for exclamatory astonishment—traffic-cops act towards visitors
as if pleasing them was the sole purpose for their official creation.

All this has been good for Durban's economic health; it
has been equally beneficial to the character of the citizens.
This annual invasion of a million people from a thousand other
centres has eroded the surface of Durbanites' psychological
insularity. If it had not, the typical Durban citizen would
have been insufferable. Any group of average citizens has a
terrifying effect on the detached observer when he visualises
what it would have been, unleavened by the mental attitudes
of a million incursionists each year.

If there were any doubt that South Africa consists of four
"countries" with four distinctive types of citizenry, Durban
would shatter it completely. As in each of the other three
provincial centres, so the character of the people of Durban
is the product of their history. Named after Sir Benjamin
D'Urban, it has always been an "English" town—while the
proportion of Afrikaans-speaking to English in the Cape and
the Transvaal is 100 : 48 (in the Free State, Afrikaans is
predominant) it is 100 : 16 in Durban.

Quite a considerable portion of the population is made up
of this-generation immigrants. Many of them are "remittance
men" in one form or another. A notable percentage is

composed of—their own description for themselves—"British Loyalists" who persuaded themselves that they could demonstrate their loyalty to Britain in no more convincing manner than to export themselves, and their capital, away from Britain and so avoid the embarrassment (accepted by the forty-nine million, not self-described as "Loyal", who remained) of contributing to Britain's welfare by paying tax on the wealth with which that country had provided them.

To sit, as I have so often had to do, in hotel lounges, cafés and tea-rooms, unable to avoid eavesdropping on the babble of insipidities which passes for conversation among the "Durban Dowagers", the wistfully troglodyte ladies from some antimacassared era indulging in an orgy of resurrected sentiment, is an experience in past-peeping that cannot be excelled either for amazement or resentment. From the aviary-chatter emerges unbridled condemnation like canary-snarls of the country in which they are guests and noxious nostalgia for the country from which they have escaped with the loot. They are more English than the Queen, although they, in fact, belong to nothing more specific than the human race.

"I wonder what the dear Princess will wear at Ascot," is a typical specimen from a Dowager weighted down with necklaces of decidedly semi-precious stones—the nicely-corsetted accents made the question sound like words in a comic-strip cartoon, and as emptily provocative of intelligent reply. Mental processes, such as the "Durban Dowagers" are subject to, have created a psychological climate that, while it can become oppressive, is not pervasive enough to be unduly effective. The dear old dears are probably only reacting to the effort of carrying the "White Woman's Burden"—maladjustment. It is not that they are unable to adjust themselves to the South African way of life: with a quaintly-demoded air of supercilious antiquity, they just refuse to. As they are representative of a segment of the Durban population, they contribute significantly to the spiritual isolation from the rest of South Africa which gives Natal the reputation of being a persistent performer of the role of "odd man out".

Durban nurses the quaint illusion that it is Natal—it is not even the capital—and has persuaded itself that what it says, Natal is thinking. This has given Natal a reputation for isolation from the mainstream of South African thought. When all the rest of South Africa bows to the educational policy laid down by Parliament—even if the rest of South Africa did not agree with it—Natal defied it in favour of its own parochial choice and only submitted after the national authorities took law-defying Natal to court. This rebel-attitude is a matter of prejudice rather than principle because the principle involved was the Parliamentary institution, based on the democratic theory of the minority loyally abiding by—although disagreeing with—the decisions of the majority.

Without a breach of my undertaking with myself to avoid political issues in this piece of writing and employing it only as an illustration of Durban's instinctive recalcitrance with anything it disagrees with, it can be reported as recorded fact that the "British Loyalists" have frequently opposed Parliamentary decisions with a threat of secession. This threat can be reliably expected if the impending referendum produced a majority in favour of South Africa ceasing to be a monarchy. Undue importance should not be placed, overseas, on these adolescent fits of the sulks. They are merely the outbreaks of temper often seen when children cannot get their own way. Their effect on the stability and economic strength of South Africa are as substantial as trying to pat smoke into shape.

Adult-minded Natalians do not talk of "seceding" because

either the "independent" Natal would have to finance, educate, defend and generally welfare itself or it would "secede" to somewhere else. To where? It would be like the county of Wiltshire or the state of Idaho seceding. I interpolate this part of the description of Durban solely to inform overseas minds of the inconsequence of childish braggadocio and the ability, stability, of South Africa in face of it.

Another characteristic of Durban people is their organic inertia. This is not a product of their history but of their climate. What "the altitude" is to Johannesburg the humidity is to Durban—Johannesburg's rarefied atmosphere energises; Durban's humidity enervates. For much of the year, the people of Durban have to live and work in a sticky, muggy, stifling atmosphere; vital, sultry, intense, with a suggestion of the crackle of electricity which neither fans nor sport attire can sufficiently alleviate. It can become physically debilitating so that it is almost inescapably easy to assume an attitude of neck-sagging listlessness and acquire a hedonistic urge to indolence.

Durban people tend to become *mañana*-minded—"tomorrow" is always their busy day. Under the atmospheric pressures of humidity, the foot-pounds of energy get cut down so that the effective work-hours curve well below those of any other province on the labour graph. If some scientist were to devise a method of "humidity-control", the per-man-hour rate would shoot the mercury out of the top of Durban's productivity thermometer.

Not that production is a Durban problem apparently. In and around the city, the Corporation's policy of encouraging industrialisation has been one of the most notable testimonies

to South Africa's phenomenal expansion. Hundreds of new
and flourishing industrial establishments are taking advantage
of Durban's undoubted facilities. While the range of industries
shows a catholic taste—capable of producing anything from
generators to cups for flying-saucers—there are one or two
industrial concentrations which make Durban distinctive. For
very good reason, the paint industry is focused in Durban,
while the food-processing industry has had its roots in the city
for some years. Perhaps the biggest capital turnover and
output is made by the sugar industry.

In its 110 years of existence the Natal sugar industry has
expanded steadily until now it produces more than a million
tons every season. Wide rolling plantations of sugar-cane
cover much of Natal's eastern seaboard from 90 miles south
of Durban to 170 miles north and swathing well into the
interior. Although, with the exception of 60 miles between
the Umgeni and Tugela rivers, it does not form a continuous
strip, the area is known as "the sugar belt" and comprises a
cultivated area of 800,000 acres, in some parts traversed by
deep ravines, the courseways of rivers and streams.

It is usual to reap three or more crops from each planting
and as between eight and nine tons of cane are required to
produce one ton of sugar, the production of last year's
1,128,187 tons is a reflection of the vast area under cane.
Because of the nature of the terrain much of the work has
to be done by hand, necessitating a large labour force. This
has produced one of South Africa's human problems.

Nearly a century ago this labour-demand was outbid by the
gold-mines and Bantu from adjoining Zululand were attracted
to the Transvaal, leaving the Natal sugar-plantations seriously
undermanned. As the sugar planters could only make the
kind of profits they desired by keeping production costs low,

cheap labour was imperative. The same problem faced the Rand gold-mines and was temporarily solved there by importing Chinese labourers. Natal went to India for sugar-plantation workers and a very considerable number of Indian labourers was brought in under indenture.

Unlike the Rand, where the gold-masters repatriated their coolie-labour on the fulfilment of their indentured period, the Indians in Natal remained. For many years they have been thorny in South Africa's flesh and for more than one reason. They have remained a cohesive group which the Natalians have not assimilated and which the Bantu have rejected. They have thrown up a social classification marked by internal legal squabbles (to serve the searchers for legal assistance, a young lawyer came from India to settle among them; he became a notorious stormy petrel: his name was Mahatma Gandhi) and contrasting wealth and poverty. They have resolutely refused repatriation and, as they are in the non-White category, have come under the Colour legislation of this Government and its predecessors.

Durban has become, in fact and despite its ultra-English prejudices, a city of a three-race population, with the Whites in a serious minority. Roughly speaking, only one-third of the population is White, one-third is Indian and one-third Bantu, so that it can sustain the description of an Indian bazaar with a Native location and a White colony. To complicate the complicated: whereas practically all the Bantu are relatively poverty-stricken, living in slum areas of squalor beyond the limits of undisturbed contemplation, there are many very wealthy Indians whose houses and estates are superior to those of the majority of White citizens.

Indians and Bantu practise apartheid religiously—literally. They never mix. Like trees in a forest that cast the same shade but whose roots never come close together, Indians and

Bantu separate themselves from each other by religious, social and residential segregation. They are alike in one formidable respect: a profound sense of resentment. Indians go about their prosperous business, fuming with deep-burning animosities; the Bantu crouch in their wretched shacks, growling out their armageddon grievances. If both have a common object, it is expressed in an uncommon way: fights between the two are far from rare.

It is the Indians as much as the Bantu who invest Durban's insoluble problem with overtones of eruptive violence. They are not only a fervidly emotional people but of explosive fecundity. Among them, as among the Bantu, there is a dead-level of poverty—seventy per cent exist well below the poverty-line—and a very clearly defined class-structure. Unlike the Bantu who hive off in herdlike concentrations, the Indians are full of social mobility. Some of them are extremely wealthy traders and a wedding among the crust of Indian society usually takes place in the huge City Hall with squads of police directing hundreds of limousined Indian guests. It is the knowledge of social superiority that adds to their sense of frustration and isolation from the other population groups.

All these racial factors produce, in Durban, a subconscious, if suppressed, state of fear as if living on the tip-toe of dread, which the repeated rioting of the Bantu, when law-enforcement officers attempt to prevent illegal activities—such as Cato Manor riots—only accentuates. It is recorded fact that all the Colour outbreaks in and around Durban have been either introvert—faction fights between Bantu tribes when the blood is churned to froth in their heads, or racial fights between Indians and Bantu—or lawlessness: revolts against the laws of the land. As most of the law-enforcement officers are White, the lawless outbreaks have been wholly misconstrued, overseas, as Black-versus-White rioting—although Bantu policemen have been assaulted or killed as well. There has never been any semblance of a rising of Black people against White people, as such, in Durban or any other part of the country. It is this revolt of Coloured races against those laws of the country that do not suit them—the normal reaction of lawbreakers in all countries—that bedevils Durban and the entire country.

Apart from that, Durban is delectable. It has all that any city could desire—much more than most have: sparkling sea, high sunshine-rate, well-designed street geography, flourishing industries, prosperous commerce and every possible favourable condition for enormous expansion. As a harbour it is vastly superior to Cape Town and, being the harbour separated from Johannesburg by the shortest rail-route, its convenience for seaborne traffic is beyond all comparison. While it is possible for Cape Town to enjoy the vicarious thrill of glorying in its glorious past, Durban has its faith-sparkled eyes firmly fixed on its rapidly-approaching future.

DURBAN stands at one end of a fine macadamised road, more than 1,000 miles long, which ends at Cape Town, the apex of South Africa's triangular stage. Only fairly approximately does this run with the coast, the first half of the distance taking in the Transkei Territories in a south-westerly direction to Port Elizabeth, the mid-way point. From there the road goes due west to Cape Town, the whole car journey only needing to occupy two days.

When towns bearing such names as Ixopo and Umtata are reached, the road is passing through the Transkei, which is almost exclusively Bantu territory. Once the stronghold of Bantu warriors, this extensive area is now the site on which a great experiment in Bantu self-government is being conducted. For that reason the Transkei is a highly significant element in South Africa's future. All the circumstances are most favourable—which is to be appreciated because if the experiment were to fail there, Bantu self-government throughout South Africa might suffer postponement or modification. There are no signs of such failure and as I write news comes in that, because of the results already secured, the second of such self-governing Bantu National Homes—the Ciskei—is to be founded this year.

About half the size of the Province of Natal, the Transkei, which is in the Cape Province, has a Bantu population approaching the two-million mark who live, in what has been a huge Bantu reserve, an almost entirely self-contained life in their traditional tribal style. Many of them are "blanket-Natives", so called because their main, if not sole, covering is a large blanket, dyed in remarkable primary colours by age-old methods known only to them. Their chief source of subsistence is by farming and as the Transkeian Territories form one of the best parts of undeveloped South Africa, a vast panoramic revelation of lushly-fertile and exceptionally well-watered land, their agronomy should be exceedingly prosperous. That it is not is due to past agricultural inefficiency which has caused wide-spread soil-erosion scarring the land with huge billiard-bald patches into a melancholy mosaic; and the fact that the male population is recruited to the mines.

Bantu in the Transkei have held their lands, untouched by the rapacities of man, on the communal principle in most of the districts. While the Bantu may give the appearance of being indolent, that is a deception: they are merely patient, believing, with Kafka, that impatience is a form of laziness. Outside of the Townships it has not been permissible for a Bantu to hold title to more than one allotment of land and that has suited the Bantu temperament which has never equated happiness with possessions. Alienation of land to Europeans has been prohibited in order to ensure that the Transkei should always be Bantu property. More than 4,500 miles of roads network the Territories which are frontiered by mountains whose cinematic sunsets are the only time-clock to give the Bantu labourers their knock-off signal. The internal control of all Bantu affairs was transferred, last year, from Europeans to the Bantu.

As the road unwinds itself, bringing East London nearer, it traverses 300 miles of terrain that is a pattern of grandeur, desolation, verdant fertility, backwoods dorps and occasional small towns. This is, to a very marked extent, undeveloped or under-developed territory—rich in potentialities; part of the South Africa with the beckoning finger.

When the Dutch East India ship *Stavenisse* was wrecked off the coast 260 years ago, 70 miles from where Durban was to begin, a party of 47 castaways struggled to shore with the intention of walking to Cape Town and unknowingly inscribed East London on the map for the first time. It assumed importance, later, as a port to supply the early British garrisons whose soldiers were bitterly engaged in Border fights with the Bantu.

Despite its lengthy past, it is the future that invests East London with a growing value. Based on the Buffalo River, with the Indian Ocean at its front door, East London has been beneficed by Nature as a natural port. Passenger ships from overseas can enter the harbour and proceed up the river to tie-up on the east bank which is now a busy dockland. Once through the dock-gates all signs of a port disappear—the tarred road winds through avenues of Kaffirboom trees and other natural vegetation into a handsome residential district until the heart of the city is reached.

It is a quiet city. Too quiet, some think. I found it a city with a seven-Sunday week—a delightful contrast to Johannesburg and Durban whose metropolitan turmoil has a 365-day year. Quietly sedate as East London is, normally content to live within the area of its own competence, it disrupts the atmosphere of calm jog-trottery during its Carnival Time when the city goes all Mardi Gras with gaiety, noise and jollity.

It is a small city. Ranking only eleventh place in South Africa's distribution of population, it has fewer than 110,000 people of whom more than half are non-White. It is a growing city. When it was first constituted a municipality its property valuation was £22,220 while today it is well over £30 million. At first it might have been in danger of being shouldered into oblivion by Durban and Port Elizabeth, the harbour-towns to north and south, but a progressive Council was determined that East London should become part of the evolutionary development that is sweeping the entire country.

Divided by the Buffalo River, the town itself is mainly on the west bank with docks on the other side, while spread out behind each are large areas that simply shriek for development. East London is now in creative throes: trembling with conceptive agony and cognitive activity. Already a large number of industrial establishments, from sweet-factories to car-assembly plants, are taking advantage of the very favourable method of municipal rating, the low land-valuation, cheap electrical power, ample water supplies, labour resources and sea-land-air transport facilities to blaze the trail of East London's wide-scale industrialisation. Again, the beckoning finger of South Africa is unmistakable.

Less than 200 miles from East London is Port Elizabeth, similar in some respects if larger, and with a more obvious air of get-up-and-go. Port Elizabeth, like Durban and East

London, presents a combination of harbour, industries and holiday resort. It possesses all the required advantages for each. Much less than 150 years ago it consisted of a fort and a settlement of 35 European civilians but the coming of "the 1820 settlers"—5,000 British immigrants—gave the settlement its impetus and its name. With a quarter-million population, of which two-thirds are non-White, and an advantageous geographical position, Port Elizabeth has now a fine harbour capable of providing anchorage to the biggest vessels afloat, excellent cargo-handling facilities including ample cold-storage, and is the hub of road, rail and air transport that radiates throughout all Southern Africa in all directions.

Industrially, the city has outstripped Cape Town and Durban with only the Rand as its superior. It shares the honour of being South Africa's motor-car centre with its next-door neighbour, Uitenhage, which is as near to Port Elizabeth as Johannesburg's airport is to that city, industry giving the basic throb to the umbilical cord. Such famous car factories as *Studebaker*, *Ford*, *Volkswagen* and *General Motors* are located in the area from which most of the million registered cars on South African roads have come.

War was the humus from which Port Elizabeth's industrialisation grew. Whatever it was that Napoleon's army marched on, South African realism could not evade the self-evident fact, during the First World War, that every army marches on its feet. To equip those marching feet, footwear was required—and Port Elizabeth's first big industry was established. The boots and shoes that have been manufactured in Port Elizabeth factories, if laid end to end, could chart the route for the next Russian satellite.

Reading the unmistakable indications of the numerous advantages that Port Elizabeth holds for industrialisation, the

Ford assembly plant was erected immediately after the First World War and *General Motors* followed five years later. These huge plants, covering a very large total acreage, attracted auxiliary industries until Port Elizabeth has proliferated, industrially, faster than any other city in the Union during the past ten years. Parenthetically, it might be noted that the past ten years crops up like a recurring decimal in this report on South Africa—it has been both the period of most sensational political change and of most phenomenal national development.

Those overseas who cherish misconceptions of South Africa as ''a backward country'' can best get an idea of Port Elizabeth —which is only the fifth largest city—if I say that Birmingham has an area only half its size. Another idea can be gained—a conception of its facilities for expansion—when I add that the area occupied by Birmingham provides living space for more than five times as many people as comprise Port Elizabeth's population. Port Elizabeth has ample room for its inevitable expansion—and equally ample facilities to make it possible.

Fully alerted to the demands of the future, the City Council purchased 18,000 acres to the south of the city, 7,000 to the north and 8,900 in Zwartkop Valley. All of these industrial estates are being provided with full municipal services and railway facilities. This is not an expression of fatuous optimism; it is a realistic assessment of an approaching certainty—it is as inevitable as the compass needle turning to the north, that those 33,900 acres, seven miles from the City Hall, astride two national road routes and immediately adjacent to the principle railway marshalling yards, will be a hive of industrial activity before five more years have passed. They form part of South Africa's beckoning finger.

Port Elizabeth is the halfway house on the Durban–Cape Town road that is the third leg in the triangle which forms the stage for the dramatic presentation of South Africa's past, present and future. The remaining 500-odd miles of road, unreeling with the coastline, traverses an area as rich in historic associations as it is in future potentialities. It ranges through the rich agricultural territory in which youthful Humansdorp has been the market town for nearly a century. It passes Knysna which has been the centre of the timber industry for as many years as some of the ancient giants in its nearby Tzizikama forest have been standing in deep-rooted imperturbability. Knysna has sheltered celebrities, from the son of George III to that other George—Bernard Shaw—for 150 years.

Standing between two great cliffs, on the bank of a narrow estuary into which the river flows at one end to be embosomed by the sea at the other, Knysna is poised in a tranquil calmcentre of the storm of cities around it. Johannesburg seems as glitteringly remote as Sirius and as undesirably crazy as an unbalanced solar system. Reciprocatingly, it is possible that the Golden City might regard Knysna as sleepwalking-by, whereas the truth is that it is going about what Sir Winston Churchill would call its lawful occasions, in an unerringly deft manner. Fishing and furniture-making are carried on, cheek by jowl, with beautiful topsy-turvy appositeness—and high profitability. If more is required for the enjoyment of life, the people of Knysna would prefer the bliss of ignorance in this intrinsically desirable postcard-still town.

When the road leaves Knysna it proceeds to George, the garden city of the Garden Route—a delightfully somnolent town of wide, oak-lined streets, half-acre gardens, luxuriating flowers and such an English-village appearance that Shakespeare could have used it for a sonnet. George, the seat of the Anglican church diocese, its cathedral stately in freezing grandeur, is as English as its name. It is, also, as stuff-shirted.

There is an air of random scholarship to George, probably left behind by the dons and students from nearby Grahamstown, home of Rhodes University among other educational establishments, with a class-room population of nearly 3,000 young men and women. Obviously enjoying the successive instants of present contentment, neither the people of George, nor George itself, are entangled in the meshes of competitive modernity, but come and go to placid John Masefield rhythms. It is a town of quiet dignity and beautiful homes which are, externally, suggestive of violins in a panelled room—a town of inner coherence; of spirit, gracious.

Englishism is woven into the fibre of the town's entire character. Even industrially, George has brought its main occupation from England—hop-growing. Imported from Kent more than a century ago, the art has become well-established on a highly commercial basis and extensive gardens flourish under ideal conditions. More than 230 acres covered with 15-foot vines yield an average of 1,000 lb. per acre which, I was assured, is more than the breweries in the entire country require. This statement lends colour to the colourless beer.

Mossel Bay is less than forty miles on and is South Africa's oldest community because it was there that Bartholomew Diaz landed at just about the time Christopher Columbus was persuading his Queen to finance an America-discovery trip. Diaz left his mail in a tree which was the recognised "post office" for passing ships and the tree still stands on a hill overlooking the little fishing town which gets its name from the large number of mussels found there.

Mossel Bay, crouching by ancient seaways, couchant but not dormant, would have been content to perform its function as a popular seaside resort and anglers' paradise but its useful port facilities proved too valuable as a business potential.

Small and large commercial concerns have been established, flourish and parade as commercial epics. They are strengthening South Africa's beckoning finger whose invitation has already been accepted by several prospering industries.

This fine national road is back-pedalling through history. It cuts through Swellendam, a dreamy Afrikaner town that can look back over 200 years to when it was once a republic. Its original drostdy—magistrate's court-house—is not only standing but standing usefully: it is a museum of antiquities that tell a tale of historical romance like beads on a breviary. Swellendam is a welcome anachronism in this fast-growing South Africa—it nods amiably at the enticements of modernity, graciously declines to grow up out of its enduring past and sits enthroned in Boer-quietness like Gautama on a lotus of untouchable calm.

In approaching Cape Town, the last stop is Caledon, with its 250-year-old roots and its age-serened eyes looking out over miles of wealth-yielding agricultural land to where the Indian Ocean, 800 feet below, caresses Hermanus, the resort-town with its quaint harbour to which deep-water fishermen drag their boats from the sea and sell their catch on the beach. Caledon with its hot mineral springs whose magic waters—the faithful are convinced—have therapeutic powers for the relief of rheumatics. Caledon with its Wild Flower Reserve, a vast natural park whose confetti carpet of pastel and harlequinaded flora, ranging the entire prismatic spectrum, attract 20,000 visitors every year.

A<small>ND</small> so on another seventy-five miles to Cape Town to complete the triangular stage of the drama of this "unknown country" with the beckoning finger. Those three national

roads, a total of 2,500 miles, form the main outlines of the
South African scene; but not its entirety. Within the triangle
is the hinterland of thousands of square miles—the midlands,
the Karoos, the platteland with their hundreds of towns and
dorps; and the British island of Basutoland surrounded by
South African territory, an anachronism that could only be
equalled if Berkshire belonged to Germany or Ohio to Russia.

Outside the triangle is a total area as large as that contained
within. Most of it is quite under-developed and equally as
promising as any that now comprises South Africa's abounding
prosperity. It includes two important cities, each of which,
in dramatically contrasting ways, is a dominant factor in the
South African drama—Pretoria, the seat of government, and
Kimberley, the diamond centre.

Pretoria was a capital when it was only a hamlet of about
fifty scattered wood-shack dwellings and a thatched-roof
church with zebra and quagga running wild in the streets.
A bushy-whiskered old Boer, when he was not chain-drinking
coffee on the stoep of his tin-roofed home, presided over a
parliament of peasants. A comparison of that with the Pretoria
of today is a graphic indication of how amazingly South Africa
has progressed during the seventy-four years since the discovery of gold turned the key and unlocked an immense
treasure-chest. It is now a city graced with the charm,
dignity and artlessness that it has gained with the years, and
which not all the ferment of war that has yeasted in its blood,
nor all the superficialities of modernity which now lacquer
it with an overlay of efficiency, could destroy or even disguise.

There is a quality to every civil-service city in the world
that stamps it like a coin. Pretoria can be seen in Ottawa or
Canberra or Washington—the mixture of cosmopolitan
suavity, subterranean intrigue and social hypocrisy that belong

to the muchymuchness of diplomacy and their underlings who live with one eye on their filing cabinets and the other on a pension. It is due entirely to the robust common-sense and uncommon sense of values which are Afrikaner virtues that those psychological blemishes which freckle the countenances of most civil-service cities are, in Pretoria, found at the irreducible minimum.

Too much of the puritanism of the Kruger era persists to cause anyone to fear that Pretoria will go the way of all Johannesburg flesh. His statue broods over the city as his spirit moods through its people. The austerity of the Voortrekkers, the strange spirituality of their incomprehensible, cold, cruel Calvinism that provided scriptural justification for unscriptural acts, have left an indelible impress on the Pretorians who proudly memorialise them in their hearts and their city.

This memorial is a giant catafalque kind of edifice, a cuboid of weather-rouged stone, that was erected on a kopje just outside the city to mark the centenary of the great Boer trek. It looms ubiquitously over the city and its citizens, none of whom can escape its memory-jogging shadow. Around it gather, every year, thousands of Afrikaners dressed in Trekker clothes and wearing *veldskoene* (veld shoes); floppy linen bonnets on the women and, on the men, specially grown mangy beards making them look something like Jehovah in his younger and more tolerant days. The monument, which thrusts its squat circumference high towards the clouds, has a central sarcophagus so scientifically constructed that at noon exactly on every December 16th—the anniversary of the covenant sworn by the original Trekkers—a shaft of sunlight falls through an opening in its summit above the insulate walls to the floor, nearly one hundred feet below, where it illumines the engraven words: "We are Thine, South Africa." That note of fanatical dedication is harmonic with all that comprises the religious *fête-champêtre* of nationalism that marks the day so that, every year and through the entire country, that week has two Sundays.

As befits a capital city, Pretoria is the shrine of the country's history. From it Kruger saw the influx, less than forty miles away, of thousands of gold-hungry uitlanders building Goldorado—a local Sodom and Gomorrah—on his doorstep. From it, later, he directed a war that began the crumble-up of the Empire on which the sun, in order to keep it well under surveillance, never set. To it was brought, as captured rebels, Dr. Jameson and other Johannesburg gold-magnates who had made treacherous war on the Government and President to whom all Johannesburg were bound in fealty. In it, also, Winston Churchill was imprisoned for a noble offence—that of reporting the truth to the world. From it, Kruger was to go into exile, hearing the clip-clop of British cavalry, sounding like the hoof-beats of the four apocalyptic horsemen, as they rode to final conquest of a brave people.

Reporting facts as I am, this national emotionalism has to be reported because it is a hard fact; so substantial as to be almost material; of such material as the garment of nationalism is cut from. Legends of the Trekkers who wrote with their lives a deathless footnote to a nation's story have gained potency by repetition, and in the hands of Afrikaner bards have, with the tumultuous years, gathered fresh accretions until they have become interwoven into the warp and woof of a people's thought as inherited lore. As infantilely unrealistic to dismiss all this as impotent mythology as to imagine that there were no tangible effects, in British actions, of Churchillian oratory or, on Americans, of the Gettysburg speech. It is quite true to report that Pretoria—and the entire Afrikaner nation—suffers from the hiccoughs of intermittent emotionalism, but untrue to state that this neurosis

has been sentimentalised down to the wispy dimensions of
impotency: it is the generator of Afrikaner power, to ignore
which is sheer stupidity.

That the existence of Afrikaner power, periodically primed
by emotional apostrophes, may not be relished by many outside
South Africa, and some within, is entirely irrelevant to the
fact that it exists. Pretoria is the shrine of its past inception
and its present generating station. On whether the Afrikaners
are competent to use that power—and to what ends—the
future well-being of South Africa depends; in that, the well-
being of the Commonwealth, if not the whole world, has a
vested interest. The first step towards capitalising that interest
is a sympathetic understanding of all the factors which affect the
investment. Afrikaner emotionalism, Afrikaner nationalism,
Afrikaner power are highly significant factors. That is why
an appreciation of Pretoria can be mightily helpful.

Without shaking off the stardust of a proud past—without
ever desiring to do so—Pretoria has decked itself out in some
of the more demure garments of modernity and attracted
industrial and commercial suitors for her favours. In lay-out,
the city is pleasantly attractive, conforming to the basic east-
west, north-south patterning of streets, practically all of which
are double-lined with jacaranda trees. On a kopje just within the
city limits has been built, of South African-quarried stone, the
handsome Union Buildings; the citadel of the civil service.
There are few grander sights—in fact, none in replica—than,
when standing on the terrace at jacaranda time, to look out towards the Voortrekker Monument on the other side of the city.
Seen from the terraced gardens of all-colour flowers, with their
chromatic scale of fragrance, the city streets form a checker-
board design of blue: the full-blossomed trees and the street sur-
faces coated with their petals as if from a hyacinthined snowfall.

Plumb in the centre of the city is Church Square in which
a magnificent but repellent statue of Kruger stands; grim,
glowering, stern, ungracious—a faithful replica. Its existence
and its position are entirely logical and—illogically—do not
detract from the surrounding beauty and the modernly geo-
metrical layout of the city. It is as if Church Square were
sitting at the very heart of an equation where beauty, and
logic, and analytical geometry become one. In that short
sentence the city is epitomised.

To leave Pretoria for Kimberley is to change spiritual and social
hemispheres. Kimberley and Pretoria are startling contrasts;
they write two contrasting chapters in South Africa's variegated
history. What is dominant in Pretoria is missing in Kimberley.
Instead of charm, crudity; instead of dignity, restlessness;
instead of artlessness, the craft of money-grabbing. Instead of
the beauty of jacaranda—the gloomy ugliness of the Big Hole.
The rise of Kimberley began South Africa's cultural decline.
It changed the face of the country and the soul of the nation.
It was conceived in duplicity, weaned in cupidity and reared
in crudity—from all of which adverse beginnings it has
emerged with far more genuine qualities than its history
portended. Had diamonds never been unearthed ninety years
ago, and the Kimberley diggings not been paraded in the black
limelight of notoriety, there would have been far fewer pages
that ought to be torn out of South Africa's history.
It was when that part of the Orange Free State Republic,
known as Griqualand West, was found to be diamondiferous
that the British High Commissioner in Cape Town arbitrarily
annexed it to the British Crown, an act of such obvious dubiety

that the embittered Free State republican Government, which had been pro-British in sentiment, allied itself with Kruger's anti-British Transvaal republican Government and the alienation of Boer and Briton was consolidated. This provided the malignant soil which sprouted the Jameson insurrection, the Boer War and the antipathies, jaundiced with the bile of racial bitterness, that have lasted into this present period.

Discovery of diamonds in 1870 initiated, for Kimberley, a decade of exploitation which showed capitalism at its worst and its best. Such men as Cecil Rhodes and Ave Bailey dominated the scene and, elementary as their commercial ethics were, they certainly did create an industry and a city. That formative period is part of the lexicon of epic exploits. Those early years of Kimberley could not fail to infect the bloodstream inherited by the city of today. Some very tough citizens laboured in that vineyard three generations ago. Fangs and claws were the order of that day and, in the insensate scramble for the priceless glass chips, there was displayed rather less morality than the warhead of a rocket.

Fortunes were acquired and squandered. Vice in all its forms had religion and culture with their backs to the wall. Valiant attempts by valiant men of better instinct were made to create a civilised community out of a horde given over to the most uncontrollable rapacities of man—and a city emerged. Most of its early foundations were laid by roughneck diamond-grubbers with fingers in many mud-pies who, out of the wealth they had secured by methods which ruthlessly filleted the Ten Commandments, supported religious charities, churches and other beneficial communal activities—a form of philanthrobbery.

Those primitive beginnings have, quite naturally, left their marks on the Kimberley of today—the Big Hole and a brittle, dissonant city of delightfully natural ebullience that repeatedly evidences a throw-back to its origin. I first saw the Big Hole from the air when the Cape Town–Johannesburg airliner very obviously went off-route. Fearing the worst, I enquired of the stewardess. "We have a VIP from America on board and the pilot is showing him the Big Hole," was the delightfully nonchalant explanation, as if when an American tycoon wanted to see "Our 'Ole" it was only proper tha tfifty passengers who knew its every contour by heart should be detoured a hundred miles to oblige him. A month later I was in Kimberley on a story and saw it myself from ground-level, getting a verti-ginous look at the desolate gorge nearly 4,000 feet below, almost to the primal ooze where life had its strange beginning. I hope the American saw it well enough to realise that it could deflate even a Texan's claim to the biggest of everything.

The Hon. Thomas Boydell, a former Cabinet Minister in South Africa, told me that when on a lecture tour of America, and he ran into anyone there who yielded, as an occasional American does, to an infrequent temptation to boast, Tom trotted out the Big Hole as the boast to end all boasts. His stock comment, whenever an American drew his attention to something Kingsize, was: "Yes, yes; quite large, isn't it? Back in South Africa we've got a hole you could drop it in and lose it." Tom cannot remember how many of America's biggest This-and-Thats he hasn't dropped into the Big Hole of Kimberley and lost.

It is the site of the original diamond diggings and after it had yielded twenty million tons of blue soil from which diamonds worth nearly £500,000,000 had been extracted, it had to be abandoned for technical reasons. There can be no questioning its dimensions—one Empire State Building of New York could stand in it, with another Empire State Building on top and there would still be 800 feet of vacant space above them. It is, as another Irishman said, "the biggest hole for its size I've ever seen".

That inverted monument to Kimberley's past achievement would require a himalayan edifice if a monument, in reverse, were to be erected to mark the present and future of the diamond industry. While writing this, I was given the latest annual sales figures—they are a three-in-one record. Last year (1959) gems and industrial diamonds to the value of £91,000,000 were sold which was £15,000,000 more than the previous record year. That combined sale was a South African record—and, for that matter, a world record. It contains two other records: gem-stone sales totalled £63,000,000 against £49,000,000 the previous year and industrial diamonds £28,000,000 which is £12,000,000 more than the previous year. I assume that there was, throughout the world, a corresponding increase in the number of romantic couples. No wonder the geneticists predict that, by A.D. 2000, the world will be over-populated—but on whether Kimberley is the cause or the effect they, who never hesitate to dogmatise, retreat into unfamiliar silence.

Diamonds, gold, agriculture, forestry, industry, commerce —these are the "furniture" for the stage setting of the South African drama. They give sparkle, colour, brightness and background to the dramatic spectacle of a mighty national renaissance. Across the dazzling décor of that scene, the performers move with purposeful stride and eloquent gesture. After all, the most ornately staged scene in the most luxurious theatre is merely a specimen of the stage-designer's art until the cast appears and brings it to life. If, to quote Shakespeare, the world's a stage, then, to paraphrase him, the players in the 300-year drama of South Africa are the people.

Entr'acte

Entr'acte

Scene I—Found and Founding

CHRISTOPHER COLUMBUS and Bartholomew Diaz—in reverse order—sailed from the Iberian Peninsula activated
by the same desire: to find a route to the Indies; not to discover new worlds. Diaz, however, stumbled on a new world
when his ships were blown ashore near what is now Walvis
Bay on the south-west African coast and never suspected that
some of those shore pebbles that his feet kicked were diamonds,
the beginnings of a multi-million fortune that has since been
made. He decided to give South Africa a miss. Five years
later, Columbus, also not finding what they both sought,
decided to settle for the substitute.

South Africa remained the "unknown country" for 165
more years, at the end of which it was the Dutch and not the
Portuguese who commanded the eastern trade route, especially to Java where the newly-established tea-trade was
centred. It was when one of the clippers of the Dutch East
Indies Company, the *Haarlem*, was forced ashore while carrying
tea to Holland, that Table Bay came to naval notice. One of
the officers of the Company who helped rescue the survivors,
a ship's surgeon named Jan van Riebeeck, reported his
observations to his superiors. A year later he was ordered to
investigate what Diaz had charted as "Cabo Tormentoso"—

89

on account of its tempestuous desolation—with a view to establishing a station where the Company's traders could put in for victuals, as a half-way house to the Indies, in rivalry to St. Helena that was already serving that purpose for the British with whom Holland was at war. In that way, a small settlement of officials began at what was renamed "the Cape of Good Hope" and Cape Town began. So also did South Africa, whose birth was connected with tea, just as a century later tea was to be an equally indirect cause of the birth of the United States of America.

Van Riebeeck stepped off the deck of his *Dromedaris* to find awaiting him an expanse of uninhabited grassland running from the shoreline to the foothills of the squatly-flat mountain and a gathering of native people—Hottentots and Bushmen who were, at the beginning of South Africa, the only "natives"; Bantu tribes were more than 1,000 miles away to the north and the east. "European" diseases, especially smallpox, eventually killed off the Hottentots and the Bushmen died out by natural elimination, leaving a remnant who now are carefully preserved by the present South African administration as sub-human curios. And so ended South Africa's only genuine native population.

There was no intention, when van Riebeeck landed, of forming a colony; his orders were merely to establish a station for servicing the Company's vessels by purchasing vegetables, cattle and grain from the natives. When, after a few years, the Hottentots failed to produce enough to satisfy the increasing requirements—or, with the Hottentots acquiring the capacity for rapacity, refusing to meet their profiteering prices—van Riebeeck relieved a few of his officials of their duties, giving them permission to leave the station and settle themselves in the immediate hinterland, create farms and sell him the produce. That was the real beginning of South Africa as a nation in substitution of a purely victualling station.

Those first burghers were Dutch and, as time passed, female Hottentots were found necessary as a counterpoise to the imbalance caused by the scarcity of Dutch women. That was the beginning of the "Cape Coloureds"—half-breeds, South Africa's present-day "tragic people", despised by the Bantu, rejected by the White people.

More immigrants from Holland arrived, and, later still, 300 Huguenots, bringing their grim Calvinist credo with them, found refuge there from French-Catholic oppression after Louis XIV had repealed the Edict of Nantes. Van der Stel, the wise half-breed Governor, recognised the unwisdom of permitting them to effect cohesion as a French colony and deliberately sprinkled them among the Dutch settlers so that natural intermarriage soon resulted in assimilation and a Dutch-French population emerged. Van der Stel rigorously suppressed the French language, and it only persists in the surnames of such Afrikaner families as Du Toit, Du Plessis, De Villiers and others of Gallic-sounding names.

Dutch control of the newfoundland, which lasted 150 years, laid the foundations of a nation. Because of the same geophysical features that limit Cape Town's expansion today —the mountain-sea contiguity—the growing agrarian population were impelled to trek eastwards for essential pasturage, fighting for every morgen they secured. Bushmen's depredations, impenetrable forests, wild beasts—rewards of 25s. for a lion, 16s. 8d. for a hyena and 12s. 6d. for a leopard were paid by the Governor at a time when his own salary was less than £2 a week—were added to the vicissitudes.

As they trekked they civilised. They ploughed barren lands into productive farms such as those at Rondebosch, now an attractive Cape Town residential suburb; they laid out vineyards, such as Constantia, which still produces some of the world's finest wines; they built a hospital to accommodate 750 patients and created small towns such as Stellenbosch, named after the enlightened Governor and whose university has since produced some of South Africa's greatest statesmen; they sent an expedition to the north and discovered the Copper Mountains in Namaqualand where now an American company mines most extensively and profitably.

Envious eyes in Europe were watching this pioneering exploration and success. What began as a Dutch East Indies Company victualling station had expanded into a significant colonising experiment whose potentialities were irresistibly enticing to those who had been too busy building an Empire by other, and less industrious, methods. South Africa's founding-fathers were too actively engaged, from sun-up to sun-down, and too mentally-insulated against external affairs, to give any attention to European covetous envy, ambushed greed and political grabology. They were colonising, civilising, building a contented nomadic community.

For a period of approximately 150 years, the Dutch-French made of that part of South Africa—at first the only populated part—a widely separated group of scattered settlements with a slowly-evolving and clumsily-improvised form of parochial government and skimpy administration. It was pioneering to the ultimate degree. At the centre of authority was the Holland-appointed Governor; magistrates travelled over the districts; towns acknowledged a Chief Burgher and local council. South Africa, the savage, was being tamed; civilisation was on the march through "the unknown country".

And news of this percolated north. Tom-toms must have worked overtime because the untamed savages, north of the

92

Zambesi, heard of the White man's newly-created farms and his sweat-won victories. As civilisation marched upwards from the south, savagery marched down from the north. Civilisation reached 200 miles north towards where Beaufort West now stands and east to Little Fish River, a distance of about 400 miles—over more than 50,000 square miles the Dutch-French pioneers were, without knowing or intending it, beginning to build a nation.

During the second half of that Dutch-French pioneering period of 150 years, these civilising farmers were engaged in no fewer than eight "Kaffir wars" against the invading savages and a continuous frontier fight against the Bantu marauders who were ceaselessly engaged in robbing and murdering the farmers and their families. It was in that harassing situation—wresting a living from a wilderness bleached by the peroxidation of the sun and blasted by the artillery of the wind, introducing civilised life into jungleland, fighting off predatory savages: a saga of unsung epics—that a new people, to be known as the Boers, was evolved.

Scene II—Britannia Waives the Rules

South Africa became a shuttle-cock in a rapid succession of European wars. It repeatedly changed hands among Dutch, French and British belligerents either as a war-trophy or as part of a peace settlement. Although having no legitimate interests in the Dutch colony whatever, the fact that France was at war with Holland appeared ample justification to Britain to surprise Governor Abraham Sluyskens by landing an invasion force near Cape Town and seizing the colony. It may have been that the British considered that, as their piratical Admiral Hawkins in a previous generation had raided

Africa at the north and grabbed the natives to sell to the Spaniards as slaves, they had a pre-empted right to do some more grabbing at the south. That exercise in Empire-building was shortlived—after holding the Cape for seven years the British had to disgorge their gains to Holland, the rightful owner.

Relinquishing the colony, after having perceived its potentialities, was too much for the British and when the Anglo-Dutch war in Europe broke out, ignoring all formal protocol and the rules of that-time warfare, Britain rushed six regiments off to the Cape—which then had no strategical value in a European war—and landed them on Blauberg strand. By force of arms they compelled the peaceful colonists to surrender the fertile lands which they, and their forefathers, had spent 150 years in cultivating. The invaders found a population of 26,700 people of Dutch and French descent, 17,000 Hottentots, several young but growing settlements, a well-equipped trading station and thousands of square miles of lush farmland. Drake and Frobisher had been highly gratified merely to grab an isolated merchantman—the standard which measured the gains of piracy had, like the cost of living, spiralled.

In his *History of the English-speaking Peoples* the caustic comment of Sir Winston Churchill is: "From this acquisition a troubled saga was to unfold."

Conforming strictly to orthodox British procedure, the sword-wielders soon gave place to the Bible-carriers: the London Missionary Society came through. It was far cheaper for Britain, and more satisfying to the conscience of the world, if South Africa were subdued by the Word than by the sword. The missionaries did their duty.

They did it so well that the whole area was soon a turmoil. The two groups of original inhabitants from whom British force of arms had wrested the country—the Dutch-French and the Hottentot-Bushmen—were thrown at each other's throats and the "divide-to-rule" stratagem was seen in its usually effective form. Until then, the two groups had co-existed in perfect harmony, having by natural process devised a mutually-acceptable way to live together. As neither of the two groups had any illusions as to their respective stages of civilisation, the natives found it both agreeable and profitable to be servant to the white-man master. This, the missionaries taught the heathen natives and tried to persuade their Calvinistic masters, was un-Christian, and the natural accept-ance of separate existence was made unnatural at a time when it was both acceptable and normal.

One effect of forcing an unnatural interpretation of Black and White co-existence instead of a time-determining, gradual and progressive policy coincident with the civilising process, was the destruction of the Hottentots—what they gained from the, to them, artificial White man's way of life was the White man's diseases. Smallpox decimated the Hottentot population. As a race they died out without—so far as records show—the White man's prayers on their lips. The arguments in favour of racial separation retained a terrible cogency.

Another effect of the missionaries' proselytising was to give South Africa its present apartheid incubus. Hottentots and Europeans had lived exceedingly well together because each recognised a clear and acceptable dividing line—one was Christian the other pagan. Because the natives were pagan —not merely because they were black—the Europeans regarded them as separated from, and inferior to, them. Hottentots agreeably accepted that separation and inferiority because their heathen minds recognised that the White man's God was greater than theirs. When the missionaries "converted" them, that basic differentiation was removed. Its place was taken by colour—the effect of "Christianising" the natives was to establish the Europeans as a pigmentocracy. From that time it was skin-hue that established separation and superiority—the colour-bar was let down.

Christianising savages can have an effect exactly opposite to the Christian philosophy expounded in the immortal words "Blessed are the meek," and the invading Kaffirs responded to missionary good-intentions with a predatory bloodthirstiness which, by-passing the instigating missionaries, made the Calvinistic colonists the devastated victims of their vulturine attacks. Five years of missionary zeal, expressed in the "Christianisation" of the "noble savage", were quite sufficient to enable the savages to demonstrate their nobility. The first Kaffir War started with the horribly fiendish murder of Lieutenant Stockenstroom and ended with the area between the Fish and Sunday rivers an abattoir-like shambles. It also signalised the birth of the Boer-Kaffir neurosis that has lasted 150 years.

Two-thirds of that time was characterised by frontier-mindedness on the part of the Boers who were compelled by the collision of identical objectives—both they and the infiltrating Bantu were seeking pastures new for their cattle—and the murdering depredations of the black invaders to regard them only as an enemy. Themselves devout Calvinistic Christians, the Boers saw nothing but social calamity in the sudden explosive charge of libertarian Christianity discharged among the natives who, they realised, would best be christianised by gradual, and therefore natural, percolation of their own Calvinistic influence. Properly imbued with the ambition to "Christianise" the heathen Bantu, the missionaries overlooked the fact that ambition can be nothing but indecent haste to arrive at some unavoidable destination—the Boers preferred the slowness of natural evolution.

As the missionaries had the full backing of the British Government, the Dutch-French settlers of a land that had been grabbed from them after they had colonised it included that Government in the comprehensive ambit of their resentments. For a century they waged a war on two fronts—against the ever-encroaching black hordes and against the governing authority which was, the Boers convinced themselves, exciting the natives' bloodthirsty acquisitiveness. Boer antipathy to the British Government was stoked by the latter's ignorance of governing a situation that they had made complicated. Ironed by a smug complacency into glossy mediocrity, the Whitehall pundits acted on the sublime assumption that all they did was right simply because they had done it, as though the Star of Bethlehem had appeared unto them. Even that gifted anglophile, Sheila Patterson, could not, in face of the facts of history, avoid the conclusion that the development of a Boer sense of nationhood was "largely as a result of the alternation of fumbling vacillation and imperialist leap-frog which characterised British colonial policy".[1]

Basic to that policy was the forcible anglicisation of the non-English population in a deliberate plan to stamp out the Dutch-French characteristics. English was made the compulsory language for all civil servants and in the courts. The currency that the colonists had employed for generations was "reformed" and English coinage introduced. Schools and churches were anglicised by monetary penalisation of the existing non-English establishments. Five thousand British settlers were imported and, with their coming, a new judicial

[1] *The Last Trek.*

code imposed that considerably conflicted with that to which the Boers had been accustomed for five generations.

All that forcible super-imposition of the conqueror's system on the established order was accomplished in the first twenty-five years of the British occupation of the Boers' homeland. During the following fifty years, the inevitable resentment of the Boers to their conquerors expressed itself in insurgent unrest or violent protest. Suffering from the claustrophobia of national youth, the Boers organised a "Great Trek" away from the British-controlled south to seek an independent way of life, that accorded with their traditions, in the north and the east where the writ of the British Crown did not run. It led to their defeat of the British at Majuba Hill.

When the Trekkers—like a second exodus of Children of Israel seeking a Promised Land—reached Natal and proclaimed it a Boer republic, a force was landed by the British for the purpose of adding it to their Cape possessions and, ousting the settled Boers, declared it another British colony. Dispossessed of that "Promised Land", the Boers trekked on again and found another in the fertile plains south of the Vaal River where diamonds were discovered; but the British had followed and annexed the Boers' new homeland, diamonds and all. On again went the Trekkers, crossing the Vaal—hence "Transvaal"—still further north where they found their "Promised Land" at last. Gold also was found there and the Anglo-Boer war resulted—the British marched in again.

During the one hundred years of British occupation of South Africa—a land first settled by the Dutch-French and which, as the Trekkers marched east and north, was progressively opened up by the Boers and colonised by them—the ham-handed methods of British "government", including the legislation which froze traditional racial separation into its stereotyped form that Britain now condemns, were accompanied by certain British contributions to the development of the country. London realised that South Africa could be a mighty asset and did not hesitate to invest men, methods and money in exploiting the asset. Had the country, at that time, been left to the Boers, who were unworldly to the point of imbecility, the South Africa of today would be more disastrously under-developed than it is. In the estimation of the Boers, the country was one huge pasturage for cattle—they were purely agrarian people with neither the ambition nor the capacity for urbanisation, much less industrialisation. Their sterling qualities and uncompromising character, if allied in friendly co-operation with the resources and efficiency of the British, could have advanced South Africa to a much further stage than it now is. That friendly co-operation was never permitted to burgeon—it was nipped in the bud by British inability to recognise that essential ingredients to co-operation are equality and respect. Compulsion took the place of co-operation and, made explosive by the radio-activity of greed, found its apotheosis in the deplorable Anglo-Boer war, which was the beginning of the ending of what General Smuts stigmatised as "the century of wrong".

Scene III—*Fifty Years of Sovereignty*

When the victorious British army had trampled the two independent Boer republics of the Orange Free State and the Transvaal into reluctant submission and all Britain was *en fête* over the end of its shameful war, most of that part of South Africa was a shambles. Kitchener, who taught the Russians the "scorched earth" policy, had destroyed the farms and homesteads of a quarter of a million people, turning them into a huge expanse of bleak desolation and creating the black devastation of domestic despair. Looking upon their grim countryside, the Boers saw the blood-dripping head of their only industry stuck on a spike of rusty ruin.

South Africa had become a vast urn containing the ashes of a nation. Phoenix-like, that incinerated nation rose again. Its resurrection was due to an electoral quirk—the Tories, with the Chamberlain imperialism, were overthrown in Britain and a Liberal administration elected in their place. Five years after the Anglo-Boer war ended, defeated South Africa won a supreme moral and political victory—to wipe out the shame of the war, to admit the immorality of it and to recognise the rights, asserted in battlefield valour, of the vanquished, the British Government granted the two defeated republics responsible self-government co-equal with that which the British-owned Cape and Natal colonies enjoyed. It back-fired somewhat because of Afrikaner reaction which regarded British repentance to the injured as more infuriating than the injury.

General Louis Botha, who had been Commander-in-Chief of the Boer Forces, was elected the first Prime Minister, and two other Boer generals—Hertzog and Smuts—were in his ministry. Theirs was a colossal task. They had not only to build up from the ashes; they also had to effect, between Boer and British, a reconciliation of spirit that would obliterate corrosive rancour. They were more successful in the first than with the latter. In the space of the half-century that followed the union of the four colonies—the establishment of the Union of South Africa—a great and prosperous nation has been created; not even fifty years have been sufficient to damp-out the embers of bitter resentment.

Some thoughtful observers now strongly hold the view that victorious Britain was too generous too soon to the vanquished. They assert that the people of South Africa were not, five years after the normal carnage and the abnormal atrocities of the Anglo-Boer war, fitted for the gift of what that war had been fought to deny them—fitted neither materially nor spiritually. Some add that if one British Government was right to give them national status after defeat, its predecessor was wrong to take it from them with bayonets. Others assert that to give South Africa the half-loaf of Dominion self-government was an unrealistic feeding of the appetite for the full loaf of complete sovereign independence.

Ignoring all opinions on the matter, the hard fact is that in 1910 the Union of South Africa was created, becoming a full self-governing member of the Commonwealth of Nations with immediately limited authority but with unlimited powers for future complete independence. Nothing can prevent South Africa exercising those powers except the will of the people. That is the 1960 position.

In arriving at that position, a half-century of statesmanship and democratic development has passed. Statesmanship has been provided by five Prime Ministers and administrations of every gradation of political policy from near-subservient pro-Britishism to extreme anti-British republicanism. Democratic development has been shown in the progress of a defeated Boer-minded people to a nation of high ideals, modernised outlook, widespread industrialisation and social responsibility—completely competent to govern themselves completely. This metamorphosis is in the same category as that of America after the War of Independence and of Russia subsequent to the Bolshevik revolution. And, as in their cases, it has only been produced from travail and trial and torment.

At times, failure seemed imminent, the obstacles too high, the problems too intense. Botha, Hertzog and Smuts, as sequential Premiers, were sequentially rejected by the Boer population they had led in war and served in reconstruction. National unity was shattered by schisms. Armed rebellion broke out and brother slew brother. Strikes were caused and ruthlessly suppressed by cannon and bomb in the streets. Economic depression rained down its red-hot coals of disaster like some evil nimbus of Dantesque spray. Two world wars were participated in and split open the half-healed wounds of their predecessor. Two-thirds of the population formed a seething cauldron of over-boiling discontent. Extremes of indecent wealth juxtaposed filthiest poverty. Political crises chased their own forked tails in a crazy-pattern of efforts to reconcile irreconcilables—the perpetuation of white all-supremacy together with the building of a nation in the contentment of security and the security of unity.

Fifty years is not long enough. Another generation is required for the erasure of memories and the removal of prejudices. Men are still living who, as babies, were the victims of the disease and humiliation of Kitchener's concentration camps and, while their envenomed memories are sneerfully dismissed as mythological legends the details of which are lost in the long perspectives of recollection, they still exist as actual facts in a factual situation. Such memories are being woven into national lore, and the histories of many other nations—including Britain and America—show that such legendary lore can become the highly coloured threads in a national tapestry. The existence and the effect of the insubstantial pageantry of such memories and myths italicise the astounding South African renaissance.

From the bloodstained and oppressive past is emerging a

e young bull"—son of the tribal chief, a fine figure of a Zulu buck.

An urbanised Bantu boy—in the messenger uniform of a city firm.

hosa belle of the Transkei Territories caught in a characteristic pose.

An important moment in her life—Zulu baby-girl getting her first hair "do".

Aerial view of the city-heart of Pretoria as it has developed from Kruger's rustic capital.

Durban city-centre with the clock-towered General Post Office and the City Hall edging in on the left.

new South African generation—the protoplasmic stockpile which replenishes and refreshes a resurrected and reconstructed nation. This people, second-generation post-Boer war, are the determinants of South Africa's future. And if they are to determine it, that future is assured because the present South African generation are keen to follow the advice of Kruger who, in one of his rare moments of liberalised enlightenment, farsightedly counselled: "Take everything that is good and noble from your past and build thereon your future."

Now, as through the past fifty years, South Africa is bedevilled by politics. These are not, as in other countries, concerned with international affairs or even such important national issues as social conditions, economics or fiscal policies but concentrate on such purely localised matters as "the colour problem" and national symbols. Momentous as these may appear when removed from comparison with the issues that occupy the waking thoughts and haunt the dreams of people in other countries—world over-population, international blocs and nuclear warfare—they secure an overblown importance under the bellows of party politicians who stagger to Government and to Opposition under the tattered banners of racialism and nationalism. If the "colour problem" and the "constitutional issue" were removed from party election manifestos—as being essentially national and, therefore, bipartisan—the progress of South Africa, the nation, would jet-propel forwards freed from such inappropriate brakes.

Fifty years of struggle from national defeat, through the rationed-out quotas of self-government, to near-complete sovereignty have been negotiated until a resurrected nation can assert itself with a supreme distinction. Positive progress has been made on that road to complete sovereignty—the abolition of the supra-authority of the Privy Council in Westminster over decisions of the South African courts; the hand-over of the British naval base of Simonstown in the Cape to the South African navy; the relegation of the British national anthem and the Union Jack to secondary status; the massive industrial revolution since the British evacuation which has made South Africa self-supporting to a very significant extent. An entire people have got up from their knees and emancipated themselves almost completely—only the past puts any shackles on them.

It is a polyglot people—a South African race has yet to emerge. To that national crucible a dozen nationalities have made contributions: Dutch, German, French, British, Irish, Scottish, Welsh, American, Italian, Greek, Portuguese, Jews and, numerically greater than all these combined, the various Bantu tribes. All these, both past and present, have provided, are providing, the multitudinous cast of characters for all the roles in the dramatic performance enacted on the vast stage which is South Africa, against the historic backcloth of three centuries.

Dramatis Personæ

Dramatis Personæ

PEOPLE, not things, constitute the basic to every country. Industry, commerce, agriculture, economics, the entire structure of society, are the outgrowths of the people. People matter. People are decisive. People produce the wealth. People have the power to make the wheels of industry revolve —and to brake them. People have the power to fight the wars —and to refuse. It is impossible to depict the material aspects of a country—as this piece of writing sets out to do—accurately and meaningfully without the pre-requisite of a picture of its people. That is true of any country; it applies with underlined emphasis to such a complex country as South Africa whose complexities derive from its complex people.

People are, in South Africa, a more significant factor than in most countries because—as America—South Africa is the melting pot for a population of many national origins but— unlike America—the various national types in South Africa have not completely shed their origins and become entirely identified with South Africa as a South African people. In a fairly precise sense it is true to say that while the polyglot population of America has, by natural evolution, produced from within itself the *homo sapiens* known as American, from the similarly variegated people of South Africa has not been evolved the archetypal South African.

This may be denied because the average "South African" is

proud of his citizenship and nationality. He may be only a second-generation citizen or he may trace himself up through soaring genealogies to the Great Trek or look down the long lines of his ancestry until they meet in the fo'c'sle of the *Dromedaris*. Genealogy does not make race. While the family-tree provides visible evidence of ancestry, it is the buried roots from which racial life derives its existence. And when the roots of any South African's family-tree are examined they are found not to be South African; they are Dutch, or French, or Jewish, or Portuguese, or British, or German, or Greek, or Italian, or Bantu—or a mixture of more than one of those. Some particular one of those racial fundaments provides the basic character of the individual who, in claiming to be South African, is most manifestly Dutch or French or British or of some other race.

Let all be agreed on the primary but simple fact: the decisive element in any country is its people. Decisive because ultimate power—to give a nation its character, to expedite its development, to bestow a distinctive quality, to impede its national progress—ultimate power resides in the people. One of the internal contradictions of democracy is that it does not permit the sovereignty of demos. While all-power resides in the people, real power is exercised by the élite—the financial, political, social and cultural few. Maybe that is just as well —assessing the I.Q. ratios of the mass of the people is more than enough to prove that, as the majority are not fit to be trusted with real power, it is advantageous that an élite exists to exercise it for them. That does not detract from the fundamental truth—that it is the people who not only make a nation but make a nation what it is.

There has been a great deal of criticism—some ill-informed, some well-designed—about South Africa, but whatever percentage of it is justified, the burden of responsibility must be placed on the shoulders of its people and not on governments, who are the throw-up of their people. Every nation is what its people are. It is impossible for a country to be something that is not the product of its people. The word "nation" is only a synonym for "people".

Later on I will show the South Africa that I have, as a trained newspaper journalist, seen it develop to be. To do that, it is essential to see what the people are: the nation can only be the mirror reflecting the people. South Africa has been described—the description is the title of an official guide-book—as "the complex country". So it is. That is because it has a complex population. And, as I see the country, all its problems, its contradictions, its complications, its virtues and its defects are directly traceable to the fact that this "complex country" is populated by a complex people.

Take a half-dozen typical South Africans of from second to tenth generation citizenship, and what is found?—or, to ask an easier-to-answer question, what is not found?—and the answer will be: everyone is a complex, a mixture, an amalgam. One will have a family-tree whose king-root is in France, another in Holland, others in Britain or some other continental country. Since that root was first sunk, there have been marriages with other nationalities—in some cases, in more cases than will be admitted, with races of a non-White pigmentation. It is not infrequent to come across "White" South Africans—even in the best regulated families; even in the highest social and political strata—evidencing some unmistakable "non-White" characteristic. Even the Dutch-appointed Governor van der Stel was a Coloured man. It is not necessary to understand the science of genetics to know that racial characteristics reveal themselves, in less or greater degree, in psychological characteristics.

A great deal of codology has been written and spoken about the iniquity of racialism—from anti-semitism to the Master Race—but it is difficult, without self-deception, truthfully to deny that every race reveals some distinctive characteristic. Italians are distinguished by their volatile nature, the French by their logical qualities, the English by their stolidity, the Irish by their mercurial humours, the Germans by their meticulous industriousness, the Scots by their constructive caution, the Dutch by their painstaking diligence, the Russians by their uninspired thoroughness, the Americans by their boastful flamboyance, the Jews by their self-protective shrewdness.

Going along the list to the South African, it is not possible to identify the people of that nation by any distinctive characteristic—they are a blend of many different strains, manifesting the characteristics of the several races that the people of that country have, over the dead centuries, absorbed into the family-tree. In the process of time, and by natural selection, they will breed-out the superfluities of other national characters and produce a pure strain of South Africans, with a distinctive quality. That will be the end of a complex people; the end of a country of complexities.

What there is today is a people revealing a variety of national characteristics, as their blood possesses a variety of racial corpuscles. For that reason, it is difficult to depict "the typical South African" because South Africans vary in conformity with the variety of their antecedents and, at times of emotional stress, different reactions can be expected—to accord with their basic and predominant racial characteristic. This psychological phenomenon renders difficult the task of isolating and identifying the South African, as a precise individualistic national, and explains the complexity of South Africa as a nation. Not that the result is bad because, by some process that is probably rudimentary text-book to the clinical geneticist, the general reaction is that instinctive and superior manifestation is given to the virtues, rather than the weaknesses, of the primary blood-content. South Africans who are of Dutch descent more often reveal the best qualities of the Hollander; and the same operates in the case of those who are offshoots of French or British or German or any other national forebear.

Not claiming any qualification to pass judgment, I am not so stupid or so presumptuous as to commend or condemn the people of South Africa either for their inborn complexity or their manifestation of it. Enough merely to report the facts. One is that there is a marked disposition to "group" and, as a nation derives its character from its people, South Africa is not so much unitary as an internal federation of "groups". In actual and discernible patterning the population of South Africa consists of three main groups—the Afrikaans-speaking, the English-speaking and the non-White; but each of these three has sub-divisions.

As a matter of pure fact, the descriptions "Afrikaans-speaking" and "English-speaking" are misleading if applied or accepted literally. There are, approximately, three million white-skinned people in South Africa and eleven million non-white. Just as approximately, fifty-eight per cent of the former are officially classed as Afrikaans-speaking and the remainder as English-speaking. The differentiation is based on "mother-tongue" or "home-language" and, in all probability, that is a fair method of assessment: the language that is normally used among the family.

Fair it may be; it is not adequate. A very heavy majority of the Afrikaans-speaking people can speak and read English; a much smaller, but rapidly increasing, percentage of the English-speaking people—especially among the younger generation—can speak and read Afrikaans. This means that eighty per cent of the entire White population are proficient in the use of the English language.

That fact is not decisive; what is more to the point is that the language—the "mother-tongue" test—has created two separate groups. Among practically all the Afrikaans-speaking people—the exceptional minority is negligible—there is a non-British basic history: they are of two-generation, or longer, Boer extraction. To varying degrees, they instinctively regard the English-speaking section, who, or whose parents, may have been domiciled in South Africa for fifty years, as "uitlanders", immigrants or of immigrant parentage, foreigners, almost intruders. To go, as I often have, to social parties is to see a natural grouping process set in—one section gathers, cocktails in hand, in one part of the room conversing, animatedly, in Afrikaans while the English-speakers group themselves in another part. Nothing has had me more hot around the collar than, chatting to a person, for him to address, to a third person in the room, some observations in the Afrikaans language which they know I do not understand —it seemed to me to be as ill-mannered as whispering.

It is the language, as much as politics or sentiment, which splits the White population into two groups. To state an obvious fact is not to comment—and the obvious fact is that any element which divides the people of a nation into two groups is bad for that nation. This form of division is not entirely without a mixture of politics and sentiment. It is a hangover from the stupidity and cupidity that characterised

British control of South Africa in the past. It is all very well for English people in South Africa to say to me, as they so often have: "These diehard Afrikaners are living in the past." What are they expected to do when the past is too recent to expunge from the mind?

"They're constantly harping on the Boer war and the concentration camps." Naturally—the Boer war is not sixty years old and the parents of many of the Afrikaners of today endured the atrocities of British concentration camps which gave Hitler the idea for his. It cannot be expected for the memory of Britain's disgraceful war on the peaceful Boers, and the disgraceful conduct of it, to have been wiped out by the "conscience-money" payment of partial independence. How long will it take the Jews to forget—never forgive—the Hitler atrocities? When can anyone expect the Irish to cease "harping on" their nation's seven centuries of British over-lordship, marked by constant bloodshed, leading up to the Black-and-Tans disgrace? Even the Americans often revert critically to their "colonial" misfortunes. These are the politico-sentimental factors that, because they remain in the minds of the people, condition the course and colour the character of a nation.

South Africa's ethnology is best viewed in the three main-streams of Dutch-French, British and Bantu origins. This somewhat haphazard categorisation makes it necessary to include the Coloureds in the last group although, such is their tragedy, they exist in an ethnic no-man's-land. (To avoid confusion with "the coloureds" of America, who are of negro blood, I should explain clearly that the Coloureds of South Africa are not negroid—i.e. Bantu—but half-breeds with a percentage of White-blooded parentage or ancestry which varies so considerably that some of them successfully "play white"). However diffuse the individual origins of those in these three main groupings may be, predominant characteristics—of psychology, customs and conduct, way of thought and life—unmistakably identify them and indicate, as members of the cast of characters, the roles they perform in this national drama.

Cast of Characters
(in order of appearance)

THE DUTCH-FRENCH

Enter the Dutch-French group, direct descendants of the original immigrants, the forebears of the Afrikaners of today. Three centuries of propagation have produced a people in whom all the major characteristics of the nation's founder-fathers are fused. They are explicable and readily understood if it is constantly remembered that they are the modern derivatives of a race of frontiersmen who, gun in one hand and Old Testament in the other, had to hold increasing watch and guard over the frontiers of their land, with its thatched earth-and-reed huts, wagons, cattle and homesteads, against marauding black savages. This incessant vigilance, dawn-to-dusk labour and life-or-death warfare, combined to develop, on the sub-structure of Dutch and Calvinistic heredity, a unique character whose genes and mores have passed into the bloodstreams of generations.

If it were possible to distil an archetypal synthesis from all male Afrikaners he would be revealed as violently opinionated, loud-voiced, defensively aggressive, chauvinistically enthusiastic, ancestor-worshipping, mythologically religious,

politically factious, inferiority-conscious, self-reliantly independent, tenaciously obstinate, crudely courteous, instinctively
hospitable, incurably unimaginative, physically restless and
mentally conservative. Above and below that hypothetical
norm there are gradations that run from the retarded and
uncouth to the cultured and fastidious. Into whatever
adjectival classification any individual Afrikaner falls, this is
true of him and of all others: he is, they are, nothing but the
ultimate product of distant forebears. All the present-day
Afrikaners can be readily interpreted in terms of their
ancestral history. To find the explanation, the thoroughfares
of the past must be retrodden.

When the Netherlands Government decided that the Dutch
East Indies Company trading station on the Cape of Good Hope
needed the supply-house of an agricultural colony instead of
relying on the Hottentots, "assisted immigrants" were sent
out. They were poorly educated, socially inferior, uncouth
and uncultured—but enormously industrious and devoutly
religious. And, above all, consumed with a deep, passionate,
unquenchable animosity for the British nation, then at
the peak of its blood-stained power and at war with their
own.

They had known of the introduction into warfare of
"frightfulness"—as Sir Winston Churchill, in his "History"
described it—by Cromwell, two years before van Riebeeck
sailed from Holland for the Cape, when, with calculated cold-
bloodyness, that "Great Englishman" had placed an iron
foot on the neck of the Irish race and in the process wiped out
almost every man, woman and child in Drogheda—of which
feat Cromwell unctuously reported: "They made a stout
resistance. We refused them quarter. We put to the sword
the whole number; I do not think thirty of the three thousand

escaped with their lives. I wish all honest hearts may give the glory of this to God.''

These founder-fathers of South Africa arrived at the Cape when Britain, under the same ''Great Englishman'', was making war on their native land with the same ruthlessness, the same God-invoking blasphemy; and also on the peaceful Dutch colony in America, named New Amsterdam, changed to New York after the British had conquered it by force of arms. They deafened Cape Town with a loud ''Hallelujah Chorus'' of rejoicing when news came through that the Dutch navy had sailed up the Thames and brought the British to their knees.

All the many instances of the blood-thirstiness of the ''Great Englishman'' took place during the first decade of Dutch settlement in the Cape and it is no exaggeration to say that the accoucheur at the birth of South Africa was bitter anti-Britishism. Such a feeling was the expression of patriotism— the founder-fathers were Dutch and the British were their country's enemy. Born in anti-Britishism, it is not surprising if its echoes have reverberated down the corridors of South Africa's history and may even now be faintly heard by Afrikaner sons.

Forty years after van Riebeeck's landing—and, therefore, thirty years after his departure because he only stayed at the Cape for ten years—nearly three hundred French Huguenots arrived. Most of them had come from Holland, to where they had escaped from religious persecution in France, and they brought with them to the Cape a Calvinistic zeal which ''put teeth'' into the Dutch settlers' more quiescent conception of that forbidding creed; and great skill in viticulture. It was the Huguenot immigrants, rather than the Dutch settlers, who established Calvinism as the faith of the new colony.

That was the most lasting ingredient they contributed to the way of thought of the modern Afrikaner; to it, recalcitrant independence and disputatious resentment of authority were added by the Dutch founders.

Isolated from the governments of their native lands, they could not regard the authority of the Dutch East Indies Company officials as a satisfying substitute. Rather than accept that, they would accept none. They openly revolted at the minimum of control introduced by van der Stel, the wisest and kindliest of van Riebeeck's sixteen successors, and when they discovered that his son, who succeeded him, was making a "corner" in the colony's wine and meat contracts, they adopted a rebellious anti-Company attitude. In retaliating, the Company took action to reduce the colonists' power by reducing the Company's dependence on them—slaves were imported.

This had an effect which time has done little to reduce— from then on the line separating White and Black was clearly defined: when Black was the colour of slavery, the White-skin was the imprimatur of aristocracy. The founder-fathers were compelled to define the inferiority of slavery and found no apparent alternative to establishing their own separation from the slaves with a colour demarcation. And through the years that were to follow, that differentiation would persist until it became a mental stereotype, ingrained into the character of the Afrikaner people.

Anti-British sentiment, religious fanaticism, ever-insurgent independence and a profound White-Black consciousness became fundamentals to the founder-fathers during the first fifty years of the new land's life. They became part of the people's character and that fact does much to explain the Afrikaner of today—he, like all human beings, is the repository of those inherited characteristics which condition thought-processes.

If that first half-century can be termed "Genesis", the second should be "Exodus" because it marked the departure of the Dutch-French immigrants from the Cape Town environs in search of pastures new and, in addition, better. That exodus coincided with the black invasion from the east and north; two mass-movements of peoples engaged in the same search. Clashes were inevitable—the wandering Boers found themselves engaged in perpetual frontier war. During the century that followed—a century of restless pursuit of pastoral security obtainable, in that vast sun-pierced bowl, only by incessant frontier war—the mould was formed from which the Afrikaner character has been patterned.

It was also "the century of wrong". As they trekked north in search of the security of independence, resented authority followed on their heels. And during that century all authority emanated from Whitehall; its couriers wore British army uniforms. Wandering in the wilderness, like the Israelites whose 19th-century equivalent they believed themselves to be, the Children of South Africa strode through their own Red Sea—the British conquerors on one side, the black hordes on the other. Only the most hopeless of fools is capable of imagining that three generations could live that kind of pincer-entrapped life without bequeathing its psychological effects to the generations that were yet to be born.

Here were a people, who had made of themselves a race apart, as insular as troglodytes. They had submerged their Dutch and French and German nationalities into a new one—they were South Africans and South Africa was, now, their true and only homeland. In a sense, they had de-patriated themselves; they had renounced their natal lands and their

Architecturally serene and placidly elegant—Libertas, the Prime Minister's official residence in Pretoria.

Parliament in session—this shows the scene at the first sitting of the first National Government.

Hostels for Bantu workers in Anglo-American mines—modern version of the old "compounds".

Aerial view of Meadowlands, the modern Bantu township just outside Johannesburg.

national birthrights to acquire a new homeland and a new nationality. They had severed the umbilical cord with their mother-countries: South Africa was all. To it they had devoted every pulse of the heart, every fibre of the muscle, every passion of the soul. Their foreheads sequined with sweat, they fought the sandglass to scratch crops out of iron soil which they irrigated with their blood and their tears and their sweat. Fortified by that dedication of mind and body, they would withstand the savagery of the marauding blacks and the pin-pricking irritations of a self-imposed red-tunicked authority.

If their parents had resented the mild exhibitions of milder power by the Company, the second-generation Afrikaners—legatees of a character compounded of the parents' anti-Britishism, recalcitrant independence and a fanatical religion nourished on the polar juices of puritanism—were not psychologically constructed to submit docilely to authority imposed from 6,000 miles away by an entirely foreign country who had seized their new homeland after waging war on their parents' homeland. That might have been neither logical nor natural.

Illogical and unnatural or not, the British felt justified in exercising their authority and, by the unwritten laws of conquest, they were right so to do. Untaught by their disasters as governors in Ireland and America—which cost them the loss of both—they attempted to govern the frontier-race in South Africa with traditional misunderstanding of the people and with characteristic coercion. Why should they not? Had they not "conquered" the country and were not the people their Queen's humble subjects? That being so, there must be a proper "conqueror-subject" relationship. And the British acted as if they had sworn solemn fidelity to that principle—with a regal negation of the manyness beneath them.

A people's entire culture was wiped out. A foreign language was forced on the children's tongue. A rejected form of religion was State-established. Aliens were imported to unbalance the rightful population. Strange and repugnant customs and practices were introduced and made compulsory. Taxation was levied for the benefit of the conquerors. Whenever the land disclosed hidden wealth—diamonds and gold— it passed into the hands of the foreigner. Powers of defence, education and self-government were taken from the people and transferred to the invaders. Everything, and more, that the Caesars had done to the Ancient Britons the Modern Britons did to Afrikaners. And, like Caesar, the British created a monolithic administration which they deluded themselves was immutable whereas Caesar showed that the only immutable law of a monolith is the immutable law of its inevitable demise.

No profound knowledge of mass-psychology is required to estimate the effect of this suzerainty on a Boer people who had inherited their parents' character. Britain is not so foolish these days. Britain began to realise—not too long after its unforgivable war on the peaceful Boers—that no force had yet been created powerful enough to suppress the power of the people. Recognising that eternal verity, Britain has given self-government to a long list of her "subject" nations— beginning with South Africa and ending, without doubt, when the last "subject" nation is subject only to itself. To learn that great truth Britain had to wade through blood and tears —on the veld, in Flanders, on the North African desert, in blitzed London, through the passive resistance of India and the blood-riots of Cyprus. And as a result, Great Britain has become greater; the God who made her mighty has, because of godly ways, made her mightier yet.

On the veld the victory of arms went to Great Britain; to South Africa the victory of spirit. It was a war of which I have never heard a Briton boast. Wars before and since have been fought for principle; the British fought the Boers for gold. When diamonds were unearthed in a part of the Free State, the British simply annexed the territory. When gold was discovered in the Transvaal, annexation of that independent republic was only possible at the point of nearly half a million British bayonets.

This piece of writing is a factual report and reports the facts of the Boer war which have become clearer as Time wafted away the fog. These are those facts: gold was found in the Transvaal and was pounced on by British speculators and exploiters. Kruger decided that some of its value should revert to the people of the Transvaal and so taxed the gold output. Sitting in secret conspiracy in the head-offices of the British gold companies in Johannesburg and presided over by Cecil Rhodes who had only just previously been Prime Minister of the (British) Cape Colony, the leading gold-tycoons conspired to devise a plot to overthrow the elected Transvaal Government by force of arms and grab control of that independent republic. They were operating with the knowledge of Joseph Chamberlain, the Colonial Secretary of the British Government in London. The armed raiders, led by Dr. Jameson who was to become Prime Minister of the Cape Colony under the British a few years later, were defeated by the Transvaal Government forces. Kruger, distrustful of the sullen silence that followed, demanded the withdrawal of British forces elsewhere in South Africa—Britain refused. And the Boer war began—with 87,000 untrained Boers fighting for their homes and homeland against 450,000 of the armed might of the British Empire.

It ended with 6,000 dead Boers and 22,000 British fatalities —but 26,000 Boer women and children died in the British concentration camps; more Boer civilian victims than British soldiers killed in open warfare. Those are the death-roll figures that marched over grief's immeasurable territories but they do not represent the total of war's frightful balance sheet. By the end of the war, the whole land was devastated by Kitchener's "scorched earth" war on civilians—hardly a farmhouse was left standing; stocks were driven off or destroyed; the basic economy of an agrarian nation shattered. And in the heart-soil of the surviving Afrikaner people, a deadly herbiage grew. "It was a vast tragedy in the life of a people," Smuts said of the Anglo-Boer war—"an epic struggle between the smallest and greatest of peoples."

That "century of wrong" has burned itself into the minds and hearts of the religiocentric Afrikaner people and created a national psychosis which exists as one of the hard facts that no report on the drama of South Africa can ignore and remain factual. To understand the latest acts in that drama, it is necessary sympathetically to understand the character of the present-day Afrikaner and the forces of the past that have etched that character. Those forces explain the bitter suspicion, self-defending aggressiveness and consciousness of an inferiority complex, caused by oppression and suppression, which are the distinguishing characteristics of the Afrikaner in the South Africa of today. Only their elimination by gradual amelioration can ensure that the South Africa of tomorrow is as great and prosperous as its human and material wealth indicate to be possible.

It is at that point that statesmanship and true political science enter—a subject far too fertile in controversy and opinion for this detached report beyond the statement, which remains in the area of fact, that the necessary reorientation can only be achieved when each of the two main groups of characters possesses an intelligent assessment of the factors that have created the outlook and aspirations of the other.

THE BRITISH

Enter the British group who first edged their way on the stage not long after Nelson had given the French fleet a real Trafalgar of a thrashing which had a misproportionately tonic effect on the morale of the British people. They were not only cock-a-hoop; they felt cock of the world. That mental attitude of international superiority marked the entire British psychology and promoted a feeling of arrogance which became almost as much a virtue as a vice. Holland had been crushed by the French, to whom the British fleet had been leased for the occasion, and it was in strict accord with triumphant British arrogance to seize a Dutch possession before the prostrate owner could get back on his feet. That same British arrogance and sense of unchallengeable superiority marked the British occupancy of South Africa for a century. What could have been nothing but a vice, the intelligence of the British transformed into a virtue. If it was "a century of wrong" it was also a century in which British genius brought order, law, system, methodology, organisation and development to the country and its people, laying the foundations on which a nation was to build itself.

All the facts of history assemble to assert that had South Africa been left to the Afrikaners during that century, it would be one of the backward countries of the world today.

Devout, obdurate and enduring as they were, the Afrikaners, never over-stimulated by the insidious drug of thought, did not possess those qualities essential to the scientific organisation of a modern nation. Their virtues focused themselves, naturally, on other achievements—those in which the disorderliness of independent action, "rugged individualism" and unimaginative enterprise are more modestly productive. It was the capacities for ordered progress, for intelligent organisation and for calculated exploitation of natural resources which the British introduced and skilfully applied, that gave form and substance to an inchoate country and a factious people.

Colonists as the Dutch-French were, they were not genuine colonisers. They practised a nomadic economy—eating off the land until it was exhausted and then moving on to repeat the process. Settlers as they were, they did not really settle —they remained long enough to re-group for further wanderings. It was not until the second decade of British occupation that serious town-planning began with the official migration to South Africa of 5,000 British settlers, who were that, not merely in name. Historic now as "the 1820 settlers", those British families of 5,000 people, the nucleus of tens of thousands to follow, began the real South Africa of rooted communities and permanent civic organisation.

That this perfection of colonisation was not altruistic in intent; that Britain regarded South Africa as an investment; that large-scale immigration solved British domestic problems; that Britain expected to take out of South Africa more than it put in—true as those facts are, they are somewhat irrelevant to the greater fact that it was the British, and not the Afrikaners, who created the conditions which made the South Africa of today a feasible possibility. Their achievement was at the expense of Afrikaner sentiment and national independence, but the historian would utter falsely if he failed to state that Afrikaner sentiment and independence were then being directed into ultimately unproductive and futile channels.

Trekking is a commendable declaration of independence; but the direct opposite to building a nation because a nation is a combination of settled communities, rooted and domiciled, organised and efficiently directed, productive as well as consumptive, practising the precepts of permanence rather than indulging the instincts of wanderlust. Trekkers can blaze trails; they cannot build cities and remain trekkers. Those sterling qualities that turned the Afrikaners into pioneering trekkers, nomadic adventurers, vigilant frontiersmen, produced exactly that spirit of restless striving, thrustful progression and unsatisfied mobility that is the negation of city-building.

As they trekked they left behind the dead camp-fires, the consumed land, the unexploited resources which the constructive efficiency of the more intelligent British took over and made over. Where there had been the crude justice of the frontier, the British introduced legal codes and enlightened administration. Where there had been the anarchic hit-or-missism of "rugged individualism", the pedantic British established control and order and the restraints of democracy. Where there had been superficial scraping of the surface, the British developed, organised and exploited the buried resources.

Behind and beneath the manifest evidences of the Afrikaner way of life, with its Old Testament economy, South Africa was gaining all those virtues of character and qualities of mind that made the British justifiably great. Some of Britain's most skilful administrators accepted the responsibilities of true colonisation; some practised its worst devices. Accompanying the glorious accomplishments were some detestable methods the memory of which tarnish and diminish the glory. Basically, the many British errors derived from the errors in British character—the superiority of arrogance, the denigration of anything non-British, the smug complacency, the uplifting conviction of self-rightness. These psychological defects inevitably produced a massive blind-spot—complete inability to understand other peoples; a myopic condition not lessened because it was expressed with a set of highly-polished vowels when contradicting the virile aspirations of an uncouth people.

That did not detract from their supreme ability to understand their own selves and their own purposes. Fundamental to all the immense good they did—and, possibly, to all the evil that lived after them—was what appeared to them as the all-transcending, all-pardoning purpose of making mighty Britain mightier still; of adding another lustrous jewel to the Royal crown. All their beneficent achievements were primarily motivated for that end; if the invaded people benefited as well, that gave the lustre another polish; if they suffered, their sufferings were a regrettable necessity to that desirable end.

A century of this thinking cannot quickly be un-thought. Logical as it was for the British to consider Britain's welfare as predominant, to make that consideration so painfully apparent to its victims could only create a psychological climate in which the fruit of even the best actions would wither on the vine. Fifty years after the end of that "century of wrong"—and century of accomplishment—the Afrikaner finds it easier, because natural, to remember British motivation than to recognise British benefaction.

In brooding over that past, nursing ancient grudges, mutter-
ing meaningless and verbose shibboleths, it becomes difficult
for the Afrikaner to appreciate that he owes his modern
South Africa to the British, despite the latter's lengthy
inventory of disastrous errors. He glories in his remarkable
railroad system—one of the greatest achievements of its kind
in the world—forgetting that it is a monument to British
engineering skill and efforts; as was also, in the *Union Castle*
steamships, overseas transport. He takes not-so-secret pride
in the excellent banking system that networks the entire
country, overlooking the fact that the great *Standard Bank* was
a British institution. He boasts of his country's solid financial
position, ignoring the British enterprise which made mining
the basis of the nation's wealth. He has increasing pride in
the expanding industrialisation of his country, oblivious to the
heavy investment of British techniques, skills, experts and
money that made it possible. Also can be added to that
catalogue of British contributions—and this fact is as firmly
entrenched in history as the preceding ones, and worthy of most
candid thought—the fact that the "colour-bar" principle
which the Afrikaner regards as unalterably wise and just,
was part of the British legislative and administrative policy,
officially recognised and accepted by Westminster when the
only form of constitution for the new Union of South Africa
that the British Parliament would approve documented the
principle of "apartness" for the Bantu.

Odious as are the accusations that Britain can sustain during
"the century of wrong"—which no official apologia has
yet succeeded in clothing in garments of improbable glamour
and romance—and enormous as their errors and malpractices
were, the South Africa of today, and present-generation
Afrikaners, if a balance sheet were struck, will find that the

credit side heavily outweighs the debit. If that fact, inescapable and irrefutable, is recognised by the Afrikaners—and its twin, the culpabilities of the British during that century of forcible occupation, admitted by the non-Afrikaners—the reconciliation of spirit, essential in a dual-population country, can be attained and South Africa shake off the dust of its past, stride into its ever-better future.

That is not yet the position and for that both Afrikaners and those of British stock share the blame. This reluctance by both to employ the past only as a teacher of essential lessons persists and, as it does, it creates a "group" patterning. This will continue until the two sections cease to be sections, the two "groups" group no longer, and there is a unified South African people. That is not so now.

On one side are the Afrikaner people, as reluctant to part with their centuries-old resentments as a spinster is her virginity. On the other are the English-speakers, with traditional and characteristic everlasting implications of superiority; still thinking of South Africa as "ours"; still colonial-minded; still unable to recognise the historic and unalterable fact that South Africa is a sovereign state, as politically separate from Britain as Belgium or Brazil; in the Commonwealth of Nations (which they persist in mis-calling "the British Commonwealth") as one of the full partners with no one partner—not even Britain—superior to the others.

It is this outmoded concept, held by many English-speakers in South Africa and often expressed by some of them, which I found to be the irritant that creates the noticeable disunity among the people. It gets under the skin of the majority like a splinter.

This ubiquitous and old-fashioned Britain-über-alles attitude has to be recognised as one of the existing hard facts of the

actual situation. It cannot just be pooh-poohed away. A fact
is not rendered non-existent by acting as if it had no existence.
Even some of the more South Africanised settlers from Britain
manifest, to an extent that varies with individuals, some form
of this anti-South African attitude. Afrikaners are very sensitive—possibly super-sensitive—to the nuances; that is due
to the inferiority complex which is a national trait. When
they hear someone—perhaps away from England many years
and who claims, with justification, to be "a good South
African"—refer to a holiday in England as "grand to be going
home again, if only for a month", they wince. They know that
they, themselves, have no other home than South Africa—all
their eggs are in that basket; all their love and loyalty devoted
to that land; all the heritage of their past and the promise of
their future pin-pointed there. They, quite naturally, do not
regard "as one of us" the settler who—having come to South
Africa not for South Africa's benefit but for his own—has
his body in South Africa and his heart in some other "home".
A ducking will always be the reward for the man who stands
with one foot in the boat and the other on the shore.

This is one of the differences between South Africa and
America—the two countries which have so much in common.
Millions of Americans, or their forebears, are from other
countries but America is now their one homeland; they
boast of being American citizens and are proud to bring up
their children with singleminded loyalty to and love for their
nation. Somehow or another, it has not worked out that way
with a preponderant section of English settlers in South
Africa—they carry with them more than an understandable
nostalgia for the land of their birth; they add to it a critical
attitude to the land of their adoption.

When they were "home" they would instinctively act on

the principle—when other countries attacked Britain with hostile criticism—"I'm for my country, right or wrong." When they become domiciled in South Africa—because they are better off there than in Britain, otherwise they would not have come, or coming, remained—they openly side with, or secretly applaud, overseas critics when they pound and punish South Africa for South African national methods. That is because, in their hearts and minds, they do not regard South Africa as "home"—they have divided interests, divided sentiments, divided loyalties.

It has taken me twelve years trying to understand this—and I have not succeeded. I never experienced it in Canada, for instance. There, every Canadian citizen is a Canadian first, last, and all the time. He may only have lived there five years, but let someone in England sling stones at Canada and he will rush to champion Canada and tell the English critics, in expressive North-American idiom, that England is a vulnerable glasshouse. I well remember Charlie Prater, the comp on the Toronto *Evening Telegram*, when I was facing him making up the paper "on the stone" and incautiously, even if justifiably, said: "Back in London we did it this way." Charlie, his parents immigrants from England, said: "You can pipe down on that, chum. I know how you do things in London. I was there during the war and I saw how you do things there." He proceeded to inventorise the "things"—from the street cars to the street-walkers, from the cafés to the cinemas, from the slummy houses to the slatternly housewives. I piped down.

It is the supercilious suggestion of superiority on the part of many English-speakers that, together with the Afrikaners' emotionalised resentments, divides the South African people. Not that the former is entirely without justification. Using a by-and-large assessment, it is seen that, in the majority of occupations, man for man and job for job, the South African resident with overseas training and experience is superior to his "opposite number" who is equipped with only South African training and experience. That, of course, excludes South Africa's important gold-mining and diamond industries —because Britain has none—but includes every type of human endeavour with which I became acquainted. There are exceptional exceptions, such as Dr. H. J. van Eck, Mr. Anton Rupert, Dr. M. S. Louw, who would be giants among giants anywhere. The trouble is not centred in the fact that the settler from overseas is better than the South African equivalent but that he tells the latter he is. Or shows it by his manner—the English snobocratic superiority.

And it is all so childishly stupid and ignorantly unrealistic. After all, the English-speakers are in South Africa to live, work and die here. Where is the sense in making it unnecessarily difficult for themselves? South Africa is the South African's country. They did not force English immigrants to come; the majority came because they made up their minds that there was more in South Africa for them than Britain had to offer. If any one of them were to deny that, he would be accusing himself of acting mindlessly. They came to take something out of South Africa and, if they do that, they are in honour bound to put something in—their work, their loyalty and their full co-operation. That is how a growing number of British settlers regard their responsibilities—it is to be deplored that so many give Afrikaners a contrary impression.

Both this attitude and that of the insular Afrikaners are to be deplored—but not misunderstood. They are historic inevitabilities. And the effects of history on any people cannot be ignored—they can only be modified by sympa-thetically seeking a reconciliation. Only along the route of mutual understanding of the basic origins of conflicting thought-processes can the complexities which bedevil South Africa be removed and a true "South African race", unified and merged in a common nationhood, be evolved.

Historic influences, mental approaches, language, religious creeds, social contacts and ideological conceptions divide the two white groups. Even their conceptions of government differ—Afrikaners reject the British concept of plutocracy in favour of a theocracy. They are divided by differences; they are united by a unanimity—the almost completely national conviction that, in a multi-racial state, there must be White supremacy: the traditional South African policy of separation, apartness, which came with van Riebeeck, was perpetuated and given legal administrative form by the British and is practised, to varying degrees, by every Afrikaans-speaking and English-speaking citizen at this day. That is not White versus Black—it is White plus Black: the groups which form the complete cast who are responsible for portraying the Drama of South Africa.

THE BANTU

Enter the Bantu peoples who provide the background chorus—sometimes shrilly pleading, sometimes murmuringly plaintive, sometimes ominously growling—to most of the 300-year drama. These are South Africa's most important people—their importance is centred in the facts that they constitute South Africa's only serious trouble-spot of any magnitude; and hold the key to the country's prosperity. All other problems are accompanied by conceivable solvents; the so-called Natives constitute a problem of such interwoven complexities that no mental genius has yet been created who is able to "solve" it without, from such solution, other equally tantalising problems proliferating. When all the manifold ingredients of the present problem are courageously consulted it will be apparent that many of the proffered "solutions" are but a foamy cataract of theories dashing over the vulgar rocks of fact.

They are South Africa's most important people because they carry, on their sweating bent shoulders, the heavy end of the golden cross on which they have been, are being, crucified. They have been the bane of South Africa's past; they are the stanchion-support of its present. Remove that, and the whole three-pronged productive economy—mining, industry and agriculture, with their parasitical fungus—would totally collapse. It is that hard fact which accentuates the present problem and tinctures much of the condemnation of that problem with unrealism. That is because it can only be resolved—not necessarily solved—by an utter revolution of the existing system that has caused it, employing two theories which, if followed to their logical conclusion, become illogical in modern South Africa.

Socialism is one. Part of the socialist philosophy is the social ownership of the means of production. Another is the principle that the first charge on industry is not profits but wages. Application of those philosophic precepts would, Socialists claim, solve South Africa's greatest problem. They say that they would deal with the root and core of the problem —the poverty of the Bantu people. They do not concede, what their opponents assert, that even if that solved the problem, from the solution other massive problems would emerge. This is all too apparent if the population structure, in its economic terms, is examined.

133

Using exact official statistics only approximately, this is the set-up: of the total 11,000,000 Bantu people, 4,250,000 are still living on the Reserves; 3,000,000 work on farms; 3,000,000 work in industry, commerce, transport and the mines in urbanised conditions; 750,000 live in rural areas. Their total cash take-home amounts to about £365,000,000 per year or, including non-cash payments, an average of less than £14 per month per household.

If they had to be paid more, farmers say they would give up farming because their profit would not equal what their investment could "earn" elsewhere; the ramified structure of industry would collapse because, industrialists say, increased wages, loaded on the per-unit production costs or deducted from profits, would make their enterprise unattractive. And mining would explode an atomic bomb under the Stock Exchanges of the world because, as the gold-price is fixed, the new costs caused by a wage-increase would knock the bottom clean out of present gold-share values.

Socialists, who have their own corrective formula for all those effects—the social ownership of the means of production, distribution and exchange—would contemplate those results of their "solution" with equanimity. Those who reject Socialism and yet recommend "social equality" as the solution to South Africa's problem, must—if they have the intelligence that qualifies them to make any recommendation—realise that "social equality" cannot be achieved in a quagmire of poverty. If they are sincere and intelligent, they must be aware that "social equality" is related to economic equality—that the average income of every Bantu home would be made equal to that of every non-Bantu home: an increase from £14 per month to at least £28 per month or doubling the deduction that wages make from profits—because profits are the surplus-value of labour.

"Social equality", which can only involve economic equality, would do to the entire South African economy what doubling the wages of America's steelworkers or of the workers in Britain's motor-car industry would do to those countries. That is the factual representation of the economic aspect of South Africa's problem because there is extremely little White manual labour performed in this country. That must be repeated to those overseas who are accustomed to the concept that all labour dignifies man—in South Africa extremely little manual work is performed by White workers. They are the aristocrats of labour, monopolising the skilled jobs and supervisory positions in mining, industry and agriculture. Manual work—the genesis of production—is the Black man's almost inviolable preserve. Socialists, who are not amenable to the law of sufficient reason, can permit themselves to advocate such "social equality" but for non-Socialists to do so is a very notable excursion into unrealism.

There is another section which is justified in telling South Africa how to solve a problem that has defeated some of the greatest British statesmen—including Disraeli and Gladstone; some of the most skilful British administrators—including Lord Somerset and Sir Garnet Wolseley; and all of the better-informed South Africans from van der Stel to Dr. Verwoerd. That permissible group—infinitesimally small—consists of the completely sincere and consistent Christians of this world such as are to be found among the ministers and nurses, devoted and dedicated, who labour in the bundu.

They are those who put the teachings and philosophy of Jesus to work—they do not necessarily include all those professional Christians who are more competent as preachers than as practitioners. They do not include every prelate and cardinal—those humble followers of He who had not where to lay His head. Nor the goodly company of those who interpret the Sermon on the Mount to mean blessed are the meek for they shall inherit a bishop's palace of many mansions, a chauffeur-driven Rolls Royce, an over-stocked cellar and a chef-provided table groaning under three good octagonal meals a day.

Pure and undefiled Christian philosophy is a condemnation of South Africa's colour situation. Only the pure and undefiled practitioners of it are in a position to prescribe a formula from their special algebra of spiritual experiences. Apartheid in all its forms and under its varied nomenclature—separation, segregation, White supremacy, apartness-with-justice, parallel development, political-rights-with-qualifications—that have been used by British and Afrikaners, collides with and cuts clean across the basic principles to exemplarise which Jesus lived and died.

Only those who accept and practise all He taught are justified in selecting from the whole the part that condemns South Africa's traditional policy. Merely to detach from the whole that part which, because it applies to others, is easy to apply to South Africa and regard other parts, because they are inconveniently self-applicable, as "unreasonable and inappropriate in the modern world" is an action that is, to avoid the word hypocritical, inconsistent. South Africa's colour situation challenges South Africa—it is also a challenge to Christians to apply the whole Word to themselves.

As neither Socialism nor the pure and undefiled Word has been applied to South Africa those two recommended "solvents" must remain theories—anæmic subtleties which earn a connoisseur's appreciation of romantic absurdities. There are others. These can be best outlined by quoting those who have proposed them to me.

"Give the Bantu some political concession to keep them quiet because they cannot be held down for ever." This is a fascinating mixture of humanitarianism and cynicism. Its unavoidable inference is that the Bantu have a perfect right to the whole loaf but, as they must not have it, buy them off with half a loaf. It is "peace in our own time". It is "look after ourselves". It is "never had it so good". It is "preserve the present and let the future take care of itself"—what has posterity done for us, anyhow? Anyone who cannot see its cynicism needs a Seeing-Eye dog.

My interviews with literally thousands of people in South Africa prove to my mind beyond any doubt that the opinion which most closely approaches unanimity is that "there must be a show-down sooner or later". This is usually accompanied by the view that it will be sooner rather than later; that the solution to the problem has been postponed too long; that the "sometime" of Bantu pacification has become "never" —there's one cherrystone too many on the plate. It is, also, expressed in such terms of pessimistic fatalism that the only possible interpretation is the belief that the show-down will be—suddenly: alagazam!—a blow-up.

I discovered no genuine grounds for this fatalistic outlook. To whatever extent there is, or has been, a Black-White hatred in North African territories, there is no such feeling among the Black people, as such, for the White people, as such, in the south. There is not even a desire for social integration among the Bantu—they strongly prefer the enjoyments of a self-contained community to the embarrassments of inter-racial social life especially as that, in their opinion, would possess certain features which compare unfavourably with their own. As a people they have always preferred and practised apartheid—it is the methods by which the principle of apartheid is applied that infuriate, because they humiliate, them.

Apartheid—apartness—is traditional to them. It was the rigid policy throughout their tribal history—the aristocratic Zulu tribe lived distinctly apart from the Xosas and they from the Lesothos and the Mashonas and the Felcani and the Tembus; and all the other tribes from each other. They practise apartheid against the Coloureds and the Asiatics today. It is not the principle against which they protest with groan-ings that cannot be uttered, but the inhumanities and injustices with which the Government apply it. Their animosity is not directed to the White man but to the White man's laws. To base on it the fear of a "blow-up" is as fallacious as construct-ing perfect syllogisms on a palpably false premise.

"They're human beings and should be treated as such" is another expressed attitude, one that is often used by the "one man one vote" advocates. That is countered by opponents who rely on genetics, anthropology and zoology for their opposition. What makes a member of the animal kingdom a human being? they ask. Is it nostrils and lungs for breathing? If so, all animals are so equipped. Is it bipedism? If so, apes walk erect on two legs. Is it a form of intelligence? If so, the loyalty of the dog and the integrity of the horse are intelligent reactions. They go so far as to doubt if a not inconsiderable proportion of the Bantu are far enough removed from their inherent savagery—"they are instinctively jungle-minded"—to have yet become, in respect to civilised minds, more than children.

I well remember, when I made my first trip to South Africa, seeking information on and advice about the country from the

South African High Commissioner in London, the late Heaton Nicholls who died two years or so ago. Heaton Nicholls was a liberal-minded man—he broke from the United Party, the opponents of the present National Government, because they expressed their opposition in, to him, a too benign and amiable fashion. He said to me:

"But all the time remember this—the Bantu is still, basically, a savage. He cannot be otherwise. His grandfather was living among the forests and mountains, wearing a leopard skin, brandishing a hide-shield and waving an assegai, shouting blood-curdling war-cries. That ancestral blood and its emotions cannot be completely bred-out in merely eighty years. He cannot avoid, in moments of emotional stress, reverting to the deep, black recesses of his inherited mind, no matter how much he may have acquired the superficialities of civilisation. I firmly believe that even such a grand and civilised man as Paul Robeson would, if the theatre he was singing in burst into flames, go berserk."

Whether it be true or false, the existing fact is that a not unsubstantial percentage of South Africans view—to varying degrees of intensity—many Bantu as semi-civilised. It is irrelevant to the existence of that fact to assert that the Bantu have been given far too limited opportunities to develop to a higher stage. True as that is, it does not alter the fact that, for whatever reason and from whatever cause, most South Africans are convinced that the majority of the Bantu are below the mental and spiritual level that civilisation regards as average.

There is a disbelief in the civilisation of the mass of the Bantu as being anything more than a cultivation of surface textures; an almost invisible integument. Even among the most thoughtful South Africans the opinion is expressed that it is unfair to expect a people who have only been learning to write during the past thirty years to have had time to erase all the stigmata of a neolithic age or remove all the treacherous roots from the dark loam of the mind. The belief is sincerely held by many intelligent people—British and Afrikaner—that emotional agitations from either liberalistic or nationalist quarters are bad for the Bantu mind, causing the smudge-fire of a dying savagery to burn more sootily under the up-draught of emotion. They declare that politics and economics and social philosophies cannot override the genetic inheritance which must regulate Bantu evolutionary advancement down to a tempo that is much slower than that which other beneficiaries of the civilising process have been able to maintain.

That the Bantu are, as a mass-people, at a lower stage of civilised development is—if it is true at all—much less a reflection on them than a criticism of the British and Afrikaner administrations which over the past 150 years have deliberately, and as a conscious act of policy, devised the situation. Chickens, released during those 150 years, darken South Africa's skies and eclipse the sun as they come home to roost.

Clotted nonsense has coagulated around the so-called "right to a vote" wherever the Parliamentary system operates. Seventy years ago Cecil Rhodes advocated "equal rights to every civilised man south of the Zambesi" and the British Governor of the Cape, before that, had proposed extending the vote to every person, of any colour, who had a specified educational qualification. This latter is the furthest that the most libertarian political group in South Africa today—the Progressive Party—will go in the forlorn hope of exceeding the limits of a formula without destroying it. Imposition of an educational qualification was dropped by the British Governor when he realised that it would cause the disfranchisation of many White voters of that day. If the Progressives succeeded in the same objective, the result would be similar—unless the educational qualification were made so low that every White person now equipped with the vote could pass through its wide mesh.

Democracy does not now work effectively simply because the ideal of "the right to vote" is fallacious. No one should have that right who has not the intellectual ability to employ the vote with an intelligence that thoroughly understands the multifarious and far-reaching political issues by which his vote can affect the progress of the world and influence the destiny of mankind. Not only for the Bantu but for every person in every country of the world, the imposition of a high educational qualification would make the democratic principle truly functional. There are millions of people in the world exercising the most potent instrument yet devised—the vote, superior to the inter-stratospheric ballistic missile, because controlling it—who are not competent to arrive at the considered judgments their votes blindly implement.

South Africans, practically as a whole, vociferously react against the "one man one vote" proposal. That they are wrong, in the view of many people overseas, is quite irrelevant —the hard and existing fact is: they do. Their attitude is derived from the entirely logical processes of the first natural law: self-preservation. "One man one vote" places electoral power in the hands of every man merely because he is a man; it completely ignores any other possible qualification, either economic or educational. Applied to South Africa, it would mean the rule of three million White people by eleven million Black people, because three million adult Black voters would swamp one million adult White voters.

Of those three million adult Black voters fewer than 20,000 are at all competent to run—and fewer still to rule—

the country. South Africa is the highly-complicated piece of machinery that every other modern nation is—Government is but the managing director's office. It manages and directs not only the administrative complex but legislates for the entire mechanics of the national economy—the mines, a huge industrial organisation, finance, banking, the Stock Exchange, vast commercial ramifications, a highly-developed modernised agronomy, scientific research and activities, an extensive professional structure. To run only one of those vital operations —the mines—more than 100,000 experts and technicians are required. Government and administration—both national and provincial—require 30,000 men and women experienced in that science. Finance, banking and the Stock Exchange system are now the intricate and delicate operation they are because 60,000 skilled and highly educated people control them. In the conduct of commerce, scientific development, the professions and agriculture more than 150,000 experienced and completely qualified experts are engaged.

South Africans of all classes and opinions declare that the "one man one vote" policy would plunge the country into ruin and destruction. There is not, among the Bantu, a sufficiency of educated, completely civilised people to direct the destiny of even the nine Bantustan states which the National Government proposes to establish—and that fact is used as an unanswerable argument by the opponents to that proposal. To place this highly-complicated country under the direction of —at most—20,000 educated Bantu, the overwhelming majority of whom are educated no further than Standard VI levels, would result in such catastrophic chaos that the economy of the entire country would stagger to a stupendous disaster under the impact.

"This is the National Government's doing; let them get out

of their own mess" is another attitude that has been considerably expressed to me. It is not without a percentage of validity. This present Government inherited a legacy of confusion, devised by 150 years of maladroit British and Boer government which panhandled the future—and the present Government has essayed the stupendous task of carving intaglios out of backyard pine, with more zeal than sense, in more haste than speed, more like visionaries than men of vision. All the evidences point to two facts—the task is too immense for rapid completion; the methods employed on it are too precipitate. History cannot be unwound so easily.

This colossal problem is not of modern construction. It no more belongs to the present era than to the Smuts or Hertzog or Botha or Kruger or the Milner eras. It is the culmination of historic processes. It began 300 years ago and has been developing, like an inflamed boil, as the years pass until now its pus is ready to burst and only a lancet can relieve the massive accumulation. In its attempt at therapeutic treatment, the National Government has employed the inadequacies of mustard-plasters and the cruelty of unanaesthetised surgery. In flinching from a major operation which would remove the root of the inflammation—economic injustice—the Government has had recourse to the quack-nostrums of fatuous ideologies.

For the planting of that root, the British cannot evade all of the incubus of responsibility. History stabs an accusing finger. Only if the tablets of the past could be expunged would present British condemnation of South Africa be feasible and the reason for it cease to exist. It began and continued because capitalist Britain and British capitalists only viewed South Africa as an area for exploitation—to apply Bismarck: "a city to loot". That is asserted, repeated and reiterated on every bloodstained page of South Africa's history during the "century of wrong". South Africa's "colour problem" is as much a British as an Afrikaner legacy.

History, with its ineradicable facts, tells the unmistakable, undeniable story. It was the British administration that introduced the technique of Bantu apartheid—separate islands of Black population from which to draw cheap labour-fodder: the present Black "islands" of Basutoland, Bechuanaland and Swaziland, designated British Protectorates, are the remaining relics; and evidential proofs. Criticism and condemnation of the present Government in South Africa is warranted and appropriate—but not on official Britain's lips.

WHEN the founder-fathers landed from the *Dromedaris* at Cape Town there was not a Bantu nearer than 1,000 miles away. Ancestrally their home was at the savage birthplace of mankind; in fact, some of the christianised Bantu, in later years, were to trace their forebears back to Ham, the son of Noah, whose other son Shem founded the Semitic race, and claimed to be directly descended from original man. Apocryphal as that may be, there is ample proof that the Bantu warriors acted on the vulturine principle that wherever there were others doing better than they, that was the place for them to pounce. Their progress from the Congo and north-east Africa, during the first ten centuries of the Christian era, has been traced, defining a constant advance to reap where others had sown.

From the east coast which looked out on Arabia and India they rolled down like a black miasmic vapour over the land, responding to the smell of other people's prosperity as it reached their broad nostrils. Masses of dry-stone ruins mark where they found, and destroyed, earlier civilised people; geologists have traced their predatory march in the ashes and debris that tell the tale of the passage of medieval Bantu down to and through the centre of the continent. They have deciphered from the 1,000-year-old remains the advance of the Mashonas to the area north of the Zambesi where ruins of ancient buildings, block-houses and excavations testify to a pre-Bantu occupation which the marauding savages from the north exterminated. Signs of this Kaffirisation chart the Bantu advance on every outpost of civilisation and it is possible that had their search for the fabulous if not fabled King Solomon's mines succeeded, it would have halted there long enough to spare the infant South Africa the terrors of a series of Kaffir wars.

When the Portuguese mariners, diverted from South Africa by the storms of Cabo Tormentoso, established a settlement along the east coast, the black vultures with assegai and poisoned arrow for talons were attracted by the blood-smell of White men. Under their chieftain, Monomotapa, the Makalanga tribesmen poured into the fever-sodden interior, living in wattle and daub huts over an area that stretched down the hinterland towards what eventually became Swaziland, raiding Mozambique and murdering any White men who ventured inland. Waves of Bantu invaders swept down like locust-plagues, indulging their cannibalistic appetites on a diet of Portuguese until Quiloa (now called Kilwa) was destroyed and Mombasa sacked. That murderous victory by the Bantu savages took place exactly 60 years before van Riebeeck landed at Kaapstad, nearly 3,000 miles' marching distance away.

Stretching from the mouth of the Zambesi to Angola in the

west, a black mass bisected central Africa; but it was a movable girdle: the blood-fevered Bantu were on the war-march south. Most progress was made on the east with other tribes striking through the Great Lakes until, when news reached them that the White man—their "lawful" prey—was settling at the furthermost southerly tip of the country, it became a competition in plundering speed for the prize.

Only if the whole continent of Africa is regarded as the rightful possession of the Bantu can they be correctly described as the South African native population. If occupancy is the test, the Hottentots and Bushmen—now virtually non-existent—were the natives; the Bantu invaded the Cape many years after the White population had settled, cultivated and established it as their home. To speak of South Africa as "the Bantu homeland" is to deny the historic and recorded facts. There were no Bantu when the first White men arrived and where they settled.

Nor were the Hottentots and Bushmen an advance corps of the Bantu invading army; they were its first victims. Bushmen possessed no Bantu physical characteristics except non-White pigmentation. They were the final relics of the Stone Age, having once been the only inhabitants of all Africa south of the Zambesi and were, for a century, the victims of Bantu cannibalism. They were not Bantu in appearance; not black but of sallow complexion; not big-built and burly but dwarfs; not Congo-negroid but with triangular, fox-type faces, broad upright foreheads and deep-sunken eyes. Hottentots, whose ancestral home was around the Great Lakes, were driven south by the advancing Bantu from whom they were, physically, most distinctly different with physiognomical indices fundamentally unlike them. Slight of build, hollow-backed, small hands and feet, their skins varied from olive-yellow to near-white. As a race they cease to exist, either destroyed by the Bantu or by European diseases or absorbed into the Coloureds' twilight fraternity.

From the north and the east the Bantu tribes converged on the Cape—which was all that then comprised present-day South Africa—waging incessant war, blood-lusting and conforming to no rules other than those of jungle savagery. They advanced on the scattered farm settlements like hordes of crayfish in crustaceous armour brandishing fiercely-waving pincers. When there were not pitched battles, there were constant and murderous attacks on isolated farmsteads as they sought mindless satisfaction of animal desires. White farmers were slaughtered and their womenfolk assaulted; cattle driven off and homesteads burned to ash-heaps. For a century, the White population was engaged in a war whose frontiers shifted with the advance or retreat of the Bantu savages. That long state of self-protecting belligerency channelled and canalised Boer thinking into an attitude that needs no atomising to understand it and is one explanation of the bar that divides the South African population.

It was not until 1770, as the Boers extended from around Cape Town eastward to the Mossel Bay area, that they made their first contact with the Xosa vanguard of the invading Bantu and so began a century-long battle against the advancing hordes. They had come from the Congo forests and from the north-east swamplands, murdering other tribes as they war-marched until the fierce Alambo and Amazimba tribes had poured into what is now Natal, 1,000 miles from Cape Town to the east. They were followed by the Bavenda and Bakwana tribes who came via what are now the Transvaal and the Orange Free State in search of the White men who, a thousand tom-toms through a hundred forests had telegraphed, were creating prosperous farms at the south.

Heading the invading and predatory Black multitudes were the Xosas, with the Tembus hard on their heels. Van Plettenburg, the Dutch Governor—who gave his name to the south-coast bay which is one of modern South Africa's delight-spots —conciliated the murdering Xosa chieftains by allocating the Fish River as the dividing line but this agreement was not honoured long by the Bantu, if at all. Xosas crossed the river nightly to raid the Boers' farms and capture their cattle. The first Kaffir war resulted and the Bantu were driven back across the river.

For the following twenty years the Boers kept the Bantu at their distance and a state of peaceful co-existence existed. At the end of that period, the British seized the Cape and imposed their own system of administration wherever the Boers had trekked, using the good offices of the missionaries to break up the fallow ground and sow the seeds of British policy. The most outstanding of these was Dr. John Philip who became the chief adviser to Lord Somerset, the first British Governor, on Bantu affairs. Philip would have infuriated his present-day admirers because he was a convinced segregationist and fiercely opposed the mixing of White and Black peoples. He urged on Somerset—and Somerset put the advice into effect—a policy of strict and rigid apartheid: social and residential segregation of Black from White with no rights whatever for the Bantu other than to be Christianised and be the hewers of wood and drawers of water for their White masters.

That is stated merely to keep the historic record straight. It happened less than 150 years ago, at a time when the British administration were dealing with three Kaffir wars in summary

British fashion. They also introduced the "tot" system for Bantu labour—its operation, now, is a popular target for criticism. Pass laws, relics of which are roundly condemned in South Africa, were another exercise in British administration. Hottentots were bought and sold as slaves under British administration for thirty years and when the Westminster Government reluctantly abolished slavery in South Africa they paid the farmers, who had bought slaves under the British law, only £1,247,401 in compensation instead of the £2,824,224 they had been promised, and part of that payment was made in 3½ per cent stock which stood below par and went lower. Because of their losses, many Boers had the mortgages on their farms foreclosed.

Governor after Governor employed a policy of first siding with the Boers against the Bantu and then switching to the support of Bantu against Boer for the next fifty years. They backed Moshesh, the Basuto chief, against the Boers of the Orange Free State and, when he had served the imperial purpose, threw him over and annexed Basutoland in breach of agreement. They backed the Orange Free State against the Griquas until diamonds were discovered in Griqualand and then they recognised the "rights" of Waterboer, the Griqua chief—and annexed his territory to the Cape Colony. They "shepherded" 80,000 Bantu away from Panda, a rival chief, into a reserve—and turned it into a Crown land. They established relations with Dingaan, the Zulu chief, giving him friendly support in exchange for the southern half of Natal which was annexed to the Crown; he slew Retief and his seventy Boer followers soon after. And when Pretorius set out to retaliate, British troops were sent to prevent him—unsuccessfully because the Boer victory of Blood River was achieved. They sold guns to the Galekas and Fingoes at high prices and then decreed their disarmament—"as a necessary civilising measure"—compensating them for the seized guns at current low rates. They supported the Boers of the Transvaal when they produced evidence of the depredations of Cetewayo, the Zulu chief, and then threw away the evidence, backed Cetewayo and gave him all that he asked for—at the Boers' expense.

These historic records make confusing reading without the explanation that the policy of "divide to rule" was not only traditionally British but had proved highly successful in the onward march of imperial power. That it must have confused the Bantu, whose high evaluation of the White man's conduct was an essential to their civilised development, is certain, especially when the maladministration of the British was paralleled by the ruthlessness of the Boers who had, from a long bitter experience of frontier fighting for survival, developed an attitude towards the Blacks that was compounded of feudal Uncle Tomism and inherited enmity. Between the pincers of British imperialism and Boer nationalism, the Bantu were squeezed into a docility that masked a volcanic resentment.

There was no deliberately planned policy behind the Boer attitude: it was inherent and instinctive. From the day that van Riebeeck landed, the black-skinned people were regarded as fundamentally inferior in all respects except the capacity for sweat-of-the-brow labour—and the good Calvinists could fluently quote from the Old Testament to convince themselves that they had Divine authority for an attitude which the New Testament denied. With that profound conviction as a basis, the murderous depredations of the Bantu provided sufficient material with which to build a religiocentric ruthlessness in action.

Buttressing their fearful souls with heady draughts of Isaiah, the Boers relegated the Bantu to the status of specimens of creation whom the Creator had predestined to be, for ever, the handmaiden of the White man; subject and subservient. Any deviation from the prostrate stance had to be sternly punished, as any responsible parent would a fractious child. No outrage against the Divine plan for mankind could be more heinous than for the inferior to threaten his master with force and every such enterprise had to be repressed, relentlessly and remorselessly. The actions of such virtuous Boers create somewhat cynical reactions in the less Christian mind: we know that God will forgive us our sins but our virtues will pose Him a toughish problem.

Those contrasting motivations constituted the main difference between the British and the Boer treatment of the Bantu —with one, it was part of imperial policy; with the other, it was in accordance with Divine teaching. So far as the Bantu victims were concerned, the motivation was a matter of abstract interest: the result on them was the same—repression. To the detached observer, there would appear a more acceptable quality attaching to the British than to the Boer inspiration. Empires have only been built on the bodies, blood and bones of their victims and, if an empire is desirable, the inevitable measures to secure it cannot be regarded as undesirable. In the case of the British Empire, events have proved that despite all the objectionable methods employed in its creation, it has bestowed an enormous benefaction on the world. Its sequel has been even more magnificent: after developing its undeveloped or under-developed possessions— obtained, often, over the corpses of their people—it has returned them to those victimised peoples in a far greatly improved form than they, without the benefices of imperial power, could ever have achieved. Bearing in mind the drastic key-change involved, that is a major triumph in tonal modulation.

Basic to the British administration of South Africa was the traditional "divide to rule" tactic. Bantu were worked against Boer and Boer against Bantu through the terms of office of twenty-eight British administrations. Pacification and reconciliation could never be instruments of that policy. Instigation of strife, encouragement of resentment, condonation of war were more appropriate and, because so, mark the course of events during "the century of wrong".

Apartheid—apartness: residential as well as social segregation—was the British policy with, of course, no political rights whatever. That it suited both Boer and Bantu is its entire justification and is one of the justifications cited by its sponsors for its present-day continuation. Bantustanism is of British origin. Large areas were set aside for Black occupation, delineated precisely and self-governed by tribal administrative customs: frontiered off from the areas allocated for White-only occupancy—a checker-board design of residential and social life. Temboland was one such British-created Bantustan —it is now part of the Transkei, a Bantustan of modern creation.

A well-defined pattern to the British policy of those years is clearly revealed. Two objectives were aimed at simultaneously—suppression of Boer recalcitrance against the British occupation by assisting first one side and then the other in the lengthy Boer-Bantu warfare; and preservation of the Bantu as a reservoir of cheap labour, a necessity that sharpened in the second generation of British rule when diamonds were discovered, to be followed, a few years later, by the inception of the gold-mining industry. Once that dual policy is discerned, the methods by which it was implemented are explicable and —if the justification of imperial necessity is accepted— excusable. It was a venture in classic Empire-building.

For it to succeed certain factors were required. One was that the Black labour-pool should remain just that; never be encouraged along such a dangerous avenue as ambition, self-improvement and social or political emancipation. For a full century, British administration had ample opportunity—even as late as 1910 when Westminster authorised the Act of Union for South Africa that entrenched basic aspects of the present Bantu subordination—to do for the Bantu what, if it had been done, would have secured for them some instalment of the social equality which Britons now demand that South Africa should give in full. For only half a century South Africa has been self-governed but the improvement, advancement and degree of social emancipation of the Bantu that has been achieved in that short time denudes the British, of all people, of the right to condemn.

WHILE the British were mishandling the human material known as the Bantu, the Boers were treating it with an insensitive harshness that has created a subterranean force of explosive resentment. That the Boer can justify his attitude to the Bantu with selected passages from the Old Testament and invocation of Divine guidance is exactly the reverse of justification. It is as impossible to employ the teachings of a God of Love to justify oppression as to use the Prince of Peace as the patron-saint of war. This recourse to religion disgusts most non-Afrikaners and their disgust is one of those facts whose existence is not destroyed by ignoring them.

Afrikaners have, throughout their short life as a people, been consistent in the application of religious beliefs to their Bantu attitude. Their primitive sternness, as part of the parent-child relationship, has been tempered with kindly paternalism. They believe in a God who is both just and kind: their punishment of the Bantu is justice; their Uncle Tomism is an expression of paternal kindness. On that day when Boer and Bantu first clashed, on the banks of the Fish River, the Boer first chastised the invaders and then allocated territory to them. Those related actions were symbolic. Bantu right to their own type of existence is fully recognised; they must exercise that right in their allocated territory—the philosophy of apartheid.

Even if the philosophy were acceptable, the present Government is undoubtedly rendering it repugnant by the methods of application. Somewhere, during ten generations, a streak of sadism has crept into the Afrikaner mentality. Only that could explain the unnecessary human cruelty that disfigures the application of apartheid by some officials and makes apartheid repulsive even to many of those who might be prepared to accept its philosophic content. It is, my investigations convince me, the lengthy catalogue of small and large inhumanities characterising the individual implementation of apartheid which has made it a dirty word to most people and among whom many Afrikaners are included. Among many who adhere to the policy of segregation that has been traditional to South Africa—under British as well as Afrikaner rule—there has developed a rigid rejection of its modern form because of the sequence of human cruelties which has deformed it with a hideous scarification.

It would seem as if a deep, ingrained bitter antipathy to dark pigmentation has been accumulated during the years and now overflows the pent vial so that its century-long concentration oozes out in uncontrollable retribution for long-past evils. That may well be the case. History is too unmistakable on the point: for decade after decade, generation upon generation of Afrikaners suffered sorely from Bantu tribes who were bereft of any of civilisation's restrictions. That could, and in all probability has, resulted in an inherited neurosis which now seeks compensation in unleashed harshness.

It is as if the core of a guilt-consciousness was built into the Afrikaner race at conception and only the emulsion of civilised counter-thinking can cure that psychological sickness. There are unmistakable signs that among the new generation of Afrikaners that mental therapy is at work. T. S. Eliot once wrote: "For all that happens began in the past and presses hard on the future." As the present jostles the past out of the consciousness of the new Afrikaner, he can be seen as making sincere and intelligent efforts to reorientate the inherited Boer-Bantu relationship. His traditional paternalism is being revealed and expressed in certain improvements in Bantu conditions—pathetically limited but, compared with anything previously done, extremely significant—that have been effected during recent years.

Less than 100 years ago, Bantu savages were marching on Afrikaners, breathing fire and slaughter, shrieking unintelligible war-cries, bloodlust frothing in their uncivilised minds. Less than 300 years ago, Bantu tribes were making their first contact with White men and the White man's civilisation. Three hundred years is an eyelid flash compared with the time it has taken other peoples to become civilised. Three hundred years after the Romans had brought civilisation and Christianity to Britain, the Brythons were still clothed in skins—hence their name—their faces daubed with woad, and they worshipped pagan gods: this could be a description of the Bantu at the same stage of development only 300 years ago. It took more than 1,500 years for those Britons to get even partial, very considerably qualified, suffrage, and "the right to vote" was conceded to all British adults less than two generations ago. When it was first proposed to accord that "right" to others than the gentry, Wellington told the House of Lords that he opposed "the outrageous idea", being convinced that the existing Parliament was sufficient and satisfactory, as it consisted of "a large body of the property of the country and in which the landed interest has a preponderating influence". As it took the British more than 1,500 years from the time when their ancestors were running around in skins and with woad-daubed faces to reach that minimum stage of "political equality", Afrikaners advise them to consult their own history when they demand that South Africa should operate the "one man one vote" policy towards the Bantu who were pagan savages much less than 300 years ago.

Only this year, Mr. Harold Macmillan, the very first Prime Minister of Britain ever to visit South Africa, even if he was only here for ten days, delivered a speech to the members of Parliament in Cape Town, which included much admonitory finger-wagging at South Africa for its misdoings. Had his moralistic lecturing and heckling come from Mr. Hugh Gaitskell, his Socialist opponent at Westminster—for whom and whose "one man one vote" policy most South Africans, of all political colourings, have expressed deep abhorrence—South Africa would have accepted them as being, at least, consistent. Coming from the leader of the Party which had, for more than a century, been mainly responsible for the power-politics of British imperialism that had left to South Africa a legacy of resentments; that had practised apartheid, initiated Bantustanism and the Pass Laws; exploited the natural wealth of the country and then left it in ruins—such moralising was considerably too much for the stomach. Despite the generous doses of bicarbonate administered by the English press, many South Africans just puked.

Criticism, they said, might be appropriate from every other Commonwealth country, from America and from Socialists; from the British Tories it came as if atheists were condemning others for the collapse of moral living that godlessness caused. On the lips of a British Tory, self-righteous criticism of South Africa for the way it is handling the problems that British Toryism created was so unctuous as only to be explained as the protective coloration to a bad conscience. South Africans know their history. They take the view that history is not yesterday's newspaper that is torn up and thrown away: it is an imperishable parchment on which is recorded the facts of the past whereof the present is constructed; incontro-vertible, ineradicable, irrevocable.

They lost no time in relating the Macmillan lecture to those facts. They recalled that it was a sequence of Tory administrations at Westminster which had forcibly seized South Africa, destroyed the Afrikaners' culture and suppressed their language, seized territories when South Africans had transformed them from wilderness to fertile lands, annexed Griqualand so soon as diamonds were found there, took the goldbearing Transvaal from its elected government at the point of half a million bayonets; by maladministration and definite policy, made of millions of Bantu one huge problem. It was a Liberal Government at Westminster—not the Tories, who fiercely opposed it—that, by returning to South Africa the self-government its Tory predecessor had taken as an act of robbery-with-violence, indulged in the mystic rite of expiation for that "century of wrong"—a soothing coda to a tragic sonata.

South Africans listened to the new Tory leader as he piously reprimanded them for the efforts to solve the "Colour problem" by methods which, however reprehensible in detail, are considered to be good in intention; they listened—and looked at the "Colour problem" that misgovernment by his own Tory predecessors had dumped in their lap. They compared what South Africa had done to undo Tory misdeeds in fifty years with what Tory government had done in the previous one hundred years. They compared the complete ignorance, primitive living conditions and lack of social welfare which the entire Bantu were suffering when Tory Britain ended its century of government with the educational advancement, continuous Bantu housing schemes and social services far in advance of anything the British Tories are now doing in those Native territories they still administer.

Had the criticism of their efforts come from a Socialist leader, South Africans could have understood it, even if they rejected it, because Socialism is the antithesis of the Tory policy of economic exploitation that is the cause and root of South Africa's "Colour problem". Economic justice, being blasphemous in the Tory credo of exploitation, the Macmillan holier-than-thou sermonette sounded to many in South Africa as belonging to a text-book of abnormal psychology.

That reaction was expressed to me by South Africans of varying political opinion and outlook. When a man of such deep-seated antipathy to the present Nationalist Government as Mr. J. C. (son of General) Smuts finds himself forced by Mr. Macmillan's speech "reluctantly to agree with Dr. Verwoerd" the adverse effect of the Tory Premier's homily can be measured. Mr. Smuts, who said he is "a warm and affectionate admirer of Britain and an inveterate opponent of Dr. Verwoerd's Government" synthesized the views of the Macmillan speech that numbers of other thoughtful South Africans expressed to me. Of the Tory Premier's basic premise—that all men are inherently equal—he said: "This is a sound Christian concept but is in every other respect unproved and probably fallacious and contrary to the teachings of anthropology and evolution. It would take a very great stretch of the imagination, for example, to put the primitive Bushmen of the Kalahari or the pigmies of the Ituri Forest on the same level as the Western European. My feeling is that we delude ourselves if we work on this simple belief of equality."

Mr. Smuts also published a full commentary[1] on Mr. Macmillan's conception of the temperament, aptitude and ability of the Black peoples. He said:

"It is incorrect to assume, as overseas people do, that the African native is merely a White man in a Black skin; that his reasoning and responses will be the same; that his reactions to problems that confront civilised society will be similar; that his political and administrative abilities will be subject to the same trends.

"In fact the Native is as different from the European as the horse is from the zebra and their responses to extraneous influences will differ as widely. To believe that the Native will measure up closely in development pattern to the peoples of Western Europe would be a gross and dangerous delusion. Already this fact has been brought home sharply in the hard practical world of the dismembered British and Dutch colonial empires.

[1] *The Star*, Johannesburg.

159

"To many of us it is clear that the vast bulk of Black peoples are not concerned with political rights and nationalistic aspirations, nor in fact with any ideologies, but are far more preoccupied with work-a-day matters like full stomachs and happy homes."

That is the realistic assessment of "the Colour problem" that many other South Africans expressed to me. They believe that the politically-inspired demand for Native "independence" has no genuine depth; that it is an artificial demand cloaking the real fact that the Bantu, as a mass-people in South Africa, are much less agitated by an upsurge of nationalistic emotion than a desire for "full stomachs and happy homes". That, in itself, is a revolutionary demand: to grant it would cause an economic revolution. For that reason, every Government—including the present one—tries to evade it by substituting for the most practical solution of the problem evasive ideologies and ideology-inspired policies.

To the South African governing class of today, as to the sequence of British administrations, the Bantu is primarily regarded as a vast and valuable labour-pool. It is conceivable that present-day South Africans are convinced that it becomes a much more productive labour-pool if its denizens are dealt out doles of development. However much that motivation may be open to criticism, it is a noteworthy advance on the past policy of exploitation without any degree of emancipation whatever.

WHEN references are made by overseas commentators to South Africa's "colour problem" it can be questioned whether they are aware of its extent and depth. It is not so much a problem as problems within a problem. America has a "colour problem" but, compared with that in South Africa, it is alphabet-simple. There is much talk, in America, of solving its "colour problem" by integration. If that were done, 16,000,000 "coloureds" in that country would be integrated with—which means: absorbed by—160,000,000 White people. Integration in South Africa would have a somewhat different result: 3,000,000 White people would be integrated with—absorbed by—11,000,000 non-Whites.

My enquiries convinced me beyond all doubt that it would be extremely difficult to find 1,000 White people in South Africa who would agree with such absorption if the time came. And it is doubtful whether, in such circumstances, any other Western country would. When faced with a "colour problem" caused by the influx of 100,000 West Indians, who are British citizens, Britain was conspicuous for red-faced embarrassment expressed in various forms of bold-faced rejection. To be equivalent to the South African integration that many British people recommend, Britain would have to integrate with her 50,000,000 White citizens a Coloured population of 150,000,000 at least—and yet, a mere 100,000 gave some in that country a choking sensation.

Integration is clearly not acceptable to the White population of South Africa, and—this is well worthy of italics—not desired by the non-Whites, as a solution to "the colour problem", which is far too complicated to sustain a sloganised solution. Involved in that problem, as the constituent elements, are not merely the Bantu, but the Indians, the Malay, the Mauritians, the St. Helenians and more than a million Coloured people. Even if the Asiatic group could be legislated for to their satisfaction, the Coloured people constitute a problem of their own—and to themselves. And even if that could be solved and the "colour problem" confined to the Bantu it propagates its own dark fibres of insolubles.

In addition to the fact that the Bantu and the Coloureds practise apartheid—when I proposed adding a Bantu housegirl to my domestic staff, my Coloured cook said that she would leave at once—the Bantu, themselves, are so diversified that the problem becomes alarming. Only those who live in South Africa for any noticeable length of time realise this complexity. Using figures approximately: of the eleven million Bantu, one-third are in the Native Reserves, one-third on farms and rural areas, one-third are urbanised or in the mines. If anyone imagines that those classifications possess only occupational connotations, he is advertising a dangerous ignorance. They form the gear and clutch of a mighty problem.

There are pronounced differentials between the Reserve, the agricultural and the urbanised Bantu so profound as almost to make them different peoples. To subject all those three main groupings to the same legislative processes—which means: to expect the same intelligence responses—would be so fantastic as to approach the boundaries of idiocy. The whole structure of existence, among the three groups, is utterly different and contrasting.

That is the stone in the furrow. A century ago, when the British had every opportunity to resolve the problem which South Africa is now demanded to solve, the sable skein was not tangled in that way. There was only one Bantu people— warlike, predatory, nomadic. The great contribution that the British made to their development—a very important and constructive one—was to get them to settle in specified regions. If that happened to be the residential segregation that is now part of apartheid, it must not be condemned on

that account. Temboland became the National Home of the
Tembus; the Zulus were domiciled in Zululand, the Swazis
in Swaziland, the Basutos in Basutoland, the Bechunas in
Bechuanaland, the Griquas in Griqualand—the six Bantustans
of that day. British-directed segregation reduced "the colour
problem" to manageable proportions.

Gold changed all that. Goldmines, like any other enterprise
in which huge sums of money—in this case British capital
mainly—is invested, are considered successful if they produce
two results: gold and profits. There was no great difficulty
in producing gold—Nature had merely secreted it for man's
discovery. The production of profits was a much more difficult
operation—profits are determined by production costs. As
every industrialist, financier and economist knows, one of the
major items in production cost is labour: its price, its wastage
and its efficiency.

After a spell of "coolie labour"—Chinese workers imported
on contract—the goldmines reverted to Bantu labour: it was
cheap; it was plentiful; it was docile. Its wastage was readily
replenished—there were millions, with Congo-chiselled
features and a high rate of fertility, available. There would not
be the goldmining industry there is in South Africa; "kaffir"
shares on the Stock Exchanges of London and Johannesburg
would not stand so high as they do; shareholders in Britain
and elsewhere would not be so comfortable as they now are
if the inexhaustible reservoirs of cheap Bantu labour were not
so accessible.

And so millions of Bantu have been transformed, by natural
or artificial processes, from a people whose normal lives
consisted of raising cattle—their only recognised form of
wealth—and either protecting or adding to them by warlike
exercises, into a huge concourse to provide the diggers of

gold-bearing ore from the bowels of God's earth; and often die by hundreds in the process either from lingering phthisis or sudden disaster. More than 350,000 Bantu men work deep down in South Africa's goldmines. Apart from their under-payment and other personal inconveniences, there is nothing to be said critically about that—millions of men work in mines all over the world. It is merely recorded here as a fact that has changed "the colour problem" during the last century.

Goldmining was a pebble thrown into a pool. Among the radiating circles was the beginning of secondary industries to serve the goldmines. Those, also, had to make profits; the cheaper the labour the greater the profitability of the under-taking. From those industries, essential to goldmining, developed the realisation that South Africa could be more comprehensively industrialised. Stimulated by war-demands, hundreds, thousands, of industrial undertakings have been established. And always there must be the correlation of production costs and profits. Thousands upon thousands of uneducated or under-educated Bantu men and women helped narrow that correlation. And so there are more than two million Bantu working in industry, commerce, transport and other occupations—and living near their work: the vast, urbanised, semi-detribalised Black population who are, mostly, so grossly underpaid that the base of South Africa's population pyramid is a huge quagmire of direst poverty providing the ideal soil in which agitational crops germinate and grow.

It is that section of the Bantu that constitutes the hard core of South Africa's "colour problem". The four million that still live a traditionally tribalised life, subject to tribal codes and sanctions, in the Reserves; the three million who live a feudal life on the farms, enjoying the paternalistic economy of

Uncle Tomism; those do not provide an insoluble problem. They have achieved some polarisation of instinct and self-discipline.

To a quite considerable extent, and within their capabilities, they are happy and moderately contented, uncontaminated with the virus of citified "civilisation" and unagitated by cravings for something they have never known. It is in the hundreds of thousands of Bantu who have been divested, or divested themselves, of the restraints, the codes of conduct, the standards and sanctions of their tribal system; who have been pitchforked into the unnatural ways of the White man whom it is their supreme ambition to emulate, that the tough nut of South Africa's "colour problem" is concentrated.

Social services in any country have to be paid for by the taxpaying beneficiaries, but all that the entire Bantu population of 11,000,000 pay in annual taxation is about £4,000,000 even after the slight increase made this year is included. Ten times that amount is spent on Bantu education, health and other welfare services. Matching that small national revenue from the Bantu are their low earnings which even prevent them extracting full benefit from the social services that the State provides. To exchange a backyard hut for a four-roomed house is not such an attractive form of domestic progress when it means £2 a month more rent. "Keeping up with the Ngolis" is no temptation so long as the income of millions of Bantu families is less than £15 when £23 per month is the official minimum required for a family to scramble to the right side of the poverty line.

A favourite diversion in pulpiteering is to declare that "all things work together for good''; that suffering and poverty can have ennobling effects on human character. That would be an unpopular evangel with Bantu people. They nurse the quaint notion that while poverty and suffering may ennoble when they are voluntary, by involuntary poverty and suffering men are made more ignoble. If ever there is a social earthquake among the Bantu, thoughtful observers have assured me that they are convinced that it will not be aspirations of political emancipation or the ''one man one vote'' demand but poverty at the epicentre. Recent international events have demonstrated that extreme nationalistic political demands have often been poverty's ultimate blow-off. When a people live a life that is not worth living, death in revolt is a considerable irrelevancy.

It is the Bantu wage-structure that constitutes the kernel of the ''colour problem'' nut which South Africa has to crack. Eleven million Bantu have an agregate total income of less than £400,000,000 which is deplorably low but, before a stream of criticism is expectorated from overseas, I should add that, when Britain handed over the ''colour problem'' to South Africa, fifty years ago, the total income of eight million Bantu was £48,000,000—South Africa has increased the British standard from £6 to £33 per capita, or, allowing for the depreciation in money-values, a three-fold increase.

Despite the manacles of poverty, many thousands of Bantu have taken advantage of the educational, social and domestic facilities provided during the past decade or two which, inadequate as they would appear, are immense when compared with those provided during the one hundred years of British administration. To transform conditions for only one-fifth of the huge Bantu population is a gargantuan achievement of which people overseas either are unaware or which they

Native shacks in notorious Cato Manor, outside Durban, scene of many faction-fights and riots, now being demolished.

One of the eight blocks of Bantu bachelor apartments, totalling 162 flats, in the Langa township of Cape Town.

Rapt attention of an art pupil at the Family Welfare Centre in Alexander, the Johannesburg township.

Hezekieli Ntuli, a Zulu modeller, at work in his hut near Eshowe in Natal.

underestimate. Whole populations of tin-shack townships have been transported to community settlements of brick-built houses, with electricity and sanitary services, each with its own neat little garden running down to well-designed paved roads. Scores of Bantu educational establishments—primary, secondary and high schools, colleges, universities—have been built. Transport services have taken the place of long walks or cycle rides to and from work. None of these services was inherited by South Africa from past administrations—they have all been created by South African governments.

Part of the actual legacy was a huge Bantu housing problem. In the main—or, at any rate, in priority of immediacies—it is centred in the urban areas, close to the chief concentrations of trade and industry. Its roots, therefore, are in the population question: it is a human problem created by the Bantu invasion of urban areas in response to the enticements of higher pay and the amenities of European civilisation.

While the White people have the lowest fertility figure in South Africa, the Bantu reproduce at the rate of 47 per 1,000 which, plus immigration—legal and otherwise—is increasing their population figure until the official estimates show that by the end of the century South Africa will have a Bantu population of 21,361,000 surrounding only 4,588,000 White people. The incursion of Bantu from their normal habitat has added more than 2,000,000 to the Reef urban areas and the official estimate is that there will be more than 11,000,000 Bantu in the urban areas of South Africa within the next forty years.

Opportunities—or, at least, a flash facsimile of them—in industry and commerce act as a magnet drawing the Bantu to the urban areas with a precocity of purpose, precipitating them, unprepared and unequipped, into the strange ways of urbanised existence. In the Transvaal alone only twenty per cent of the Bantu have remained in their own areas; the other eighty per cent have flooded into the cities. In the Free State the situation is more acute—three per cent have remained in their own home areas and ninety-seven per cent have migrated to the "European" districts.

Fifty years ago, when South Africa received self-government, Johannesburg had a Bantu population of 100,000—there are now more than 725,000 living in its metropolitan area alone, apart from the 350,000 in mine hostels. The significance of this enlarged figure resides in the fact that the city now has a second, and in many cases, a third generation of Bantu who know no other home than Johannesburg, on whom the codes and sanctions of tribalism have a weakened impact and who have become accustomed to the urban way of life as from birth. This acclimatisation to a non-Bantu outlook and the continuous, unwieldy and unregulated—often unregistered—growth of the Bantu population in South Africa's urban areas has postulated a problem in social conditions, domestic hygiene and housing such as no other country in the world has had to face. It is in viewing the extent to which South Africa has reduced the problem, rather than in solely concentrating on what remains to be done, that a fair assessment can be made by those who have no such problem to solve.

Housing for the Bantu must not depart, too tangentially, from the tribal principles that are traditional with them. That fact adds problem to problem. The nearly two million Bantu on the Reef, most of whom work in the six cities and towns, present a perfect cross-section of the entire race, and when I say that, in the goldmining labour force, no fewer than fifty-five different tribes are represented, the ethnic complications in settling a million Bantu in their own townships and housing estates should become vividly clear. Not all of the urbanised Bantu are even South African citizens. Many, probably most, come from Portuguese East Africa, the British Protectorates, the Rhodesias and even further north—and the Bantu of these varying tribal origins have customs and antipathies that are rooted in the mythological paganism of their past and in the gaping lucana of their minds.

This influx demands control. Immigration is easily controlable in Britain, a sea-girt island whose points of entry are readily regulated. South Africa has an amazingly lengthy, but invisible, boundary—and also three "islands" within the boundary: the British Protectorates—over which the Bantu could wander into South Africa and aggravate an already difficult social situation. If there were not a strict influx-control system, the cities and towns would be submerged beneath a flood of Bantu who would spawn over the land, workless and incapable of "European" work except primitive farming. Surrounding the Transvaal there are more than 100,000,000 Bantu eager to invade. If there were no influx-control and no registration cards, the housing, sanitation, health, education position—and crime, hunger, disease—would become a huge national danger.

Influx-control is not enough. Bantu workers are naturally volatile: labour-turnover in all centres of employment is very high—sixteen months is the average for any Bantu to remain in one job. To regulate that excessive fluctuation, a system of Labour Bureaux has been established which, while creating irritations and frustrations, has resulted in stabilising the entire labour force—because all Bantu workers, and all employers, are compelled to seek, through the Bureaux, their requirements.

Only through this double-decker direction—entry into the

area and work-provision after entry—did the authorities find
it feasible to grapple with the housing problem. One is,
therefore, considerably correlated to the other in an orderly,
planned perspective. There are now as many as twenty-two
townships, with 630,000 Bantu inhabitants, in the Johannesburg municipal area alone. Time off should here be taken to
meditate on what that bald statement implies.

More than 10,000 houses for the Bantu are being erected
by the Natives Resettlement Board every year. Even a small
town like Kroonstad (population: 8,000 White; 15,000
non-White) is busy erecting a Bantu township at Seeisoville
that compares very favourably with Kroonstad itself. During
the past ten years, £20,000,000 was spent throughout South
Africa on urban Bantu housing.

Ten years ago a Government survey showed that 167,000
Bantu houses were required. Ten years later more than
130,000 had been provided and by 1962 a further 185,000
will have been built. In the past ten years, more than sixty
new housing areas have been established throughout the
country and as many existing areas extended. That, by any
standard, is a housing scheme not to be apologised for.

To speak of a "new" housing area is not to refer merely
to the erection of a number of new houses: it usually includes
the demolishing of a foul and fetid shack-town that had been
allowed to grow up; and the mass-removal of thousands of
families from the old to the new. That is an enterprise in
social emancipation that not even the Welfare State of Britain
has ever essayed. Meadowlands, on the outskirts of Johannesburg, is a specimen.

Only five years ago more than 60,000 Bantu people were living
in Sophiatown, one of the worst slums that Johannesburg—or
any other city in the world—had to its discredit. As large as

Salisbury, the capital of Southern Rhodesia, it was a city within a city—and a breeding ground for disease, racial strife and crime where tsotsois, shebeen-queens and razor-slashing gangs defied even Father Huddleston's mild teachings. It was slummery in excelsis: self-made shanties constructed of old biscuit tins, canvas, wood; or rooms in tenements for which absentee landlords of other race-groups extorted excessive rents and the payment of "protection" money. Overcrowding was such that the density was 300 people to a morgen (2.2 acres). In one block of tumbledownery, 153 people "lived" in 31 small rooms. Rentals up to £5 per month were paid for a single room; up to £50 had to be paid for "key-money" and some of the landlords locked up the communal water-tap for 20 out of 24 hours each day to save their water bills.

It was decided to clear this cess-pool with its beast-pit odour by a compulsory mass-exodus to Meadowlands which was created for the purpose at a cost of more than £5,000,000. Compulsion, experience taught, was the only possible method when criminal elements found squalor profitable and terrorised others into compliance. Righteous shouts about the "liberty of the individual" bellowed out from well-meaning people living in the comfort of the Well-faring State, 6,000 miles away. Immunised against the disease and crime of Johannesburg's slumdom that was a shuddersome blasphemy against humanity and its Creator, the Archbishop of York, armed with bell, book and candle, pontificated amid a rustle of copes and clash of thuribles: "The removal of 60,000 Bantu people can be compared with the mass deportations carried out by the Nazi and Communist States."

I would very much have enjoyed taking His Grace with me, in 1955, when I toured that rabbit-warren of slums, and then again this year, when I visited Meadowlands and talked with

CURTAIN-UP ON SOUTH AFRICA

the inhabitants. That experience would be as stimulating as a sharp prod from his own crozier. If he was right in his impetuous statement, and that beneficial mass-removal was comparable with what the Communists do, then the results of his comparison can only be regarded as Communist propaganda.

Rentals at Meadowlands are from £1 to £4 4s. 6d. per month—determined by the tenants' income. That system may be, for all I know, a Communist method, in which case the Archbishop's comparison made sense. For example: a Bantu earning less than £15 per month pays £2 19s. 3d. per month—or less—for a five-roomed house with bathroom, kitchen, waterborne sewerage and services. I came across two cases where the tenants are passing through a period of serious hardship—they live rent-free.

Asked if he had had any trouble, Mr. D. C. Odendaal, the superintendent at Meadowlands, replied: "Oh yes; I have had plenty of trouble—keeping people who wanted houses away from my office." They had been living in Sophiatown slummery, where all the streets were short-cuts to the devil. Their "home" was a tumbledown corrugated-iron shack in the backyard of a shop, for which they paid £3 10s. per month.

If the Archbishop badly needs a comparison, he should compare that with a Meadowlands house. Meadowlands is away from the city, in unbuilt-up surroundings and consists of rows of small houses with gardens, on wide, paved streets. Most of the houses have four rooms, kitchen and bathroom, for which the rent is £2 10s. per month; for such, a White householder, in the urban zone, pays four times as much. Together with Protea, Orlando, Coronationville and Lenasia it forms part of a Bantu city of nearly 500,000 inhabitants.

Contrary to, contradicting, the Sinai-thunderings and liturgical fervour of His Grace, the people of Meadowlands utter their own "Te Deum" of gratitude. A short while back, 5,000 of them crowded one of the township's spacious squares, to express their grateful appreciation to the authorities. "We have asembled ourselves here," declared Mr. I. Mnguni of the Nguni tribe, "to say thanks for our deliverance from squalor in the slums and for our removal to this fine place, this model town of our own."

Those last two are the operative words—all the shops are owned and run by Bantu people; their children are educated by Bantu teachers in nearly a dozen schools; they listen to sermons by Bantu preachers in nine churches. As a mark of their appreciation, the Bantu inhabitants, at that thanksgiving meeting, presented Superintendent Odendaal with a beautiful shield, a Kerrie and several ornaments—the Kerrie, explained Mr. A. Ndela, Paramount Chief of the Zulus on the Rand, "is only for men of noble birth".

Meadowlands is not unique by any means. Nor have I singled it out as a show-piece—in fact it was a prototype from which lessons were learned and applied beneficially elsewhere. Springs (population: 26,000 White; 80,000 Bantu) has a model Bantu township, named Kwa-Thema, which is superior to many White towns in South Africa if only on account of its lighting system—it cost more than £140,000 and provides lights in side streets and more light-standards per mile in the main streets than most White towns. More than 80 miles of overhead lines have been strung up and 30 miles of underground cable laid to serve its rehoused Bantu population of 35,000 living in 5,749 model houses—all of which have been erected by Bantu labour.

It has an impressive civic centre, seven schools, a modern clinic, shopping centres, nine churches, library, cinema and every other modern amenity including a crèche where 200 children have expert care from 7 a.m. to 5 p.m. at a cost, to the parent who goes to work, of 4s. a month. Rentals at Kwa-Thema—named after a former Bantu leader—range from £1 12s. 6d. per month for a two-roomed house to £3 for a six-roomed house. More than 1,500 houses are being tenant-purchased—for £250 payable over 30 years.

Or there is Daveyton—which cost £7,500,000 to establish —with 8,000 model homes for its 46,770 Bantu inhabitants who are located in ethnic groupings. Every group area has a Ward Committee, each member of which represents a block of houses, and one of the Committee's functions is to settle all disputes according to their ethnic laws and customs, except where tribal law and custom conflict with public policy and justice. Daveyton, which covers 2,400 acres, is planned to more than double that acreage and house a total of 180,000 Bantu.

Or there is Alexandra which five years ago was a chaotic tumbledownery, a black-spot—known as "the Dark City"— notorious as the focal point of crime, squalor, poverty; terrorised by gangs which could have given points to any combination of Wild West and old-time Chicago that America could conjure up. The old bad Alexandra was on Johannesburg's door-step like a fly-infested dog-turd.

Although it could only accommodate 25,000 people, 148,000 "lived" there. No water or sanitation was provided to the "houses" although Alexandra supplied Johannesburg's industry and commerce with much of its labour force. Hygiene and health were a duo of unknown words. The streets were mish-mashed mud. Life consisted of merely a marking time between being squeezed out on to some confinement rag-bed and being lowered into some unhallowed hole. It is impossible, without recourse to a blending of Dante and Dickens, to describe Alexandra as it was five years ago, the home of tens of thousands of Bantu who, in the hopelessness of their frustration, oozed bitterness like a pustulated pimple on the mind.

Then another "Great Trek" was begun. Thousands of families were uprooted from "the Dark City"—where terror-stricken inhabitants paid "safety-fees" to gangs of ruthless Bantu terrorists—and transplanted into the new township. A section known as Mokoka, which had housed 70,000 Bantu in 12,000 mud-tin-and-sack hovels, was the first to be evacuated to Meadowlands and the humane living conditions which high-voltaged engineering had there created. First established under the British administration, and named by them after their reigning Queen, the township of Alexandra was South Africa's worst shacktown—terrible to observers, terrifying to its inhabitants. If nothing more had been done but erase that black spot, South Africa's rehousing policy would stand under heavy commendation.

I could proceed until the point of boredom and repetition was passed with this report on South Africa's enormous achievement in Bantu housing and, in doing so, I would not be axe-grinding but merely stating established facts in order to get the record straight. Such as these: In less than ten years, 300,000 Bantu have been rehoused in 59 urban townships outside the Johannesburg area; and 13 Bantu towns have been created. When the British handed South Africa over none of these existed. Is it nothing to you, all ye that pass by?—that tens of thousands of Bantu people, whose mental outlook has been forged in the furnace of terrorism and hammered on the anvil of poverty, have been transplanted to conditions in which human dignity and personality have an opportunity to develop?

Bantu housing has ceased to be a vast running sore; it is now a well-controlled problem. In dealing with a minimum of two million wretchedly-housed people and replanting them in their own towns, a time-period of ten years is light-speedy. It took a hundred years of misrule to create the widespread Bantu squalor in the interests of Bantu exploitation and, while the exploitation has not been eradicated, the squalor is being progressively reduced. This may not be proceeding fast enough for those critics who want cream before the cow is pastured but, when Rome required more than a day, the building of Bantu cities must be seen as an even greater accomplishment.

WITHIN the rehousing of the Bantu another noteworthy achievement is being accomplished—a natural sequel: a social, cultural and business existence, essentially Bantu, is being made possible by the encouragement of communal life. Like rehousing, this is not proceeding fast or far enough. There is far too enormous a back-log. Measured by British and American standards, the progress may not be so impressive as South Africans regard it, but there may be some unwisdom, some unfairness, some unrealism, in measuring it by an over-seas yardstick. Certainly some foolishness, because neither Britain nor America is qualified to comment—they have never had to face such a colossal human challenge. I have met, in South Africa, scores of eminent British and American visitors who, at the end of their visit, made despairing exclamations which can be fairly synthesised into: ''Boy-oh-boy—I'm glad it's your headache and not ours.''

South Africa is handling probably the biggest problem in

human relations since Moses came down from the mountain-
top and did some high-pressure personnel work on the Jews
to make them give up worshipping the golden calf. From the
uninvolved spectators on the side-lines, South Africa thinks it
has the right to expect sympathy, if not encouragement. They
rather resent it when bottles are thrown at the players on the
field—especially when some of those bottles leave hands under
whose finger-nails are deposits of past grime. They say: No
doubt we are here and there making a botch-up of the job,
but let the critics remember three things: we did not
originate the mess that we now have to clear up; if we are
falling down on the job, being baited by destructive criticism does
not help; we are still waiting for those who do the baiting to come
across with just one sound and workable alternative proposal.

This policy of creating Bantu townships in which White
traders are forbidden and which have their own local administration is—objectionable as the word has become—a process
in apartheid. I have been to some trouble to get the opinions
of those who matter far more than anyone else—the Bantu
inhabitants. Not one whom I questioned criticised it; practically all were gratefully appreciative; the dissidents were not
opposed to separate townships: their grouses were either about
their inability to pay rent or directed to purely parochial
matters in the same way that people everywhere always manage
to find some reason to criticise the local council. Makgona
Tsothe is a well-educated Bantu who, as a working journalist,
is in close and constant contact with his own people. I will
just quote him from *The Star*, the leading anti-Nationalist
newspaper in which, only this year, he wrote:

"In so far as apartheid affects his political, social and
educational interests, the urban Bantu regards it as most

abominable. But I can recall no thinking African who would condemn residential apartheid. It is this particular segment of apartheid that has been, and still is, a blessing in disguise.

"Prior to the enforcement of the Group Areas Act of 1952 many African families in Johannesburg lived in the backyards of their White landlords. They led an aimless life. And the few who showed signs of striving for an idealistic way of life soon had their aspirations woefully bedevilled by the concomitants of the freedom they enjoyed in the backyards.

"In contrast today, the African in his present townships, where he has been allowed to trade among his people as he pleases without any fear of foreign competition, is achieving an epoch of economic self-realization.

"Not only has he been given the privilege of renting a house indefinitely in the townships, but he is also authorised to build a house of his dreams in some areas. Few, particularly among the Whites, realize that places like the Dube township are miniature cities where the people have come to realize their real selves in practically all walks of life— something to which they could not have attained were they left indefinitely in the backyards of the White landlords in White areas. That is the advantage residential apartheid has brought. But I must not be taken as favouring apartheid in general—it is simply that we should face reality as it presents itself."

When they try to solve the "colour problem" South Africans have no illusion: they know it is a toughie. They take over where others left off. They listen to advice about "integration" from those who when, for 100 years, they had ample opportunity to practise it, did the reverse. They know that the Bantu are out-breeding them—47 per 1,000 Bantu birthrate against 16 per 1,000 among the White population. They know that "integration" could only mean—every anthropologist confirms—the surrender of minority culture to majority culture: the supercession of the basic aspects of White civilisation by Black aspects. From that maze-pool they see only one exit—encourage the Bantu to develop their own culture among themselves.

And that is just what is happening. Under that encouragement—or as an escape from suppressive measures; no matter what the inspiration, the result is the same—a Bantu culture, and the expression of it, are now marked features of their segregated social existence. That development has this significant feature—instead of White culture either completely dominating, or being completely dominated by, the Bantu, the latter are improving their cultural expressions by substituting certain White aspects for those Bantu manifestations which they now realise to be defects.

To appreciate this it must never be forgotten that the Bantu are not only the descendants of heathen tribes; they are still, to varying degrees, tribalised. Witchcraft, polygamy and certain a-moralisms are blood of their blood and only to a limited extent has blood-purification taken place. Witchcraft, polygamy and certain quirks of moral thinking still remain; to a declining extent, it is good to report, but no-one would be so foolish as to build hopes of complete elimination of basic tendencies in two generations.

Because of their historic background, tribal customs and moral standards, the Bantu code departs frequently from European appreciations of right and wrong. What is reprehensible to the White employer—such as lying and petty thievery—can be justified by custom or necessity by his Bantu worker. To change inborn concepts is a miracle in character-reformation which demands the space of time in which to operate; and the remarkable developments in that sphere bestow the accolade on the civilising power of religion and education.

Crime figures are high but no higher than might be expected under the economic goads of low wages, hunger and poverty. There has been a compensating drop in those curves as the graph of income has improved. Bantu crime, like other aspects of South Africa's "colour problem", has an economic root and when this is removed, when the investors of £600,000,000 British and £200,000,000 American capital can bring themselves to face a dividend-cut in order to pay wealth-producing Bantu labour a proper wage, the entire picture can be changed. My extensive investigations have produced over-whelming evidence to confirm that contention.

Neither religion nor education has completely eradicated all the manifestations of heathen ideas from the Bantu mind and, probably, not even a doubled wage-packet would, either. It is this hangover from heathenism that has given the Bantu an instinct for violence. When the *Drum*—newspaper for the educated Bantu—invited its readers to enter a short-story competition, violence, cruelty, ferocity and destruction were the themes of most of the manuscripts submitted. Psychologists may interpret this instinctive thinking as a manifestation of an inherited zest for dangerous living and the spirit of desperation with which centuries, that began in the jungles and swamps, have been marked. Mr. Tom Hopkinson, the editor of *Drum*, a most understanding sympathiser with Bantu aspirations and a zealous opponent of everything that de-humanises the Bantu people, put it differently: "Thwarted by

social and political obstacles, and the fact that he lives in the
20th century, the Bantu," said Mr. Hopkinson, "can only
expend his emotional energies and inner tensions in the
hurly-burly and violence of the township's daily life." It
may be that both Tom Hopkinson and the psychologists are
right but their opinions remain opinions; the fact is that the
crime-state among the Bantu is comparatively considerable and
has faced the police with frequent challenges to law-enforcing
authority that have resulted in sternly repressive action.

Both the Afrikaner and the Bantu are, by inheritance,
violent-minded. And with the same derivative: a century of
frontier warfare. Among the Pedi tribe, formerly a very
warlike people, the tribal education of their boys is still
deliberately directed to the development of a violent aggressiveness. Severe and frequent "corporal" punishment is
inflicted on Pedi boys who show signs of pacifist tendencies.
When they become urbanised they carry into that new life the
inherited vice of violence which has been developed within
them as virtue.

Bantu people, even when highly urbanised, are unable
completely to denude their minds of tribal superstition. That,
in its urbanised form, finds an outlet in religious variants—
there are seventy-four licensed sects. Their religious concepts are focused on the magic and mythologic contents of
their faiths: a belief in some Supreme Being capable of the
most impressive miracles at the drop of a prayer transmitted
through a hierachy of ancestral spirits; and an equally profound, if bewilderingly contradictory, belief that man can
manipulate supernatural forces in his own interests. They
regard sorcerers as evil but accept, as supernaturally potent—
or supernatural potentates—the witchdoctors who can, they
unshakably believe, cure their sick, protect them against

harm, make their self-eroded lands, and their barren women, fertile.

For several recent years the State-provided health services have been seriously impeded by the belief in and practice of witchcraft. A few months ago this provoked the Government to introduce the Suppression of Witchcraft Bill which, *inter alia*, provides the maximum sentence in cases where persons lose their lives following a witchdoctor's "cures". That such action was necessary—and admitted by the Government's political opponents—must be accepted as an eloquent commentary on modern South African life. Parliament recognised, and admitted the recognition, that witchcraft still plays a significant part in present-day Bantu culture, despite the effects of urbanisation, model townships, education and religion. Sickness and misfortune are ascribed to mischievous imps and evil spirits. Lucky charms, taken from another man's body —preferably alive—are greatly sought after; those in greatest demand are the heart, blood, bowels and generative organ because they are regarded as sources of his power.

Many of the more enlightened Bantu expressed appreciation of this new law to eradicate witchcraft. Even if cynics may sneerfully attribute an absence of altruism to it, I must report that the first group to make such an expression was the Orlando school for Bantu herbalists. They, quite rightly, pointed out that "people were inclined to confuse witchcraft with genuine herbalism" and they felt that "the Bill would ensure a secure future for the herbalist in the Bantu townships".

Potential patients of herbalists and witchdoctors were not so forthright—or so forthcoming—with their appreciation. Most significant was the attitude of the National Council for the Blind who welcomed the legislation, pointing out that

Bantu worker in the Natal "sugar belt" wielding the fearsome-looking knife on the canes.

Dr. H. H. W. Hermanus and Dr. H. L. Z. Njongee, the first Bantu to qualify at the Witswatersrand University.

Venda girls performing a Domb " initiation " dance in the Northern Transvaal.

Student nurses of Baragwanath Hospital at the entrance to the Nursing College.

their work was seriously hampered because Bantu people visited witchdoctors who prescribed such "infallible remedies" as the removal of one eye to improve the sight of the other.

Opinions do not enter into this factual subject: too many statements have been made to me by actual participants to make that necessary. The existence and persistence of witchcraft among the Bantu are accepted by South Africans as conforming to the tribalism which only lengthy periods of education and Christian indoctrination can completely eliminate—and even then there are many thoughtful people who wonder whether it is possible or wise to exterminate such a basic characteristic as tribalism.

One witness to the influence of witchcraft is cited here. He is the Rev. J. L. Reyneke of Rustenburg, the delightful "capital" of the Transvaal orange-growing country. To enable him to write his thesis for a doctorate in anthropology Mr. Reyneke spent much time with no fewer than thirteen witchdoctors, studying their technique and learning their "secrets"—if possible. He watched one thaumaturgical ritual when a witchdoctor, wearing a rakishly-decorated headdress of ostrich plumes, treated a young Bantu—"the insane one".

With his magic knuckle-bones at his feet, the witchdoctor ripped open a living sheep with a razor-sharp tipa, slashed out its heart, dipped it in a bowl of weird medicine and ordered "the insane one" to lick the blood-gushing heart. Contact of the man's tongue with the still-throbbing heart would, the witchdoctor explained to Mr. Reyneke who must have listened with hang-jawed amazement, make the Bantu's heart realise that "it is ticking too fast" and that it would slacken-down its tempo to that of the sheep's. "The medicine-man," commented Mr. Reyneke, "has to be careful not to let the sheep's heart stop beating in this cure for insanity. He believes that if it does, so will the patient's heart."

Bantu in the urban areas, making claustrophobic descents into the abyss of a mind-dark past, still believe that the ceremonial slaughter of sheep or goats will make a barren woman fertile. This superstition is so ingrained that the Town Council of Vanderbijl Park—"the steel city"—decided, only last year, that the slaughter of livestock, for ceremonial purposes, should be authorised on its own Bantu locations. "There is no doubt," the Finance Committee of the Council declared, "that the majority of Bantu still believe that it is absolutely essential to slaughter either a sheep or a goat at weddings and births to make a barren woman fertile and to honour dead heroes and parents. Since the ceremonial slaughter of live-stock forms part of the Bantu way of life, we think that, as in other towns, it should be allowed."

Polygamy has always been the Bantu code in marriage, subject to the ability of the marrying man to pay "lobola"— originally cattle, now cash—to the bride's father. Bantu society is still definitely orientated to polygamous marriages, although monogamy is increasing. To the Bantu mind, a fundamental requirement of any male is the propagation of children and as—they assume—the number of children would increase parallel with the number of wives, the more that a Bantu has of the latter the greater will be the number of children. A childless marriage is as despised as an infertile woman; hence, birth-control is anathema; regulation of fertility is condemned. One of the "benefits of civilisation" is that, while polygamy still exists, the urbanised young Bantu female is acquiring knowledge of, and skill with, "European" techniques in contraception.

Drunkenness is a considerable accomplishment with Bantu

people, both men and women. "Fire-water" is in great demand despite Government action to control its availability. Wine and brandy are mainly consumed; whisky is not generally appreciated and beer is regarded as both commonplace and innocuous. Non-enthusiasm for the latter may be due to the fact that its consumption is permitted—usually a wholesome nutritious beer made mostly from millet and with a low alcoholic content. Most of the police actions which accompany "riots" are efforts to enforce the law designed to prevent the Bantu becoming a willing victim to the ravages of high-octane liquor.

CRIME, drunkenness, witchcraft and polygamy only illumine, by their existence, the vast enterprises in cultural life that are now conspicuous in Bantu urban areas and townships. It is as much a testimony to official policy as to the social emancipation of the Bantu that such a remarkable development has been achieved by a people who, only three generations ago, were almost completely submerged in paganistic customs and the darkness of savage heathenism.

A people who, only fifty years ago when South Africans took over the government of their own country, had an indigenous culture which stepped from ancient superstitions, have now acquired forms of artistic expression of such high Westernised standards that their public performances are seriously reviewed by the leading music and drama critics of the press. "Full" notices appear outside any Johannesburg theatre in which Bantu artists are presenting a stage show, a band concert or a choral performance. *King Kong* was such a first-class dramatic performance that it filled the University theatre nightly for a season, the season had to be extended and my old friend, Jack Hylton, a foremost London impresario, after seeing the show, booked it for West End presentation. *King Kong* is one of many such.

Bantu choristers from five Rand township choirs, totalling 225 voices, with full orchestra, packed the 2,000-seater Johannesburg City Hall night after night with a performance of Handel's *Messiah* of such high quality that a famous gramophone company made long-playing records of it. These stage and concert artists are not professionals—they come from the model Bantu towns which have now been established; they were, five years ago, living in the degradation and tin-shacked squalor of Sophiatown and Alexandra.

This cultural development is symbolic of a renaissance in Bantu artistry which the massive rehousing plans have released. It is a symbol of denial—denying that the riotings, gangsterism, violence, shebeenism that the world hears so much of are representative of the modern Bantu way of life. No truly objective picture of "the colour problem" can be obtained if only a one-dimensional effect is presented. Against the century-long accumulation of cruelties and inhumanities perpetrated on the Bantu by former governments in the interests of imperialism and forty years by more recent Afrikaner governments in the interests of racial-segregation, the emergence during the past ten years of a Bantu people capable of indulging with utmost success in Western arts has, in all fairness, to be set.

No one with whom I have discussed this—neither Bantu nor Afrikaner—is content with its extent. Both share the same conviction: that the establishment of modernised, hygienic Bantu townships is making its extension certain. This remarkable growth of cultural expressionism could not have sprouted from Sophiatown's ugly soil—only crime and immorality and bestial living and a soul-destroying existence were its products. Before another five years have passed there will not be one Bantu slum-spot on South Africa's entire map. Instead, there will be a widening and deepening of Bantu artistry and its expression.

There is nothing surprising about this. Other countries have had similar experiences. Art has not burgeoned in their slums but followed their slum-clearances. I worked on Fleet Street newspapers when London, Glasgow, Liverpool, Manchester and other big cities were pock-marked with black-spots. I saw an enlightened Government erase most of them —and the artistic abilities and appreciation of the denizens had their first real chance to bloom. South Africa is doing the same with the Bantu slums—because there are no others in this pigmentocracy.

As the slums go, their places are taken by model townships where, because apartheid forbids White traders to operate, a new Bantu commercial class is creating itself. That is an effect of apartheid to which, quite naturally, White traders object. It is, however, one of the new forms of Bantu self-expressionism that is a feature of South Africa's present system and whether it is good or bad determines how much there is on the credit side of the apartheid balance sheet.

New towns mean new homes; new homes mean new outlooks; new outlooks mean new aspirations and ambitions. These are revealing themselves in a desire, among the Bantu, to emulate European standards and habits. In the science of salesmanship, "create desire" is the first principle of customer-behaviourism. Animated by a powerful desire to emancipate themselves, socially, the Bantu people are Europeanising their consumer-habits. Not every European would admit that his "civilisation" is worthy of slavish imitation but the fact is that the Bantu are changing from their "mealie and meat" dietary to European foodstuffs and most of their cupboards are now stocked with potted meats, canned fruits, jams, tinned fish, tea and even cartoned baby-foods.

Cosmetics—the hall-mark of being Europeanised—are in enormous demand. Mr. Nimrod Mkele, M.A. from Natal University, can be quoted as declaring that he found twenty-three different kinds of beauty preparations on the dressing-table of one Bantu girl. Their use comes natural to the Bantu who do not consider that they are aping Europeans, but vice-versa: their Bantu grandmothers painted their faces when Victorian matrons considered the application of rouge a sign of immorality.

In the new homes of township Bantu families, where once were nothing but sugar-box chairs and beds of straw, is modern furniture. Sewing machines are in almost all their homes; radio sets and radiograms in many. Brightly-curtained windows and tapestried chairs encourage the curled-little-finger niceties of the occupants and give a stertorious lie to those who opposed rehousing with the fallacious contention: "Put a pig in a parlour and he'll turn it into a sty." Just as I used to hear Tories in Britain declare: "If you give the working class a bathroom, they'll only keep coals in the tub."

From this new "consumer-habit" has emerged a new Bantu commercial element of nearly 7,000 traders and several whole-sale associations. Already a millionaire class has begun in the person of Mr. Khoto Sethuntsa who has made a fortune from highly-effective herbalism, lives in an Oriental-style "palace", owns houses and farms and runs a small fleet of American cars. Runner-up is Mr. Eric Ngobeni, the wealthiest Bantu in the Transvaal, who began in Johannesburg as a 15s.-per-month garden-boy. There is also Mr. Daniel Miolamu who now owns a 780-morgen farm and admits to being worth £3,000 a year. I have seen, in Dube township, the luxurious £8,000 house of Dr. A. B. Xuma with its double garage and servants' quarters. I have seen Mr. Ephraim Chabalala supervising his service station in another township—100,000 Bantu are registered car-owners—which he took over from a European four years ago. He now has a petrol through-put that makes him one of the biggest car-fuel sellers in South Africa, pumping 80,000 gallons monthly into Bantu cars and £1,000 monthly into the bank.

These are the exceptional surface-features of a Bantu social revolution. Underneath is a far-reaching sub-soil of poverty —the majority of Bantu family incomes are well below the £23 per month that is officially estimated as the minimum. That situation is not due to Government action but to Government inaction—failure to establish a satisfactory minimum wage. There is a growing number of large employers— such as Mr. Harry Oppenheimer, the mining magnate, and Mr. Sam Cohen, the progressive head of *OK Bazaar*, a nation-wide chain of stores—who fully realise that poverty depreciates working ability through malnutrition and causes absenteeism through illness; they are, without Government action, regularly increasing the wage-standards of their Bantu workers.

Instead of State regulation of wage-structure, the Government has introduced a considerable range of Bantu welfare services. These are entirely of South African origin; none of them existed at the time of the hand-over, fifty years ago. They also exceed in extent and cost the welfare services now operating in those neighbouring African territories for which the British Parliament still has responsibility.

Statistics, usually wearisome, become dramatic in this

particular case. South Africa spends £2 2s. 8d. per head of the Bantu population on Bantu education and health combined. That is fourteen times as much as is now being spent on similar services for the natives in Nyasaland, a British responsibility. In the three British "protectorates" inside South African territory, for which the British Parliament is directly responsible, an average of 10s. 3d. per head is spent, compared with South Africa's 42s. 8d. per head, on education and health combined. To see that social operation in comparative terms, here are the figures for annual expenditure, per head of the Black population:

	Education		Health		
	s.	d.	£	s.	d.
South Africa	15	9	1	6	11
British Protectorates					
Bechuanaland	4	10		5	0
Swaziland	5	7		5	11
Basutoland	5	6		4	4
British Responsibilities					
Nyasaland	1	7		1	6
Uganda	2	5		2	6
Kenya	4	0		5	1

None of these figures—including those of South Africa—compares with overseas standards but, if disgrace attaches to that fact, it should be apportioned pro rata to the countries responsible. South Africans are not only conscious of their shortcomings but conscience-stirred. That makes them super-sensitive when Britain indiscriminately criticises South Africa for its treatment of the Bantu population. South Africans feel that, when their country is spending more than four times as much on their Bantu as Britain is on her Native people, criticism will come much more convincingly when that disparity has been removed and the British welfare services come, at least, up to South Africa's standard.

South Africans point out that their expenditure on the Bantu benefits tens of thousands from the three British "protectorates" who have left that protection for South Africa who spends four times more on their health and education. That may account for the fact that Bantu in the "protectorates" clamour for passes into South Africa and, when these are refused, thousands smuggle themselves in either surreptitiously or on forged passes for which as much as £50 has been paid—more than 30,000 enter Johannesburg illegally every year. South Africans wonder why there should be this frenzied ambition to get away from the "protectorates" into South Africa if the former are so excellent and South Africa so forbidding as they are depicted. And some rather crude South Africans are even tactless enough to mutter something about "mote" and "beam".

Considering that, at the time of the hand-over, Bantu education was negligible in those parts of South Africa where it was not non-existent, the educational facilities now provided are, by comparison, fairly impressive. Bantu children are taught by Bantu teachers who have been trained in State-provided Bantu colleges and universities. That fact—although it is part of the apartheid policy—is worthy of unprejudiced consideration. It is a significant proof that—despite the objectionable aspects of separate development—the Bantu are now at least in process of being educated and having the darkness that has been buried in the portfolio of their minds banished.

There are now—I have to emphasise the present tense because the numbers are expanding monthly—7,138 Bantu primary, secondary and high schools. They are attended by nearly 2,000,000 Bantu children who are taught by 25,811 Bantu teachers—426 of them with university degrees—earning more than £8,000,000 per year. To that number can be added more than 6,000 student teachers at 43 Bantu training colleges. Those figures are regarded with some pride by South Africans because they are the statistics of a purely South African achievement and I quote them here in order that no fair-minded person overseas should be denied, by ignorance of them, the opportunity of approving that pride and applauding that achievement. Should there remain any hesitation, it may be dispelled by this clincher: during the past five years only, the number of Bantu candidates who entered for the matriculation examinations has doubled, and nearly forty per cent passed.

Before the hand-over, fifty years ago, an exactly similar claim and boast could be made—because double nought equalled nothing. That zero would also have represented the number of Bantu students admitted into Bantu universities—and the number of the universities. This year 580 Bantu students are attending the three Bantu universities in addition to 290 at teachers' training colleges. Within a generation, illiteracy, which stood at 91 per cent of the entire Bantu population, has been reduced to 58 per cent—mainly elderly people—and will be entirely non-existent among the next generation. Illiteracy now stands at 99 per cent in French Equatorial Africa and a Unesco survey reported, last year, that there were 700,000,000 adults in the world who cannot even read or write; and 100,000,000 of them are among the 150,000,000 in other parts of Africa—less than 5,000,000 are among the 11,000,000 in much-condemned South Africa.

On the education of the Bantu an average of more than £10,000,000 is spent annually. This may appear a small sum in this era of astronomical figures; for South Africa it is far from inconsiderable and its full significance would only be discerned if it could be compared with expenditure on Bantu education throughout South Africa fifty years ago—a figure which British records, inconveniently, do not contain.

At the Bantu universities—which cost £353,000 a year to maintain—2,000 students have taken such advanced courses as anthropology, philosophy and psychology, as well as the more practical subjects of economics, commerce, chemistry, administration and physics. A modern medical school costing nearly £500,000 has recently been erected at Durban, associated with the University of Natal, for the training of Bantu doctors and is among the four best equipped medical training centres on the African continent.

Educational problems in most other countries are, by comparison with South Africa's, rudimentary. Practically all the Bantu children come from homes where a hopelessly low educational standard is the norm. When they return home from school, there is little, if any, parental assistance to encourage them to retain, at night, what they have learned during the day. Both at home and at school, linguistic difficulties impede progress. At home a tribal dialect is spoken; when all the children assemble at school they bring with them seven different tribal dialects—it is not necessary for me to elaborate the obvious. I can add, as a piece of embroidery to the obvious, that the Braille system has just been applied to five Bantu languages; no fewer than 70,000 words, taken from five dialects, were broken into symbols.

Education is both helping to solve "the colour problem" and aggravate it. As the Bantu become more educated, they acquire an intelligent appreciation of the complicated structure which is South Africa's traditional way of life. Instead of feeling themselves to be blind victims of a senseless force, they are obtaining a realisation of the sociological and ethnological factors in a multi-racial society. Such understanding removes the infuriation that derived from the fatalistic conception of a predetermined, and therefore unalterable, destiny which was common to the Bantu two generations back. In its place is developing a passionate desire to escape from their traditional position of inferiority and to claim rights from which previous generations considered that their ignorant condition precluded them.

As the Bantu become better educated, and education becomes more widely applied, the "colour problem" will take on a different aspect. Ignorance made the Bantu accept an inferior position as warranted by the White man's superior education. This relationship is changing every year that the Bantu schools and universities turn out Bantu youth with varying degrees of educated minds. It is at this point that apartheid meets its greatest challenge and achieves its most poignant defeat. My houseboy, Sidney, told me with great pride: "My wife got her B.A. yesterday." I congratulated her vicariously but Sidney, a mournful expression chasing the pride from his eyes, said: "But what can she do with it?" The number of frustrated young educated Bantu, the utilitarian employment of their education stultified, can only be estimated in the light of the number of students the Bantu universities produce.

Apartheidists say: "When the Bantustans are established, there will be ample scope for them among their own people."

Apartheidphobes retort: "No matter how many Bantustans are created, there is only a maximum number of teachers, doctors, lawyers and other professionals they can require—what becomes of the rest, if they are not allowed to practise among the White population?" It is not my function to comment on facts; only to record them—and one fact is that the blessing of education that the Government is bestowing on the Bantu is shaping a new problem in human frustration which it is the Government's duty to solve.

It is the Bantu health service that absorbs a large number of the newly educated. There is a rapidly growing number of fully qualified Bantu doctors so accomplished that they now wear a bedside-manner like a second skin. There is a large number of nurses and midwives but still insufficient for the demands which are ever-increasing with the education of the Bantu away from their traditional reliance on witchdoctors, fanatical "healers" and home-prescribed herbal "remedies". Institutionalised medicine has far to go yet—there is a paucity of hospitalisation in comparison with the size of the Bantu population. Recent additions have been an anti-TB hospital in Johannesburg which is completely all-Bantu—the entire staff: medical, nursing and administrative—and a new Maternity Home near Pretoria.

Most of the distinguished visitors to South Africa are taken to see the Baragwanath Hospital, just outside Johannesburg, adjacent to the chief Bantu townships. Not only is it a show-piece; it deserves to be. Standing on eighty acres, it is one of the biggest specialist hospitals in the world, providing medical and surgical services for half a million Bantu on the Rand and specialist services for the four million Bantu throughout the entire Transvaal.

Originally built in 1941 by the British military authorities as a TB hospital for servicemen in the Middle East theatre of the last war, it was purchased from them for £500,000 six years later. Various additions have since been made and more than £1,500,000 annually is expended in maintenance alone. In addition to treating 500,000 Bantu outpatients every year it has 1,975 beds which are constantly filled, emptied and refilled with Bantu invalids. A staff of 192 White and Bantu full-time doctors and more than 900 Bantu nurses are on duty in the 46 wards and nine of the most modern and best equipped surgical theatres in the entire continent, wherein an average of 1,400 operations are performed per month. All services to the Bantu patients are free and that includes the delivery of more than 5,000 babies annually in the excellent maternity department.

Baragwanath is a highly institutionalised hospital. There are fully-equipped laboratories, physiotherapy, occupational and speech therapy departments, orthopaedic appliance workshop, a paediatric unit which deals with 100,000 under-nine children yearly, and the largest training school for Bantu nurses in all Africa as well as post-graduate courses in radiography for registered Bantu nurses. In the X-ray department an average of 65,000 examinations are carried out each year. The surgical department is housed in a separate block which cost £240,000 to complete two years ago and contains, in addition to the nine operating theatres, two plaster theatres, a recovery room, and a central sterilisation unit.

Medical and surgical skills are constantly challenged at "Bara" because Bantu patients arrive with conditions which are totally unknown to text books—peculiar to their way of life and tribal customs. With no precedent to guide them, surgeons and physicians evolve skilful methods of treatment— when confronted by such unique clinical situations—that are positively miraculous and become case-histories in the world's lexicon of healing. Many of these mystery-illnesses are the results of the quackery of the "muti-men" who play on Bantu ignorance with "secret" methods to end pregnancies. They employ a powerful, unknown poison in the medicine which they compel the women to drink—it ends the pregnancy by killing the women. Those who manage to get to "Bara" in time are terribly ill and, as the secret poison has never yet been identified, the doctors fight in the dark to save their lives, usually with remarkable success.

Baragwanath stands on the veld, unique in the world—a temple of healing for 4,000,000 Bantu people whose forebears, only two generations ago, knew no other medicine than witchcraft. It ended its first decade as a Bantu hospital last year. In ten years, nearly 5,000,000 patients have been treated, 50,000 babies brought into the world and tens of thousands of lives saved. Proudly conscious of the immense work that this one hospital, alone, is doing for the Bantu people, South Africans get a little restive under overseas criticism respecting the "inhuman treatment" of the non-White population. They are not insensible to the fact that the operations of the apartheid philosophy are disfigured by numerous executive details that well deserve criticism for their cruel thoughtlessness or inhuman harshness; but they feel that the monotone of that criticism depreciates its validity when it is unbroken by well-deserved praise for the other aspects of South African treatment of the Bantu.

INHUMANITY also characterises some of the applications of the apartheid principle to the Coloured people who form that section of the population which is, or should be, constantly pricking South Africa's conscience. They are a tragic people, the victims of schizophrenia of the blood, and what has amazed me has been to observe that, while there are constant outpourings of mixed sympathy and indignation both by South Africans and from overseas in respect to the Bantu, very little of either is generated on behalf of "the Coloureds".

These live in no-man's-land—apartheid cruelly labels them non-White and the Bantu make them the victims of their own form of apartheid. They are crushed between two segregational millstones. Their very existence is a challenge to the conscience of White South Africans because they are the progeny of their forebears' miscegenation. They are more South African than the Bantu because they began, as a people, with Jan van Riebeeck and his original settlers before the Bantu arrived at the south. These half-breeds vary in pigmentation from the palpably negroid to those so light-coloured that they are tempted to "try for white"—a fairly understandable desire that often has a piteous, in some cases a literally tragic, sequel.

This pathetic ambition is never experienced by the Indians, Malays or Bantu for an all-sufficient reason—they do not suffer from any mixture of blood. It is the "White" blood—the heritage of miscegenation by some White forebear—that, in being responsible for the existence of the Coloured people, teeth-grates the conscience of Afrikaner and British alike with history's accusing repercussions.

There are nearly one and a half million Coloured people in South Africa and, until the harsh arbitrariness of apartheid interfered with tradition, they had always been regarded as, because non-Bantu, part of the White population. Concentrated mainly in the Cape, where the responsible miscegenation originally took place, they did not constitute a "colour problem" because the Cape had grown up with them and accepted them as the vestigial evidence of White ancestry. Apartheid has changed that, places them in the general classification of non-White and treats them as Bantu who, for their part, reject them as of mixed blood. That is the tragedy of the Coloured people.

They are the responsibility of the White people and the insensitive refusal of Afrikaners to recognise that Afrikaner blood flows in the veins of many Coloureds may be the defensive reaction of a guilt-complex. Van Riebeeck's original party only included a few women, all married, and one of the first appeals received at the Dutch East Indies Company head office was: "Send out some lusty farm wenches." Very few arrived in response and to ease a troublesome situation van Riebeeck introduced the Company custom of mixed marriages.

Marriage was not the only form of miscegenation and the promiscuity that was generated by blind biologic urges reached such a stage that, eventually, it had to be made a legal offence. By then the damage had been done; a generation of mixed-blood children had been born in and out of wedlock. It started in van Riebeeck's own home. He had introduced into his household a Hottentot girl, whom his wife named Eva and who, before she was twenty-one, had given birth to two illegitimate children, one of which was South Africa's first half-caste. There is no official record of the child's father but the Company handsomely rewarded Pieter van Meerhof when he made an honest woman of Eva, and so in resolving a domestic problem, created for South Africa a greater.

Although hybridisation between races is condemned by all geneticists—it is an animated footnote to the advocacy of segregation—from that officially-blessed beginning the Coloured people emerged. An entire tribe, the Bastards, who had, through White miscegenation, lost their negroid purity and become—as their name, sometimes also spelled Baster, but both sustaining the Afrikaans meaning of half-caste, betokens —a people of mixed blood and confused parentage. Bastard pride forbade them to mingle with the Bantu; they wore European clothes and assumed their paternal parents' names of van Wyk, of Maasdorp, of De Freitas, of Smith, of de Villiers, of McNab and similar indications of the consanguinity of their birth. These and many others are the family-names of thousands of the Coloured people today.

A noticeable increase in the half-caste population took place when Malays were introduced as slaves, and during the thirty years of British occupation before slavery was abolished in South Africa considerable illicit miscegenation was practised which increased when abolition gave to the slaves a slightly higher status. Slavery was abolished in South Africa well before America followed suit—after a civil war to prevent it. Afrikaners of today wince, under American criticism of South Africa's attitude to present-day Bantu—especially when they read Winston Churchill's *History of the English-speaking Peoples* and learn there that fifty years after the Act abolishing slavery throughout the British Empire had been passed, its retention in America was championed in American pulpits "as a system ordained by the Creator and sanctified by the Gospel of Christ".

That defence of slavery, approaching Philistinian hypocrisy, recognised few ecclesiastical boundaries—which is not surprising in view of the further fact disclosed that Episcopalian parsons owned 88,000 slaves, Baptist ministers owned 125,000 and their Methodist brethren-of-the-cloth owned as many as 219,000 slaves. Afrikaners now wonder whether the fierce denunciation of their present-day "colour-bar" comes fittingly from Methodist ministers who, they say, while unaccountable for their Church's past and the fact that more than 5,000 Methodist ministers in America justified slavery as being "sanctified by the Gospel of Christ", ought not to act as if that past could be atoned for by vilifying South Africa for the position of present-day Bantu.

Slavery and its abolition in South Africa were part of the origins of this country's Coloured people. With the waiting of centuries on their faces, they have occupied a position as pathetically tragic as any unwanted illegitimate child ever since. White people, some of whose blood is in their veins, reject them; the Bantu despise them for that reason. For them life is a landscape haunted by a forbidding past and a formidable future. Until fairly recently, they enjoyed a few specific "White" privileges denied to the Bantu but the more rigorous aspects of the apartheid laws have robbed them even of those, as if the deliberate intention was to detach them completely from the White section of the community and force them into the Bantu ambit, there to live in the fuzzy outer frontier of the human race. As this succeeds, the traditional respect of the Coloureds for the Whites will recede and the evil logic of bitter hatred may take its place.

In this way is South Africa intensifying the complexities of its "colour problem". It did not require such intensification, as my attempt to break it down into its component elements should show. In the showing, its background is clear because nothing can be more foolish than to upbraid modern South Africa as if the problem is of South Africa's unaided creation. More foolish still is the mental state which views it as having been hatched-out during the past ten significant years.

Leafing through the centuries it is clear that it began when

Jan van Riebeeck landed and initiated the Dutch-French period; it developed into a stereotyped form under a hundred years of subsequent British rule and has been given serious legislative treatment, to regulate and control it, during the fifty years that South Africans possessed and exercised self-rule. Given wise administration, South Africans will deal with the problem in South Africa's way but, if so, I am quite convinced that the way will not satisfy all overseas demands. It is possible that South Africa could make more headway in its drive to a solution if its concentration on the job were not modified by the necessity to listen to continuous back-seat driving. An essential pre-requisite to swallowing well-meant criticism is that the pill should be well coated with praise for what is praiseworthy. And that is the cue to raise the curtain on what modern South Africa has accomplished.

The Performance

The Performance

WITH that cast of many characters, on that vast geophysical stage, with action covering a time-space of three centuries, the dramatic performance of modern South Africa is presented in a spectacular world-première. Never have the eyes of international peoples fully witnessed, or their minds completely realised, all that marches under the jaunty banner of South African development. There have been profile glimpses: short, sharp scenes like those in some revue and, like them, usually exaggerations of true life: grotesqueries, silhouettes, vignettes—each compressing one aspect into a short photographic and distorted exposure.

And, naturally, the mental effect on the observer is equal to that obtained from an irritating peep-hole view of a few of the bits of coloured glass which comprise a kaleidoscope. Emphases are inverted; Euclidian principles are defied so that the part becomes greater than the whole; and from the darkroom of misinformation emerges a grotesquely out-of-focus picture. To see South Africa, it must be viewed in its entirety: the worthy as well as the discreditable, the meritorious in addition to the ignoble, the accomplishments and not only the defects. Tapestries of phantasy must be pulled aside and a casement opened on the leafy world of fact. Actuality is then identified and truth revealed in inviolable isolation.

South Africa's present story can only be adequately

appreciated by a reading of its preface: the Anglo-Boer war which was sequented by self-government. That decade cannot, with any sense of realism, be dismissed as of the past, past. There are events in the lives of man and nation which are employed by destiny to shape their rough-hewn ends. They are the finger-posts of fate, standing at the Y-road of human existence; whether the right-hand or the left-hand turn is taken is the stuff of which history is made. To retrospect is to recapture significances; to reject the perspectives of the past as merely "the dead hand" is to voyage into foolishness.

That decisive decade in which the twinned events of the Anglo-Boer war and the inception of self-government reside was the overture to the drama. A land had been laid desolate; those of its people who remained alive, scattered or home-lessed; an economy was shattered; the mind of a nation was in nervous breakdown; a way of life was fragmented. And, in that supine position, South Africa was handed the res-ponsibility of self-government. Fervently desired as it was, fought and died for as it had been, it could not have been obtained in more unpropitious circumstances—a devastated nation had first to struggle to its own battered feet. When the fact that self-government immediately followed a "scorched-earth" war is placed in position, the South Africa of today— a mere five decades later—can be accurately evaluated. In whichever guise this modern South Africa is seen—to some an object of unrelieved criticism; to others a new Jerusalem, to yet others a combination of some of the characteristics of both —whatever it is, it is a Phoenix-like resurrection. Only those with neuralgia in their sense of proportion can fail to see the true vista.

Viewed materially or culturally—the things of time and sense; the things of the mind and spirit—modern South Africa is only of fifty years' growth and capable of being compared favourably with the U.S.A. a half-century after the British had been forced out of that country. Materially, it can show an ever-spreading industrialisation, a comprehensive and carefully-contrived finance system, economic stability, a wealth of reserves and resources which have enabled it to survive economic depression when disaster wrote its capricious signature across other countries' balance sheets. It is seldom noticed—or, if noticed, the full significance not appreciated —that, during those fifty years, South Africa has effected one of those solar-plexus achievements: a fundamental change of economy.

When the Anglo-Boer war came and went, the economy was based on agriculture and mining—in that order. So it remained during the first decade of self-government. Today, mining and agriculture take second and third place to industry which now makes the major contribution to the national income. Goldmining provides income that represents 12 per cent of the whole, agriculture 16 per cent; but the manufacturing industries provide 30 per cent of the national total —equal to goldmining and agriculture combined. When modern South Africa began, 50 years ago, that sector of the economy which, last year, produced 30 per cent of the national income only produced 6.8 per cent. Few countries can show that enormous advance in the first half-century of their nationhood, and when overseas iconoclasts verbally assail South Africa the unanswerable retort can be expressed in incontestable statistics.

Where there were fewer than 200 manufacturing establishments 50 years ago—and all those small-scale affairs like some gimcrackery sired by Heath Robinson out of O. Henry—there are now, ignoring the up-to-50 labour-force units—more than

16,500 factories, many of them with more than 1,000 on the payroll. Output of what is inaccurately termed "secondary industries" has jumped from £295,000,000 to £600,000,000 in the past ten years—a more than 100 per cent increase. It is extremely doubtful if there is another country in the world that can show such a result during the same period. It is not only an industrial revolution nor merely higher-echelon progress—it is the sign and symbol of conversion from an agricultural to an industrial economy.

That fundamental transformation has been marked by three phases. First there was the necessity to utilise the ever-increasing agricultural products—and that brought into existence a food-processing industry, mainly located in the fruit and vegetable growing Cape where, now, most of the canneries are located. An industrial dawning out of the hurtling night of war followed, creating manufactures of footwear, textiles and steel in order to reduce South Africa's dependence on highly-inconvenient imports. As these two wide-scale industrial experiments succeeded, they proved to be the keystone to the arch of an inclusive industrialism embracing a wide range of general products from heavy engineering to hair-pins.

Despite that expansion, South Africa is still importing a vast quantity of goods that it could produce itself. Consumption-levels are such, in a country of high living-standards and low income-tax, that the home market depends considerably on imported goods for which gold—South Africa's most remunerative export—pays. Total imports amount to £566,000,000 annually, which means that in relation to national income South Africa is the second largest importing nation in the world—31.5 per cent as compared with Britain's 20 per cent and America's 3.5 per cent. That fact gives tongue to a clamant demand for increased industrialisation.

Everything is inducive and conducive to such an expansion in order to correct that imbalance. There is ample space, cheap land, low rateable valuations, a remarkable system of internal transportation, an inexhaustible pool of labour and unlimited raw materials. In fact, more pre-requisites to a low production cost, concentrated on one site, than can be found in any equivalent country.

Steam-coal at a pit-head price of ten shillings a ton is the cheapest in the world—one-third of the American and one-sixth of the British prices. That gives South African industrialisation its basic advantage because from it derive ample supplies of cheap electrical power. Official estimates place the unmined coal reserves, so far located, at 75,000,000,000 tons —and mining costs are the world's lowest for several reasons: in addition to labour-costs, there are two other contributory factors—coal seams are at convenient depths, in regular formation; and mining operations are considerably mechanised.

Coking-coal is the basic element in South Africa's remarkably inexpensive electricity supplies. Escom—the Electricity Supply Commission, a public corporation—generates more than 15,000,000,000 units per year to serve a territory of nearly 200,000 square miles. This figure is increased by municipal undertakings so that South Africa, with a White population of 3,000,000, has an installed capacity of more than 4,000 megawatts—compared, for example, with Holland (population: 12,000,000) of 2,400 megawatts. Dry as statistics are, these give a lively indication of South Africa's success in keeping abreast—at least—with better-known countries.

In order to give a more graphic touch to the figures, I will add that the average cost of electricity in South Africa is less than one half-penny per unit. I forget what the cost was when I lived in London but I well remember the strict economy that all had to exercise in the home, switching off the lights at every possible moment. In my Johannesburg flat, if I happen to realise, when going to bed, that I have forgotten to switch the bathroom light off, I climb in between the sheets: it's not worth the trouble of going down the passage to switch off. The flat is almost over-supplied with light-candelabra, standard lamps, wall-brackets, fluorescents in the kitchen, desk and bedside lamps; the cooking is done on an electric range; there are electric heaters in every room and constant, electrically-geysered water for kitchen and bathroom. Even my winter bill never exceeds £2 per month.

It is this ample supply of electricity at cheap rates which facilitated South Africa's industrial expansion, just as the coming of steam permitted Britain's industrial revolution. Escom itself induced numerous industrial establishments to come into existence: machinery, tools, plant and various services provide turnovers for a large number of establishments. For instance: during the past ten years an impressive cable-making industry has established itself and the African Cables undertaking at Vereeniging is the largest electric-cable plant in the entire southern hemisphere. Most of the cable now used in South Africa is manufactured in the country.

Specially favoured with advantages that are peculiar to South Africa—including cheap land, power and labour—an extensive system of "secondary industries" has mushroomed up during the past two decades. Other countries have experienced industrial renaissance but what makes the South African achievement so distinctive is its background: industrialisation could not commence until a war-devastated land had been renovated and all the mechanics of a suddenly-acquired self-government given time to be devised by the processes of trial and error. Those circumstances, only matched by those surrounding the formative period of the United States of America, throw up in graphic relief the transformation of an agricultural economy with its ox-wagon standards to widespread industrialisation in modern terms. South Africa's industrial revolution is not so much technical as pyrotechnical.

Outstanding in this development is the industry of food-processing which was the logical first-entrant of that transformation. In the Cape a score or more canneries provide hundreds of farmers with an outlet for crops whose market is guaranteed before the vegetable seeds are planted or the fruit-blossoms spray the trees with colour. Canned fruit and vegetables—and other audible edibles—have taken the gamble out of light farming. Canning has also become a major rivet in the national economy: it helps to provide foreign exchange by exports which underwrite imports. The industry now processes every conceivable commodity until it looks as if the day were approaching when it will be possible to buy even the lilies of Avalon and the sunsets of Cockaigne in a can.

Footwear manufacture is among the few veterans of South Africa's industrialisation—the First World War gave it the creative impetus. Seventy factories now produce 20,000,000 pairs of boots and shoes each year. That is equal to the production of Australia—from 470 factories. Not only are South African factories able to supply South African requirements; in addition, ten per cent of the output is exported.

Here again there is a link between a flourishing secondary industry and the primary of agriculture. South African tanners, who used to be active in importing hides and hiding imports, now employ domestic hides and skins almost exclusively. In the production of 20,000,000 pairs of shoes, South

African footwear manufacturers consume, in any given year, nearly as many million square feet of lining and upper leathers. If there were no such local factories, South Africa would have to export one cattle hide to pay for every pair of shoes imported whereas that same one hide, retained in South Africa, produces an average of eight pairs of shoes. This particular industry makes a South African raw material worth eight times its export value.

South Africa's other chief industry is textile and clothing manufacture and it is significant of the switch-over from the basic of agriculture to industrialisation that the three largest new industries are alike in two respects: they use agricultural raw materials; they produce exportable goods which substantially benefit the foreign-exchange position. On the great rolling farmlands of South Africa a sheep-population of 38,000,000 grazes, enabling South Africa to be the fifth largest wool-producer in the world. Apart from the very considerable quantities of wool that are exported, no fewer than twenty-two spinning and weaving mills in South Africa process the local product into textiles. This, like much else in the lengthening roll of South Africa's industrial developments, has been perfected, in the main, during the past ten years—the pioneer worsted spinning and weaving mill was established in 1946 at Uitenhage.

As the textile industry develops so the local clothing factories increase their consumption of South Africa's raw materials; so also does clothing-manufacture expand. During the past ten years, more than 200 new clothing factories have been established until there are now nearly 700 comprising an industry which, when self-government began, did not exist. It employs nearly 50,000 workers including more than 25 per cent of the White women engaged in the whole of

South Africa's secondary-industrial complex. In these factories clothing to the value of more than £50,000,000 is produced annually. Some of the most beautiful curves in this country of beautifully curvaceous women are found on its production graphs.

If the entire economy of a nation is to be switched from an agricultural to an industrial basic, it is both wise and natural that its industries should absorb its agricultural products. That must be the first stage in the transition unless the agricultural community is to be plunged into the deepest abyss of disastrous depression. It was that policy which South Africa has followed with the result that its three chief secondary industries—food-processing, footwear and textile-clothing— are not only highly successful internally but, within a network of circumscriptions, are maintaining and widening the success of agriculture. Only by an integrated development which, in displacing the primary industry from first position also strengthened it, could industrialisation be a national asset —the external symbol of inner values.

By creating, or comprehensively expanding, those three secondary industries which consumed agricultural raw materials, the necessity for others, to serve the new industries in meaningful concatenation, revealed itself. It was like a miner uncovering a vein that led to the mother lode. A demand set in, rich with overtones of tremendous possibilities, for machinery and light engineering and, in response, further industrial undertakings had to be established. Without invoking State direction—a socialistic device which free-enterprise South Africa stoutly rejects—these pool-widening circles of derivative developments were canalised by the more natural controls of labour-resources, import quotas and material supplies. It was a great experiment in responsible free-enterprise

CURTAIN-UP ON SOUTH AFRICA

and has resulted in the creation of an industrial pyramid, the extent of each strata of which is determined by the demands of another that necessitated, necessitates, its existence.

I could fill this and the next three pages merely by recording the classifications of the amazing range of industrial undertakings that have come into existence. It would be more significant, than interesting, reading-matter. Such a list would, however, be an enlightening index to the remarkable process of industrialisation that has, in less than fifty years, transformed the entirely (apart from the mines) pastoral aspect of South Africa into one constructed of thousands of unitary factories, conveyor-belts, generators, electric presses, mass-production, electronic devices and all the impedimenta of modernised industry.

HAPHAZARDRY adjusted to the shifting tides of circumstance is not permitted in this nation-wide transition. A delicate balancing of desire and desirability has been evolved. Without infringing the general policy of free enterprise, its implementation is consciously conditioned by a series of carefully-devised legislative acts designed to construct a cohesive and coherent overall image. A pattern of development regions has been devised which conforms to the distribution of major natural resources, the availability of labour, existing transport services and municipal facilities. This pattern embraces four categories—highly-developed regions, promising regions, moderately-promising regions and regions of limited promise. What town-planning has been elevated to in some countries, economic-planning on a regional basis is South Africa's approach to the attractive and extensive possibilities the country possesses for industrialisation. By that technique, the inscrutable becomes the indubitable.

There is a Natural Resources Development Council at constant work with a full complement of planning experts, ensuring that the industrialisation of modern and future South Africa shall avoid all the entanglements and confusion of un-correlated growth. Eager-beaver entrepreneurs are encouraged to keep their feet off the sticky flypaper of vain endeavour. This particular expression of the doctrine of "planned economy" has a basic philosophy which, according to Dr. T. J. D. Fair, the Council's chief planning officer, is: a combination of private enterprise and the provision of a variety of services by Government agencies, the latter being largely determined by "judging the priorities of development not only in the different regions of the country but also at different stages of the country's growth".

So fundamentally sound is the policy that the only criticism levelled at it by economic theorists, so pedantic that they would dispute the positioning of Shakespeare's semi-colons, is that "it is operated within the context of a free-enterprise economy"—in fact, it's too good for the capitalist system. South Africa does not appear to be unduly ruffled by otiose criticism nor diverted from the avenue of its policy. Girded by a leonine determination, it has proceeded in conformity with the plan of State-encouraged free enterprise with the result that industry has not only shot up like a rocket but stayed up like a balloon—and it is not the helium of hot-aired theories that is keeping it afloat. There is a realistic acceptance of the belief that self-interest is the gravitational constant that governs all human equations.

Economic planning in South Africa is based on the priorities of "where" and "when". That method demands some broad assessments of the country's resources and development possibilities in order that—in Dr. Fair's words—"the potentialities of its regions can be measured one against the other". From those assessments has emerged the pattern of quadruple regionalisation to which I have referred. This has become more than theoretic planning; it has now been precisely mapped.

"Highly-developed regions" are the metropolitan districts of the Rand, the port cities and four well-populated inland areas. "Promising regions" are extensive areas in the four provinces which are rich in natural resources but with facilities of varying availability for their undoubted future development. "Moderately-promising regions" are those areas which, while well traversed by railways, are at present limited in development by restricted, or under-organised, water supplies. "Limited-promise regions" are those whose natural resources are ideal for wool-sheep and meat-cattle but less suitable for industrial development. (*See map on pages 34-5.*)

Those four defined regions provide the broad outline of South Africa's development potential. It is obvious that in the second category—"Promising regions"—are to be found the more attractive and immediate possibilities. They are the economically most-advanced areas outside the major metropolitan areas and, including as they do the Southern Transvaal, north-western Orange Free State, northern Natal and the Cape Midlands, comprise the greater part of the South African triangle which I outlined earlier and cover a quarter-million square miles. And that appears to me as a very substantial development area; certainly sufficient to indicate South Africa as a treasure-chest waiting to be opened in response to the invitation of that beckoning finger.

Accepting the fact that, since self-government, South Africa has participated in, and experienced the effects of—beneficial as well as disadvantageous—two world wars, industrialisation has soared on gyroscopic wings during the past ten years. That is traceable to the fact that the previous decade contained the inception of those industries which were ancillary to agriculture—food-processing, footwear and textile-clothing—while, during the years subsequent to war's end, industrialisation has ramified out into a great diversity and variety of undertakings. This latter is seen to indicate the route which industrialisation in the immediate and distant future will follow. What started in specialisation—industries identified with agricultural products and were, in fact, considerably confined to such raw materials—is marked with a maximum degree of versatility.

It is this later development which is the key-cue to South Africa's industrialisation involving, as it does, departures from the use of solely indigenous to imported materials for processing. By that token, the potential expansion of South Africa's industrial production is, virtually, boundless, in what is practically a virgin field limited only by the enterprise and confidence of the entrepreneur class.

This enterprise and confidence does not appear to be lacking: the goldmining houses, such institutional organisations as insurance companies and building societies and other local finance houses, are so convinced of the gilt-edged values implicit in the industrial programme that their diversion of funds to that investment area caused, at one time, the Government to force it to detour the private in favour of the public sector. One result of that policy was to leave South African industrial expansion more available to overseas investors and the position is now such that American and British and German manufacturers are staking valuable claims by erecting factories producing goods which they would otherwise be compelled to export into the South African market.

Such world-famed firms as the Parke Davis Company of Detroit, who have established a $700,000 antibiotic plant, and Philips Petroleum of Oklahoma, who have erected a factory to produce 22,000,000 pounds of carbon-black, are two of many American concerns who have made a shrewd assessment of South African advantages for industrial purposes —otherwise those hard-headed, hard-faced financiers would have kept their dollars at home. More than 195 American companies have accepted the valiant challenge and now operate subsidiaries in South Africa, turning out everything from mining machinery to breakfast foods, with the result that, during the past ten years, American capital investments have jumped from $86,000,000 to the eloquent figure of $600,000,000—which is more than America has invested in all the rest of the African continent combined. South Africa was described, last year, by a journalistic colleague—Mr. Roy Vicker of the *Wall Street Journal*—after an investigatory tour of the country, as "a beehive of United States industry".

Two leading American banks have now opened branches in South Africa and the head of one of them—Mr. John Watts, international vice-president of Chase Manhattan—told me: "Considering both favourable and adverse factors, we believe that South Africa definitely rates a plus overall." This hard-headed view impressed me because, while British bankers have the gift of enclosing their opinions in an envelope of diplomatic language, Americans employ a more realistic— frank to the point of brutal—idiom. Incidentally, it is sig-nificant—of what, it is not necessary to indicate—that in a period when the tempo of British investments is beginning to slacken (according to Premier Macmillan, more than two-thirds of the outstanding capital in South Africa is British) American capital investments are increasing at an increasing rate.

"A foreign investor never need fear nationalisation here," is the official assurance by Dr. T. E. Donges, the Minister of Finance. "He is always free to repatriate his profits and his capital."

South Africa uses import restrictions both as a carrot and a stick to encourage establishment of American branch plants. If an American company puts up a South African plant, it usually is assured of protection from import competition. Import curbs also are a means of encouraging an outside company to locate a plant in South Africa, or, in the case of an assembly plant, of making a greater percentage of its component parts here.

Currently, for example, the South African Government is encouraging automobile manufacturers to make more of their parts inside the country, rather than importing them. The rapidly expanding range of car parts made in South Africa has prompted the Board of Trade and Industries to draw up a ten-year scheme that will have far-reaching effects on the country's motor industry. Lists of parts which can be made here to international standards and at competitive prices are being compiled. These parts are to be put into the foreign cars assembled in the eight major motor plants in South Africa.

The plan calls for these plants to add about twenty-five per cent additional South African-produced parts to their cars every year until they get to the most specialised components, which will be added more gradually. It is estimated that within the next ten years, local industry will be making between ninety and ninety-five per cent of all the parts that go into a car.

South African factories are now producing a range of

components from oil filters and car springs to elaborate electrical equipment. "Vecor"—the Vereeniging Engineering Company—recently announced the manufacture of wheels and rear-axle parts. The effect of this development is that the assembly plants—producing British, American and German cars—are now encouraging South African factories to make wider ranges of components to fit their vehicles. Overseas components manufacturers are also investing in this field.

As it is obviously impossible, in this present piece of writing, to give a detailed and inclusive survey of all the evidences of South Africa's industrialisation miracle, I can only report that it is difficult to think of any form of manufacture that is not represented by at least one factory. I even discovered in the quiet ungrown-up riverside town of Parys a small stocking factory whose ultra-modernistic character contrasts surprisingly with its external setting. It is a subsidiary of a large German organisation and is equipped with 54 knitting machines which turn out 600 dozen seamed and seamless stockings daily. Perlon thread is imported from Germany, as were also the machines, each containing 220,000 parts in addition to hundreds of delicate steel needles and costing £35,000 each.

Stockings, being suggestive of nylon, leads me to report that a £6,000,000 factory to produce nylon pulp was established near Umkomaas, on the Natal coast, two years ago by a corporation in which Courtaulds of England and Snia-Viscosa of Italy are financially interested. Basic raw material is drawn from vast eucalyptus plantations in Zululand—which represent an investment of another £1,000,000—while 8,000 additional acres are being planted in the Natal midlands. Nylon pulp exports from this factory earned £3,000,000 in foreign exchange last year.

This highly successful project was facilitated by the Industrial Development Corporation, created by the Government to "promote, guide and assist in the financing of new industries and industrial undertakings, to the end that industrial development may be planned, expedited and conducted on sound business principles". Presiding over this highly-important corporation is Dr. H. J. van Eck, an economic genius with ball-bearing intellect, with, as vice-chairman, Dr. M. S. Louw, one of South Africa's most brilliant economists of front-rank international calibre. The creation and the effectiveness of this corporation indicate the recognition, both inside the country and overseas, of the enormous, almost immeasurable, extent of the possibilities for industrial development that the country possesses and which—as that appears to be an appealing factor—can play infinite variations on capitalism's most popular theme: profits. Wherever my duties have taken me —which is a map-traversing term—seeking granite actualities with a sceptical curiosity, the Pandora Box image of South Africa has been inescapable.

In the forefront of the industrial shop-window are two highlighted exhibits—the amazing iron and steel production and the even more amazing petrol-from-coal development. If the rest of the window were empty, these two would be sufficient to halt the world's passers-by and cause them to gape in window-shopping astonishment. Both are entirely South African achievements, one having commenced twenty years after the British had left, the other being merely five years old.

Despite its wealth in gold, diamonds, platinum, uranium

and other earth-wrested treasures, South Africa would be a feet-dragging country without iron and steel; it would be a financially-embarrassed country if it had to import them as it did up to twenty years ago. Last year, by using its own products, South Africa saved nearly £70,000,000 in foreign exchange. Students of international affairs will experience no hesitation in assessing the immense significance of that statement. Iron and steel comprise the jugular vein of any country's economy.

Crude bellows-operated furnaces, which produced equally crude metal for weapons, were all that emerged under British administration and the Anglo-Boer war put out of commission the first blast furnace which the independent Boer Republic built at Pretoria. After that war, two great South African industrial pioneers—Lewis and Marks—declining to follow the path of least resistance but preferring to blaze the trail of most resistance, founded the Union Steel Corporation at Vereeniging (where the Peace Treaty had been signed shortly before) and so pioneered South Africa's remarkable iron and steel industry.

It began to take a more noticeable—in fact, its present—shape when in 1925 a young chemical engineer of the Board of Trade and Industries, infected with the malaria of earnest striving, prepared a comprehensive and detailed memorandum dealing with every aspect of the creation of a huge State iron- and steel-producing organisation. His name was Dr. F. Meyer; his thesis was adopted by the Government and he is today the chairman of Iscor—as the Iron and Steel Corporation is termed—and one of the greatest intellects South Africa has produced. Iscor was constituted by an Act of Parliament in 1928 and is one of the four Government-controlled corporations which are the pillars of the industrial edifice.

There are two great Iscor works—the first was established at Pretoria with an ingot capacity of 700,000 tons per annum; the second at Vanderbijl Park with an ingot capacity of 750,000 tons. Since their establishment the joint capacity has been progressively increased until last year ingot production reached 1,534,000 tons. South Africa used 1,814,000 tons of steel last year—Iscor therefore supplied nearly 80 per cent of the nation's requirements; and at £25 per ton less than the 20 per cent that had to be imported. A third Iscor works is to be established which will make South Africa entirely self-supporting in respect to this vital commodity.

Natural resources facilitated this achievement. Cheap and plentiful coking-coal for the seven blast furnaces which have an average total output of 12,500 tons per week is readily available. Ores are derived from the Southern Daspoort beds near Pretoria (1,000,000,000 tons reserves), the Crocodile River deposits (90,000,000 tons) at Thabazimbi in the Transvaal, the Kuruman district in the Northern Cape (28,000,000 tons) and from Dundee in Natal (3,000,000 tons) while continuous investigations are being made into ore occurrences throughout other parts of the country (6,000,000,000 tons). Manganese, chromium and limestone deposits are of inexhaustible supply. Nature shows, in South Africa, a bountiful and fully-opened hand.

With these advantages, and a vast labour-pool on which to draw, Iscor is able to produce steel at world-competitive prices. South African-produced steel is near the bottom of the international price-list. Iscor prices for all steel products have remained, for some years, 120 per cent higher than pre-war prices—American steel is about 170 per cent and British steel about 275 per cent higher than pre-war figures. So far South Africa absorbs all Iscor output—although some was exported to America during the steelworkers' strike there last year and a £1,000,000 order from Japan was also secured—but when the third works is brought into operation there will be a surplus over local needs and the impact of Iscor products will be felt on the world market as the triumphant symbol of painfully-kindled hopes. And all this progressively-increasing achievement has been recorded during the past thirty years—a frieze-like moment in time.

Five years ago the first gallon of South African petrol was produced from South African coal and went into a South African-assembled car. Since then many millions of gallons have been produced, although the oil-from-coal plant has not yet been completed. This will be accomplished this year when Sasol—the South African Coal, Oil and Gas Corporation—will go into full production. The term "full production" means 55,000,000 gallons of petrol and 6,000,000 gallons of diesel oils yearly, together with a wide variety of by-products ranging from pitch and paraffin wax to acetone and ethanol.

Sasol employs a production process that begins with the gasification of coal; the gas is converted by a catalyst into petrol, and other liquid products are obtained by the application of the Fischer-Tropsch process. Inadequately brief as that outline description is, the entire and involved operation is carried out in an amazingly complicated plant—in which £48,000,000 of Government money is invested—that stands on 3,500 morgen in the Orange Free State and where its own township of Sasolburg has been established. Here, where a few years back was nothing but wide-open, van-dyke brown veld on which wild buck roamed, stands the world's largest oil-from-coal project. In that achievement alone South Africa leads the world. Its exotic quality is breath-taking even if overseas appreciation is muted as in requiem.

OVERSEAS conceptions of South Africa are often limited to the fact that it is the centre of goldmining—which is quite true; but gold is only one component of the country's mineral wealth. In addition to the best-known—diamonds—there are uranium, coal, manganese, dolomite, asbestos, platinoids, chrome, copper and a mere matter of forty-two other minerals. Below the variegated surface of South Africa, colossal wealth is buried, a subterranean vault crammed with precious stones and glittering metals, gathered during millions of years and hoarded up by Nature as if for the Last Trump, had not South Africans, with well-riveted pioneering adventuresomeness, rifled the cache for the benefit of a needing world.

Reviewing the yields in their order of recovery, diamonds come first. Incidentally, but not accidentally, they form the most striking proof that economic law is not infallible; that it can even be defied with impunity—and profit. Whereas with most other commodities price is a figure derived from the inter-action of supply and demand, the price of diamonds is something which strides through those two economic fundamentals. Demand for diamonds, while variable, is always considerable; supply, while extensive, is controlled.

That is one of diamond's paradoxes: itself a vital element in South Africa's economy, economic law is not a decisive factor with the diamond. Demand derives from one main source: human desire. When girl meets boy anywhere in the world, the reaction will probably be felt in Johannesburg offices and Kimberley mines. Boy is far too preoccupied with a pair of sparkling eyes three inches away from his own to give a thought to a pair of sparkling diamonds in South African blueground—but the fact may well be that sparkle is calling unto sparkle. Most of the engagement rings slipped by boy on

225

girl's finger are encrusted with South African diamonds. There is a definite relationship—unromantically calculated by the cold-faced actuaries of the diamond industry—between the world's marriage rate and De Beers' profits. "Diamonds," said Cecil Rhodes, "will always hold their value while the world has beautiful women and men anxious to please them."

Love, courtship and marriage are, like many other emotional manifestations, affected by economic considerations. And while there can be love in a garret, marriage prefers a settled home, a settled income and settled security. Economic depression has a depressive effect on courtships and, in preventing or postponing millions of engagements, causes the South African diamond industry to shiver under the chill breath of falling sales and declining profits. America, always instinctively reactive by extremes, is proof—there, the sales of diamond rings in 1929 and 1932 compared with those in the intervening years of economic crisis showed how a slump in bank balances, while not causing any abatement of romantic inclinations and biologic urges, can cause a slump in that symbol of all-conquering love known as a diamond engagement ring. If it ever became fashionable to signalise betrothment with an ebony bracelet or an ivory hair-slide, De Beers would have to put the shutters up and Kimberley become a ghost town.

Only one economic blizzard to benefit the diamond industry is on historic record. That was when Hitler blitzed millions into the role of refugee—hundreds and thousands of his victims translated their money and property into more easily trans- ported, and more easily hidden, diamonds. This has been repeated, to a lesser degree, whenever the national economy of any country threatened to become seriously shaky: when those possessing wealth lose confidence in their national currency they convert money to diamonds—the stable and indestructible coin.

Demand for diamonds is, in normal circumstances, considerable and, unfortunately for the diamond industry, the unearthed supply created by Nature exceeds it enormously; so much so that the excessive supply might possibly have the disastrous effect of making diamonds as cheap as pebbles—and as profitable. And that must never be. To prevent such a catastrophe, the South African Government of nearly thirty years ago conducted negotiations with the diamond magnates which resulted in the formation of the Diamond Producers' Association with statutory powers "for the regulation and control of the sale of diamonds". In less official terminology, production was controlled so as to maintain such a suitable equipoise with demand that prices—and incidentally, of course, profits—were what economists call "stabilised". Conceived in the Gothic darkness of the Ice Age, and weaned by the alchemy of natural chemistry, diamonds are now fashioned by the new glaciation of science handcuffed to commerce.

This procedure is well explained by Professor D. J. Viljoen of Potchefstroom University who, appropriately enough in this enlightened age when finance claims a basis in religious conviction, occupies the Chair of Christian Higher Education and who, in his doctoral thesis, said: "The diamond industry of South Africa was at the outset a highly competitive industry, but its structure has since changed greatly. Formerly many thousands of diggers were found on the diggings and production and marketing of diamonds were unsatisfactory. It was soon felt that the industry would be ruined unless orderly and more efficient production and marketing methods were applied. This resulted in a long struggle, which finally led to the diamond industry being one of the best controlled industries in the world. Today it is controlled by both the Government and private enterprise.''

That is good; good for South Africa's economy and—by the great toe of Crœsus!—good for the diamond industry. Those bad old days, when the Kimberley diggers threw handfuls of diamonds on the world's market with such reckless insouciance that ''sparklers'' threatened to lose the glamour of rarity in millions of love-gleaming eyes, were ended and the entrancements of betrothment have been preserved by investing diamonds with a scarcity value superior to the pearl of great price. Diamonds in South African soil are the property of the State; the Government—being one of the two partners in the Diamond Producers' Association—retains the right to one-half of all diamonds unearthed from private land. If they are mined on State-owned reserves the Government has seven out of every eight shares. That, also, is good—the land of every country is a gift of Nature to the people and, in South Africa, the people are granted from one-half to seven-eighths right to its diamond yield.

In the very recent years, the value of the South African diamond yield has been in the neighbourhood of up to £90,000,000 per year and a total of more than £1,000,000,000 since the first diamond was discovered. South Africa produces more diamonds, in value, than any other country in the world —until Soviet Russia puts her ace of diamonds on the table— and took that premier position from Brazil, to whom India, the original chief producer, had been compelled to surrender it.

Another of diamond's paradoxes is that it is both a luxury and a necessity. Modern life could get along quite well and unhampered without diamonds; diamonds are essential if modern life is to get along unhampered. Gem-diamonds have always been the luxury; industrial diamonds are now the necessity. South Africa produces both kinds. Among several highly valuable contributions made by the diamond industry to South Africa's expanding economy—one is an enlightened labour policy which has increased wages by 148 per cent while general retail prices increased by only 64.3 per cent—was the formation of the Diamond Research Laboratory whose chief function has been to promote and extend the industrial uses of diamonds. In this excellently equipped laboratory, skilled staff crouch like sorcerers over magic crystals, experimenting with scrupulous care if only because the ingredients of research are very expensive and the methods have to be, as far as possible, non-destructive—sales-wise; diamonds themselves being indestructible. It is a brilliant example of how fundamental research into the physics and chemics of such a product of Nature as diamond can confer enormous benefits on the productivity of the entire industrial world.

Chemically speaking, diamond is carboniferous. It is an atom with four valence electrons and while others have been "splitting the atom" the Diamond Research Laboratory has been dividing the electrons. The crystal substance of the diamond has varying abrasive properties and the correct orientation of the stone to the tool is of prime importance in the industrial use of diamonds. That is where the Laboratory has achieved a supreme triumph in supra-orbital development which has resulted in South Africa enhancing the industrial productivity of the world.

Its latest triumph is the development of a miraculous process by which the colour and physical properties of diamonds can be changed. I was in the laboratories early this year and watched Mr. Harry Oppenheimer press a button which set in motion the £70,000 machine that performed a miracle comparable with a leopard changing spots. Mr. Harry Oppenheimer is the brilliant son of a remarkable father who did not emulate the example of those parents who handed on the torch without taking the trouble to fill it with the oil of genius—an enlightened, cultured and efficient man, the son of the late Sir Ernest Oppenheimer is among the world's greatest financial brains. Under his inspiration the diamond industry has made world-shattering technological advances of which this is merely the latest to date.

The machine—a high-voltage cascade electron accelerator —is the only one of its kind in the world. It was built in Holland by the Philips organisation, shipped to South Africa, and reassembled at the Diamond Research Laboratory to create hard X-rays or gamma rays, which produce new effects on diamonds. On a television screen I saw the machine go into operation. A toy train, remote-controlled, carried a tiny truckful of diamonds into the target area and I saw the gems begin to glow as a result of the radiation. Mr. Oppenheimer said that this new development could result in the discovery, within diamonds, of unknown properties. Just as Nature has not yet yielded up the secret of the diamond's subterranean manufacture, other secrets are still hidden in the glittering, glistening, glassily translucent stone.

NEXT in order of South African discovery was gold, and today it is worth much more than its own weight, because in addition to representing money it means for South Africa the wealth of foreign exchange. In this respect, the economic development of South Africa is being deliberately and con-

Harvest time in "the mealy triangle". The maize is bagged and the husks form golden mounds.

A witch-doctor and his assistants engaged in a "ritual of healing" outside a Township house.

Bars of unrefined gold being stored in a safe-room at the mines before being processed into bar-bullion.

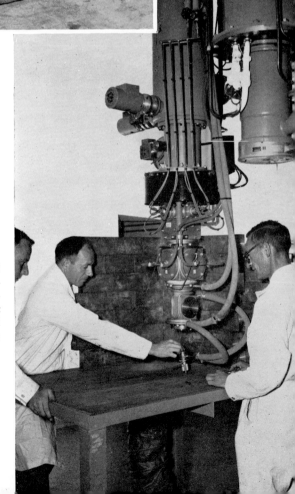

Scientists in the Diamond Research Laboratory operating the miraculous cascade-electron generator that changes the colour and characteristics of diamonds.

sciously strangled by America who, in the exercise of her monopolistic powers as the greatest hoarder of bullion, refuses to permit any increase in the world-price of gold. There are many reasons to denounce this dog-in-Fort-Knox attitude but what is beyond reason is for the same country that forces down the price of the commodity which finances South Africa's purchases of American goods to increase the price of those goods. That makes as much sense as trying to hitch the theory of space-time curvature to the principles of chess.

When practically all other commodities in the world have doubled, or trebled or more in price, gold stands where it stood more than twenty years ago. If this major South African product were permitted to achieve price-equilibrium with all those other commodities, not only would the economy of South Africa stand on a level even higher than it now is when bereft of that right, but the standard of living in all countries would also improve as a result of the increased productivity that would be created by a freeing of gold from an artificial and arbitrary price-restriction. In this matter of South Africa's basic product, free-enterprise America is the antagonist of free enterprise.

And for that departure from fundamental American philosophy it is America who, also, shares the suffering: with the gold-price compulsorily frozen, the gold-standard countries are compelled to restrict their purchases of dollar-country products. It is the firm conviction of most economists outside the North American continent, and not a few within, that America will recognise a realistic price for gold very soon— for America's sake; it is too much to expect that it will be done for the sake of anyone else. Shakespeare it was who said: "It is excellent to have a giant's strength; it is tyrannous to use it as a giant."

No one knows how much gold there is below South Africa's surface. It is reputed to be limitless; within this country's rock and lava are safe-deposit reserves that will last till moons shall wax and wane no more. Johannesburg may not deserve its name of "Golden City" but it certainly is the world's capital city of gold. Its streets are not paved with it but they are undoubtedly built on top of it. Where pavements are pounded by the hastening feet of a million people, once stood shafts which belched tons of gold-bearing ore. Two miles below the Rosettenville water reservoir lamp-helmeted miners are digging the precious ore on the stopes of the bourse-famous City Deep mine. And a hundred times a year, the pictures on the walls of thousands of homes, the pens in the trays of ten thousand offices, rattle as the city is shaken by earth tremors when some subterranean subsidence takes place, recording seismographic disturbances indistinguishable from underground atomic explosions.

Gold, like oil, is where you find it; and it has been found, so far, in a three-quarter circle of 200-mile circumference with Johannesburg midway. Last year the yield was worth £250,000,000 and as the first month's figures for 1960 showed an increase on those for the same period last year, the logical assumption is that production will score a record this year. This fabulous yield, which makes South Africa the world's pre-eminent gold producer, comes from fifty-four goldmines and as it costs between £10,000,000 and £15,000,000 to bring a modern goldmine into production the capital investment has been enormous. One mining house alone—the Anglo-American Corporation—has expended £125,000,000 on capital development in the Free State goldfields during the past ten years.

Gold is where you find it—and the search, in South Africa,

never ends. It is going on as I write this—over vast stretches
of the Transvaal and in the Orange Free State where more than
5,000,000 acres of land are held under option by prospecting
concerns. Drilling operations are incessant; not hit-and-hope
but as the logical conclusion to geological investigation. From
north of Randfontein to west of Ventersburg, from Klerksdorp
to the north side of the Vaal River opposite Parys, from
Barberton in the Transvaal to the southernmost part of the
Free State, surveying and drilling proceed day and night.
These probings into Nature's cornucopia form the rainbow
of hope—is the gold-pot at its end?

Gold is where you find it—but searching it out is a costly
and laborious procedure. "Let's sink us a shaft here" takes
only one breath to say. A year's work—more—can easily
follow. Often shaft-sinking is delayed through water bursting
in as the drill bores its diamond-pointed way through rock.
During the sinking of one recent Welkom shaft, water burst
in at pressures up to 1,500 lb.—ten times that of a city fire-hose
—at the rate of tens of thousands of gallons each anxious hour.

This constitutes a geological problem. Water-bearing
fissures are associated with fault-planes in the rock, and the
space between the walls of the fissure in which water is
impounded is generally no more than a fraction of an inch in
width. Water has accumulated in these fissures under pressure
for countless numbers of years to be suddenly released as the
shaft penetrates the lava rock. Very elaborate measures have
to be undertaken to prevent flooding, the most effective being
the process of cementation.

To effect this, a method of drilling ahead to a set pattern
is first employed. Drill holes are pierced as much as 120 feet
in advance of the actual shaft. When water is found, cement is
injected under enormous pressure into the fissure to seal it.

This method is generally successful but the famous Free State Geduld mine had to put up an epic fight against a major water inrush a few years ago. This occurred in one of the development ends on the 5,350-foot level. Cementation ranges—the pipes through which the cement is pumped—were extended and the shaft was allowed to become flooded to the level of the water station on the surface. Then additional water was deliberately pumped in so that a reverse flow-back to the development end into the fissure was induced—on the principle of the U-tube—making it possible to carry out the cementation process until the fissure was sealed.

That was not the end of the battle. Half-way through the operation the cemented fissure broke away and water rushed into the shaft with passionate prodigality at the rate of 200,000 gallons an hour. The entire process had to be repeated: the shaft was reflooded from the surface, the U-tube reverse-flow created and a 130-foot thick concrete plug made on the spot to seal off the affected area. I can give some idea of the magnitude of this task by saying that the cementation work and the casting of the huge plug had to be done by working from the surface and passing the materials, by pipes, through more than 5,000 feet of highly pressurised water.

Five hundred tons of sand had to be sent to the bottom of the shaft, followed by stone and cement, to form the giant plug—no fewer than 54,000 bags of cement were used in the entire operation. After three months of non-stop work, this major engineering feat was accomplished and the shaft successfully de-watered to the 5,350-foot level. To signalise the achievement, the Company's house-flag was hoisted; it was an oriflamme of triumph.

That triumph was followed by another—water de-salting. More than 8,000,000 gallons of water are pumped up from the Anglo-American mines at Welkom every day. One of the idiosyncrasies of Nature is that this water, from 5,000 feet below the surface, which is 5,000 feet above sea-level and with the nearest sea 500 miles away, has a pronounced salt-content. A simple geological explanation may be, of course, that millions of years ago, where now are goldmines, the sea was—but I have never got around to asking. Whatever the scientific explanation for the fact, the fact is that Anglo-American had 8,000,000 gallons of salt water on their hands every day and 8,000,000 gallons of salt water, when the sea is 500 miles away, became quite a daily problem. It could not be discharged into the Sand River nor used to quench the thirst of parched Free State farms.

How to dispose of the daily avalanche? posed a head-aching problem. That problem has been aspirined away: a special plant—Texan-like, the Anglo-American chiefs claim it to be the largest of its kind in the world—has been installed which de-mineralises saline water by the process of electrodialysis. And now the de-salted water is used in the Welkom uranium plant which requires fresh water for production. That is, to invoke the aid of Thomas Hardy, a satire in circumstance.

Another problem is air. At depths where the temperature rose above 88 degrees F., at which point human efficiency begins progressively to decline, special air-conditioning equipment had to be installed. In the Anglo-American mines on the Free State goldfields there are now 19 cooling plants operating. Each has a capacity equivalent to the cooling effect of melting 300 tons of ice a day. Extra twin circular shafts have been sunk at various Anglo-American mines to increase and improve ventilation. One shaft, of 24-feet diameter, provides upcast circulation and its twin, of 20 feet diameter, the downcast—both at the rate of 800,000 cubic feet of air a minute.

What began as a catch-as-catch-can gold-rush less than eighty years ago, with all the frenzied higgledy-piggledydom of early Yukon days, is now a mammoth industry, reflecting not only enormous investment but supreme organisational skill, a high sense of self-discipline and public responsibility. For this all credit goes to the Chamber of Mines, the internal regulatory and advisory body as a result of whose efforts South Africa can claim that there have been very few instances of goldmines failing to come up to expectations after capital had been put into them and shafts sunk. It is an industry of gibraltan stability, standing on the twin pillars of integrity and efficiency; and which last year produced more than 17,000,000 fine ounces of gold from nearly 66,000,000 tons of mined ore, providing millions of dividend money for investors and, for South Africa's national economy, an enviable foundation.

It is also contributing to the defence-material and industrial development of the entire Free World because twenty-nine of the goldmines are approved uranium-producers. A by-product of gold, South Africa's mines supply the Combined Development Agency of the Western Powers and the United Kingdom Authority with many thousands of tons of this essential component of atomic energy. Capital costs of building the uranium-producing plants were met by British and American loans—an immaculate testimonial by those two countries—and South Africa is now the third largest producer of uranium concentrates in the western world.

All this—unending gold and humanity-saving uranium— because seventy-four years ago an itinerant odd-job man stubbed his toe against a piece of rock on Widow Oosthuizen's farm. At that time the manifold activities of South Africa's goldmining industry, creating a great Goldorado, would have been ridiculed as the dream-fragments of a hashished imagination. They are, in fact, tangible evidences of the practicability of a generation of men whose devotion to the task had the invincible bulwark of a combination of dedicated service and pithy shrewdness. So equipped, they have developed a monolithic operation which is one of the wonders of the industrial world—a hive whose honeycomb of productivity forever brims.

WHILE industry marches on, with tennis-ball spring in its tread, agriculture tags along at the end of the procession with dragging feet. South Africa's first and oldest industry has been outpaced and overtaken. Changing the metaphor, it can be reported that, with roots deep-bedded in a past which began when van Riebeeck's free burghers sowed the first corn and vegetables, the sap is flowing turgidly in the centuries-old tree. It is as though the survival-struggle was draining agriculture of much of its zest, its urge, its sperm; as though it just retained sufficient vitality to inhale and exhale breath.

There are few South Africans who admit this but some of the more thoughtfully penetrative recognise the position. Agriculture is being given an appearance of vitality by regular shots of adrenalin into the bloodstream. Without the stimulants of Government protection, official cosseting and State subsidisation it would pass pantingly into more obvious decline due to its faulty pituitary. The tragedy is that it need not be.

Here is an essentially agricultural country; its people, its traditions, its history stem from the soil. To a marked degree it is true to say of South Africa that it belongs to an agricultural civilisation. If acreage of untilled land is the measure, then the South Africa of today is still a great agricultural country but, taking that acreage as the determinant, a considerable section of South African agriculture is accepting decline with the spine-sagged resignation of a mule. Compared with the tempo of advance maintained by all other aspects of the country's life agriculture is lagging.

There are contributory factors. One is climatic. While making an excellent poster for tourism "Sunny South Africa" is not ideal for farmers because the lofty sunshine figures spell for them the dread word "drought". An opening gambit for conversation in other countries, in South Africa weather is a topic of anxiety: the financial state of the farming community and the repercussive effects throughout the entire national economy are at the mercy of meteorological reports. South Africa's second problem—the Bantu constitute the chief—is water. Mr. Paul Sauer, the Minister of Lands, explained this tersely: "South Africa's development will finally be determined by the efficiency with which we use our weakest link —water."

"Sunny South Africa" is that because it has rainfall which, for farmers, is appallingly low. What there is has a bad seasonal distribution, and is dissipated quickly by a very high degree of evaporation under the tourist-attracting sun. International standards rate any country with less than twenty inches of rainfall as officially "barren"—when South Africa's figure exceeds twenty inches that only applies to eleven per cent of the country. And that small percentage consists mainly of mountainous areas which are inaccessible for livestock and inappropriate for husbandry.

Nearly ninety per cent of the country has to augment its natural moisture by irrigation if agriculture is to thrive. That is why the word "drought" conveys a dread presage of disaster and the event itself drives classic murders or Royal weddings off the front pages of the nation's newspapers. South Africa's sun does not only mean absence of rain—when rain does happen to baptise the gasping soil, the swift-returning sun dries it up almost before that parched throat can start quenching its thirst. It is a two-way disaster; first, the sun-dried soil absorbs most of an inch of rain in superficial moistening; then, evaporation quickly supervenes.

South Africans may wise-crack about "Britain's one-day summer" but they also realise the frightening price they pay for their own "sunny" adjective. One of the better rainfall places is Johannesburg so let me use that and London for a comparison. In any one year when London has an "official" drought—and that has to be a period of no less than fifteen days during which there is less than .01 inch of rain per day— Johannesburg has ten such periods. And, in the case of Johannesburg, those periods are not the official minimum of fifteen days but an average of forty-seven and a maximum of one hundred and twelve days.

That gives the rainfall comparison. Now for evaporation. Because of the high degree of moisture normally in London air, any pond in that city will, during any average year, lose twenty inches by evaporation. Its counterpart in Johannesburg will lose sixty inches. And, as I say, Johannesburg is a rainfall good-spot.

Water, it is obvious, is a major headache to South African agriculture. As it cannot, yet, be manufactured, the only cure is to make the most of what rainfall there is. South Africa has never done that. It is in the process of doing so with irrigation schemes, catchment areas, boreholes and dam-building. One step towards solving the problem was taken, fairly recently, by the Government with a new Act which made a partial return to the Dominus Fluminus law respecting water rights. Under that law, all water in rivers and streams belong to the State for allocation to the best public use. Unfortunately, the British administration, a century ago, changed that traditional South African law to one which gave ownership of such waters to the owners of the riparian lands. Private ownership of the fish in a river is an old English custom; to extend it to the water of the river was not the best service possible for South Africa.

State policy in South Africa has corrected that. It has created a series of public Water Boards who are responsible for the actual withdrawal and supply of water for domestic and industrial use in the local areas. One is the Rand Water Board who control the water of the Vaal River—South Africa's largest water supply—with its massive dam and storage capacity of 906,000 morgen-feet of water. This is a public body consisting of representatives of all Rand municipalities and such bulk-consumers as the Chamber of Mines and the railways, with a Government-appointed chairman. It now provides users with thirty million gallons of water daily. Its pumping plants, the most up-to-date in the world, raise a quantity of water, every twenty-four hours, whose weight is greater than all the ore handled that day in all the mines and lifts it to a height equal to that of the tallest skyscraper in the country.

To a less degree the operation of the Rand Water Board is duplicated by similar State-created bodies throughout the land. That system of public control governs water-distribution for domestic and industrial consumption; water distribution for agriculture is dependent on various forms of state and private irrigation. Fifty years ago planned irrigation was non-existent;

with self-government, modern South Africa accepted the responsibility of repairing the inherited omission.

In the heart of the arid Karoo a £400,000 irrigation scheme has just been established. The nearest river is the Leeu which, like all in South Africa, has a brief seasonal flow. To conserve its water, a dam one and a half miles long has been built to hold 8,000 morgen-feet of water and with a spillway designed to cope with a flood of more than 2,000,000 cubic feet a minute. It irrigates an area of about 50,000 morgen, containing 21 large farms and the water-distribution is on a basis of communal control under a Board consisting of the 21 farmers to whose lands the precious fluid is conducted by a 20-mile specially constructed canal. That is only one instance of the present-day irrigation which is solving agriculture's chief problem.

There is another away in the Free State where an irrigation scheme costing £7,000,000 is being constructed which entails the building of two huge dams, conserving the waters of the Sand and Vet rivers, that will revolutionise the province's agricultural economy. In one of these, to be completed next year, water flowing at the rate of 82,000 gallons a minute will irrigate, via 85 miles of concrete-lined canals, 9,200 morgen of new farmlands. There is, also, a £47,000,000 scheme, about 80 miles from the mouth of the Orange River, that will irrigate the extensive livestock area along the western coast.

These and similar efforts—there are 160 irrigation districts in full functional operation and water schemes on which the Government is spending nearly £6,000,000—are proceeding but having regard to the magnitude of the agricultural area they sometimes look like an attempt to subdue Vesuvius with a water-pistol.

Much more will have to be done in the way of a scientifically-

241

planned endeavour to ensure maximum utilisation of the fairly limited water supplies if agriculture is to be rescued from its handicap. Several times each year the nation is shocked to learn of drought conditions in some part of the country or another. When severe drought strikes an area, it spreads carnage across the agricultural spectrum, annihilating crops and strewing the land with thousands of cattle corpses. This spasmodic affliction minimises all other advances as if the mechanics of agriculture had been put together wrongly, like a differential installed backwards: one speed forward and three in reverse.

Beyond and beneath the water problem, agriculture suffers from another adverse effect: the quality of many of the farmers. Like most industries, the directive personnel of agriculture exposes gradations of efficiency ranging from a minimum of excellent to a maximum of indifferent. That complexion might get past in manufacture and commerce where efficient subordinates can camouflage top-flight mediocrity; in agriculture the incidence must be reversed because the farmer, himself in person, is the only key figure. There are several reasons for this widely deplored situation. One is psychological; another is economic; a third is political.

There are too many "stoep" farmers for agriculture's prosperity to be entrenched. Over the years there has developed a psychology which encourages the farmer to sit on the stoep—smoking, coffee-drinking and, I hope, thinking —while his considerable force of Bantu labourers carry out his instructions in the fields. His own physical contribution is generally confined to riding around his ranch on horseback or visiting other farmers on a busman's holiday from a busman's holiday. It is the most *infra* degree of *infra dig* for a White farmer to do any manual labour and a "working farmer" is an improbability only exceeded by that of a Muizenberg bathing belle wearing a Medici cloak over her bikini.

Added to that class are the land barons—too citified for the country, too countrified for the city. Even if they had the desire actively to participate in farming it is impossible because their estates are so extensive. When a farmer owns a 40,000-acre farm he might just as well never go near the place for all the personal attention he can give the actual operations. And there are nearly 1,000 farmers each owning from 20,000 to 40,000 acres. Baronisation to this extent cannot possibly ensure that maximum of personal oversight which is essential to practical farming.

This economic defect, demonstrated by the fact that there are 21,000 farmers with less than 500 acres each—the workable size—and as many more with farms in excess of that convenient acreage, constitutes a major imperfection of South Africa's agricultural complex. It possesses one favourable feature—in general, the larger farmers are positioned to be more progressive and modern-minded. Most farmers—and not only in South Africa—are conservative, cautious and tradition-bound; with them a febrile imagination and lusty enterprise are as likely as a secret-ballot free election in a totalitarian state. Always dissatisfied, they seldom employ discontent as the goad to revolt against the causes of their dissatisfaction or exhibit that get-up-and-go spirit of adventure which can change fighting into victory's ringing cheer. If only they were battling in another element they would know that there is only one way to shoot the rapids and that is by paddling faster than the current. Their fatal instinct for fatalistic acceptance of whatever Fate bestows is the psychological reason for the relative failure of the Ministry of Agriculture to popularise its excellent scientific facilities.

243

It required intense persuasion—so intense as almost to equal compulsion—to get many farmers to accept the Marketing Board system. The success of the Agricultural Producers' Co-operatives could be regarded as a miracle of consilience if it did not have a less miraculous explanation—their appeal to the average farmer's indisposition to do work that he could get others to do for him. When it comes to such "new-fangled ideas" as rotational farming and artificial insemination, there is a widespread reluctance to "interfere with the laws of nature".

Farming in South Africa is lagging in the march of progress because the typical farmer is, by instinct and tradition, not progressive. Farmers the world over are not famous for being vastly different. That may not be unduly important in some other countries; in South Africa, whose future will be determined by the degree of self-sufficiency it can attain, agricultural efficiency developed to a maximum is imperative. Unless the great majority of South Africa's farmers can acquire a new mental approach to farming, agriculture will languish and, in view of that potential calamity, a pressing responsibility rests on the Government who may have to forsake the glib, soft, woosy area of compromise and rationale for the more courageous territory of sanctions and penalisation.

And that is where the political consideration makes its melancholy entrance. A deplorable hangover from the recent past is the political importance that all Governments have attached to "the farmer's vote". Smuts was defeated because —among other equally telling reasons—as an Afrikaner of agricultural disposition, he failed to use his powers to correct the electoral system that unfairly loaded the vote-value of the rural community—among whom his opponents were thereby strong—in comparison with that of the urban areas where his own strength was concentrated. Had he done so, a National Government might not have ousted him. Objections of his present-day followers to the fact that "the farmer's vote" is keeping the National Government in power sounds somewhat unconvincing in the ears of an unbiased person.

Because of the decisive power of "the farmer's vote", its owner has become the beneficiary of feather-bedding consideration. Last year the benefice was worth £40,000,000 of State money to the farmer. As a result it is only natural that they should generate the idea that the Government will always be there to throw them a life-line. Welfare-Stateocracy in South Africa means State assistance for one class, but Government-aid for depressed farmers is a poor substitute for Government insistence that farmers should modernise their methods so that external aid would be unnecessary.

Because the average farmer was either outmoded or greedy the landscape of South Africa is disfigured by an eczema of soil-erosion. Farmers sowed and reaped "cash crops" of maize year after year, soaking the impoverished soil with chemical crop-forcers until it went sour and eroded into an appearance of calciniferous deposits like the fused exterior of a fallen meteor. They are only slowly being educated by an extremely enlightened Ministry of Agriculture to the anti-suicidal virtues of rotational farming—alternating "cash-crop" farming with cattle-raising pasturage so that the soil can be revitalised. On this policy of soil-conservation the Government is spending many millions every year and have now provided 579 districts embracing 14,457 farm-owners with soil-conservation work-plans. The number of farmers who implement these Government-supplied work-plans for the renovation of their soil is discouragingly small—not half of those served with plans. When all farmers realise that the

245

Government cannot always save them from the economic threats that their own incompetence or obstinacy creates, and understand that farming can only be saved by farming, South African agriculture will underwrite South Africa's prosperity —and the farmers'.

South African agriculture, despite its unnecessary defects, is a dominant, although not dominating, factor in the nation's life. It could, and should, be both. That it is not is due to the fact that the percentage of really competent, modern-minded, enterprisingly scientific farmers is outweighted by those who have, to some degree or another, lapsed into caducity. While the total production from all sources —including the millionaire-product, wool—contributes £400,000,000 to the national income, this huge sum has to be juxtaposed to the fact that it is produced on well above 2,000,000,000 acres of land devoted to agricultural purposes. An official of the Department of Agriculture informed me that this production figure could be doubled within five years if all members of the farming community farmed at the same high level of efficiency and intelligence revealed by a small minority.

Many of those 2,000,000,000 acres are tending to yield less and less every year—the soil is getting worn out and, were it not for the Government's intensive soil-conservation schemes, the heart of the fabulous "maize triangle" would become a gigantic dust bowl. There is only one remedy: stop crop growing, plant grass, bring animals to graze. Hesitating to compel, the Government encourages farmers by financial inducements to apply that remedy. A grant of £100 a year for three years is made to every farmer who converts up to 50 acres into grassland and loans of £300 to stock it with cattle.

Integration of the animal factor into the cropping system is

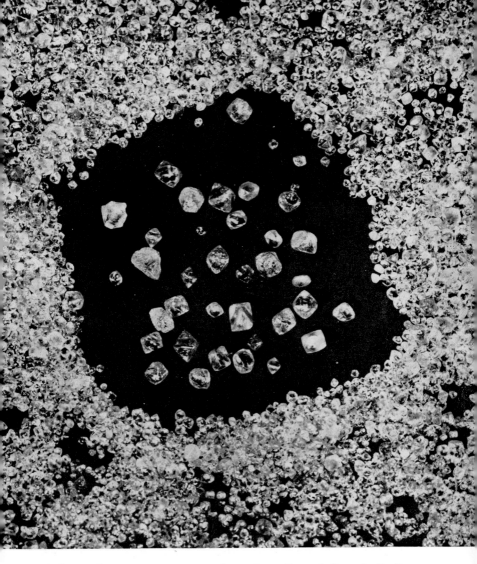

Ready for a million engagement-rings—a heap of gem-diamonds from the De Beer mines in Kimberley, all ready to be sorted, graded, ground and set for a million happy couples all over the world.

This was a wheatfield. Tragic sequel to soil-erosion on a farm at Hofmeyer in the Cape.

This is salvation. Rotational farming, soil-conservation, contour cultivation and strip-cropping provide triumph over tragedy.

essential and this has a dual beneficial effect: it revives the soil and increases the cattle supply. Very slowly farmers are co-operating in this scheme which, although it may, but not necessarily so, reduce their immediate earnings, will be the salvation of their land. Such salvation is desperately needed by many in the "maize triangle" where twenty-five per cent of farmers are getting less than five bags to the morgen whereas 7.6 bags is the absolute minimum for economic production.

Intelligent farming is entirely a South African development —it did not exist before self-government. What was almost an entirely agricultural country did not provide enough products to feed the people. It was more politic, in that era, to import British foodstuffs. In less than four decades the production of agricultural products has far outstripped the requirements of the local market and South Africa is now a food-exporting country of no mean importance. At the turn of the century South Africa was compelled to import from Britain—the procedure is now reversed.

Mealies—the South African term for maize—is a major agricultural product, a vast area being devoted to its cultivation. An average yield from more than 8,000,000 acres in an average year—because meteorological conditions are influential—is in the region of 38,000,000 200-lb. bags and the policy of the Mealie Board is to transfer about 7,000,000 bags of the surplus over home consumption to the following year and export the rest. Exports generally show a loss and this is recovered out of a Maize Stabilisation Fund which is maintained by a levy on all producers plus a contribution by the Government on every bag sold for local consumption.

Ranking as the country's second-largest earner of foreign currency, wool-sheep farming is the financially dominant feature of South Africa's agriculture. Its financial achievement is only subject to outside limitations—the fluctuation of prices on the world market—so that, with the wool farmers, jitters are always in the ascendant. On land worth £500,000,000 grazes a sheep population of more than 38,000,000, of which 28,000,000 are Merinos, who produce 789,000 bales of the fine-textured wool that makes the South African product superior.

Another agricultural success is sugar—the crop is expected to reach a record yield of at least 1,200,000 tons this year—it will have doubled in ten years—and more than one-third will be exported. More and more land is being added to "the sugar belt" which, in yielding 3.5 tons of sugar per acre, puts South Africa well into sixth place among the world's sugar-producing countries.

Among the agricultural achievements of South Africa, viticulture has won international renown. France and Germany have been producing wine for 1,500 years; South Africa for a third of that time—but the liquid joy extracted from the grapes that cluster along the hillsides of Paarl and Constantia are now as world-known as any. Napoleon was one of its first drinkers and gave Constantia pride of place in his cellars. Since then even more famous and discriminatory palates have rolled it over their tongue for the delicacy it is.

Port, sherry and table wines constitute the chief products. Hermitage grapes and Portuguese varieties, grown in specially selected and cultivated vineyards at Paarl and Stellenbosch, are the raw material for ruby, white and tawny ports. They are matured in European or Baltic oak for from five to eight years while the vintage ports are shipped to Britain for special maturation in bottle—being produced in a hot, dry climate the wine matures better in countries of a more temperate climate.

Sherry is a more recent addition to South Africa's wine list, the first consignment being produced less than twenty-five years ago. More than a million gallons are shipped overseas every year and this invasion of a market where Spanish sherries have reigned in uncontested supremacy for centuries is regarded among connoisseurs as phenomenal. Under examination it is not so remarkable when I record that geographically and climatically South Africa's sherry district closely resembles the area in which the Andalusian sherries are produced—Jerez de la Frontera is in latitude 31.41 degrees north while Paarl is 33.45 degrees south.

Table wines, not being unduly popular in South Africa, have not been so extensively produced until recently when overseas demands encouraged the introduction of improved methods of production and handling. A full range of white wines from dry to semi-sweet, and red wines from rose to full-body, are now competing strongly with continental names of historic association. What these and sherry are doing is to debunk the poseur who pretends that sherry, to be sherry, must be Spanish, and a full-bodied red wine, to be drinkable, must come from Burgundy.

Here is another truly South African product that has advanced since handicaps imposed by the former adminis-tration were removed. After only being in occupation of the Cape less than twenty years, the British subjected that district's wine exports to fiscal penalisation which drove them out of the British market and wine-growers into bankruptcy. Westminster, at that time, had politico-economic reason for giving preference to French wines and the Cape product was caught in the slipstream of international politics. This even caused the docile Lord Somerset, the British Governor, to venture rebuke at his Whitehall superiors. "The wine farmers can scarcely find any market for their produce," he reported, "and from the measures which have lately been adopted in England to facilitate the introduction of French and other wines, it is not likely that their prospects will brighten."

In fact they did not brighten for a hundred years—until South Africa regained self-government. It was the formation of the KWV—the Co-operative Wine-growers' Association—in 1918 that gave South Africa's viticulture the genuine stature that belongs only to security. In defiance of traditional individualism, the grape-farmers surrendered liberty of action to the more tempting prospects of co-operation. And they embraced that temptation with a passionate recklessness only equalled by Lady Chatterley's gamekeeper. The result is that the KWV is now almost the largest agricultural co-operative in this land of large agricultural co-operatives with very few wine-growers outside its beneficial membership. It has become a wine-growing monolith—monolithism is always the response to the cravings of the fragmented.

Through the KWV, the wine-growers now co-operatively own huge cellars in five Cape towns with a combined storage capacity of 50,000,000 gallons of wine. Scientific and laboratory skills are so organised that both the growing of the vines and the maturing of their yield are equivalent to the world's best. With assets of nearly £5,000,000 and nearly double that sum in reserves, the KWV is in an exceptionally secure position. So are its members who, last year, benefited to the extent of more than £6,000,000 in payment for their crops.

As a result of this purely South African organisation of a historic South African industry, KWV marketing has placed Cape-produced wines on the market in twenty-five overseas countries. They were not on one before self-government, and it is an ironic fact that the bulk of the wine-grower's prosperity comes from overseas because, unlike all other wine-producing countries, South Africa is not a wine-drinking country. The average South African is, in respect to the art and science of drinking and eating, in the philistinic stage: eating, gormand rather than gourmet; for drinking, harsh brandy rather than delicate wine.

Iᴛ is quite apparent to any detached student of the South African scene that the industrial and agricultural complex is underdeveloped. That obviously implies great scope for development. Only occasionally is the picture lightened and brightened by touches of maximum efficiency and the utmost exploitation of possibilities. It is this aspect that makes South Africa's future so decoratively attractive: it is not a "has been"; it is a "will be". Its glittering future is attested by its unfortunate past—for a country that only fifty years ago was still benumbed by the blitzing of a war that destroyed all the manifestations of nationhood to have made such a dazzling recovery that its industrial and agricultural accomplishments, although below optimum, are epic achievements, the future cannot be other than even greater and brighter than the present.

What was a bankrupt nation is now a country of unshakable financial stability. So secure, in fact, that when Britain was in war-caused financial straits, South Africa provided an interest-free loan of £80,000,000 without waiting to be asked. It is the rocklike certainty of its basic economy that gives its enticing future an incontrovertible guarantee. In this, the Economic Era, that materialist fact stands unmovable in face of overseas misconceptions and local problems—both of which will yield to time's infallible solvent.

Money; money—all things have to come back to that starting point. All human endeavour, all social development, all national achievement find in money their explanation and their expression. Dollars, pounds, lira, roubles, guilders are the eloquent symbols which spell out progress in an understandable esperanto. Take that alphabet and with it write the South African story—the hieroglyphics of finance make it a dramatic recital.

Like all countries, South Africa is money-minded—on the subject of money, the average South African is a gifted monologist. Throughout their three-century history, South Africans have extracted utmost relish from every piece of fluky fortune in the whole tombola of life's random repertoire, with the result that the sign of the £ has been overprinted on their instinct for cultural development. With far too many people in the higher positions, the favourite reading is a bank-book.

It has come to mean much more to South Africans, whose forebears had tasted the rancid flavour of adversity, that there has been, in the past two years alone, a decline of £65,000,000 in foreign borrowing coupled with an increase of £216,000,000 in internal savings, than that the number of books issued by the libraries has doubled in the same period. An increase of savings, rather than an increase of culture, has become the symbol of national health and the most glowing bulletin announces that the origin of South Africa's capital funds is now changing from external to internal.

In the building societies, the people of South Africa have a total of £570,000,000 invested savings, making it the largest building-society nation per capita in the world. In the past ten years, savings in that form alone have been multiplied four-fold—an infallible sign of the financial integrity of the nation. Home-ownership is an obsession with the people—more than three-quarters of the houses built during the last two decades have been financed through the building societies; that and insurance are the most palatable forms of compulsory saving.

Through the building societies, insurance companies, commercial and Post Office Savings Banks and other media for smallish deposits the people of South Africa have demonstrated their inherited instinct for providence. During the past ten years the total assets of those financial institutions have grown from £1,023,000,000 to £2,269,000,000—more than doubled by less than 3,000,000 people, if children are included, because the Bantu people are not provident even if they were in a position to be. To achieve a hundred per cent increase in internal financial strength in such a short period is a declaration of sound prosperity.

Apart from instinctive frugality, South Africans are encouraged to save by the lowest income-tax scales in the world. An average family is officially considered, in most countries, to consist of a man, his wife and two children. An average salary is around £1,000 a year. Let such an average family man in Britain or America or any similar country compare the amount he has to pay in income-tax with what a married man in South Africa, with two children and a £1,000 salary, pays —that fortunate fellow only pays £6 17s. od. income-tax. A man with three children has to wait until his income is £1,250 before he pays any tax at all. If the man with two children earned £1,500 he would pay £44 13s. od. and £87 8s. od. if his salary was £2,000 a year. It is only when he gets into the £5,000-a-year class that income-tax takes a real chunk—he would have to pay £870 in tax; but by then, the £1,000-a-year man thinks, he could afford to. A married man with an income of more than £10,000 a year pays £2,960 in income-tax and this impost provides the State with very large revenue because the South African percentage of men in that class and over is very high.

Because of the higher salary scales compared with Britain, and the much lower tax rate, the standard of personal living in South Africa is high; only the American exceeds it. Despite the heavy personal-savings figure, South Africans enjoy luxuries that would make an Englishman's—and especially his wife's—mouth water. South African domestic life more closely approximates the American, with one or two cars per family, fully-electrified homes, radiograms until TV rears its ugly antennae, and—here even the American comparison picks up its skirts and flits away in petulant envy—from one to four domestic servants to each house.

These are among the material symbols of personal prosperity. They have a national reflection. Let other comparable nations compare South Africa's public debt of £1,072,000,000 with their own. And even that low figure becomes less when it is realised that £913,000,000, of it is funded. Direct investment from overseas amounts to £1,427,000,000, with Britain, at £865,000,000, the biggest creditor; but American investors have now a £210,000,000 stake in South Africa, mainly with the goldmines and the secondary industries.

On this last fact pause for reflection should be taken. It is vested with immense significance. During the past ten years a change in the structure of South Africa's direct liabilities —that is overseas investors—has been in progress. British capital investment has been spiralling into a tail-spin and its place more than taken by American dollars. I do not suppose for one moment that South Africa has a special preference either way, although American investment is more than money

—it's dollars. If anyone should be concerned about the change it should be Britain, unless Throgmorton Street has given up the fight with Wall Street and is content to see America take over financial territories as Britain evacuates them.

No one imagines that American financiers are pouring money into South Africa primarily for South Africa's benefit. Such concerns as General Motors, Ford, Kelloggs and 190 other American concerns now in South Africa are duty-bound to their stockholders to invest their money where it will earn the most substantial dividends with the least risk. Mr. W. H. Rodkey, when he was Managing-Director of General Motors in South Africa four years ago, was not concerned about any other ideology than that of good business, which consists in pleasing the public and pleasing the stockholders. After praising the "marvellous potential" of South Africa, he told Roy Vickers of the *Wall Street Journal*: "We may not be in sympathy with some of the things that are being done but we know this country well enough to be certain that it is on an extremely stable foundation."

That same view was expressed to me by Mr. Carleton L. Dyer, the Canadian-born Managing-Director of South African Motor Acceptance Corporation, which operates in the financing interests of Studebaker and Volkswagen: "It has been my duty, during the past ten years, to examine South Africa's economic structure very carefully and I am completely satisfied that it is fundamentally as sound as the proverbial bell."

Men like Rodkey and Dyer, responsible for the wise investment of many millions of pounds, do not risk other people's money and jeopardise their trust if there is the slightest dubiety. They first of all make sure of the facts, one of which is that the U.S. Department of Commerce issued an official statement of net earnings—that is, after tax—of American investment in the manufacturing industries of other countries. Canada showed 15.8 per cent; France 19.6; Britain 18.9, but South Africa—27.05 per cent. No ideological theory affects financial facts like those with Americans, and my enquiries suggest that, just as American investors have been marching in as British investments declined during the past ten years, the next ten years might quite easily find this structural change taking on a much more significantly fundamental character.

THERE are several basic factors that comprise the financial underpinning to the structure of a nation's economy and which, in the case of South Africa, confirm Mr. Carleton Dyer's verdict. One of them is its transportation facilities. South Africa's internal transport system, while suffering under some legislative details which must be corrected, has been brought to a high level of efficiency and service that is another testimony to the achievement of South Africa, once it was allowed to manage its own affairs. Earlier in this report I indicated that South Africa's few big cities are separated by vast distances. A thousand miles intervene between Cape Town and Johannesburg, and between Durban and Cape Town, while from 200 to 500 miles separate the other large towns. These vast distances were allowed by the previous administration to keep South Africa "a backward country", self-insufficient, reliant on British imports. That has been drastically changed, since self-government, by a modern transport miracle.

Twin steel ribbons link all those towns and cities in one of the most remarkable railway systems to be found anywhere. To do that mountains have had to be tunnelled or skirted, tracks have been laid far into the desolate veld, often hundreds of miles from habitation, kopjes have been levelled and ravines filled in, extreme topographical curvature flattened and gradients reduced. What was fifty years ago an antiquated and disconnected line of short runs, operated by three companies, has, since self-government, been extended to a total of more than 15,000 miles over which 77,000,000 tons of freight are carried and 275,000,000 passenger journeys made yearly. More than 3,000 miles of the track is electrified and when the electrification programme is completed next year South Africa will have a network of electrified railway exceeding the mileage in Canada, Australia and New Zealand combined.

Instead of the ramshackle, disjointed lines operated by three companies before self-government there is now one national railway service, State-owned and State-operated. On its 15,000 miles of track connecting 3,044 stations, sidings and other stopping places 6,040 full-sized passenger coaches and 160,746 trucks are drawn by 3,259 locomotives, steam, electric and diesel. This extensive system is the biggest single labour-employer in the country with a yearly payroll of £112,000,000 and forms the chief State-trading operation responsible to a Minister whose annual budget is a major item on the Parliamentary order paper. The present Minister is Mr. Ben Schoeman whose recognised success in that capacity may be explained by the fact that he began life as a fireman on the railways of which he is now Ministerial head—a change from the usual hexagonal peg in a round hole.

Bracketed with the railways, administratively, are the harbours and air-service. The six major harbours handle cargo to a total not far short of 20,000,000 tons every year, off-loaded from an annual average of 13,121 vessels flying the flags of 21 different nations. During any year, little short of 100,000 passengers are landed at South African ports.

South African Airways planes are familiar at all big airports from London in the west to Perth in the east. In addition to that international service is the internal system which links up all the big cities of the entire Southern Africa with frequency-schedules of from two a day to once a week. More than a quarter of a million South Africans use the city-to-city air service each year, a mode of travelling that is solving the businessman's time-problem when a de-luxe journey, with meals and drinks aloft, can span the thousand miles which separate Johannesburg from Cape Town in less than four hours. A return trip in the same day, with business appointments as the meat in the sandwich, is normal routine for hundreds of executives every week.

No visitor fails to be impressed with South African road construction. Many sections of the 4,000-mile network of 100-feet wide national roads—apart from the many more thousands of lesser macadamised roads—are brilliant feats of civil engineering which have slashed into mountains, spanned rivers and arrowed across scrub-covered veld in defiance of all the eccentricities of a variegated topography. While the local authorities are responsible for constructing and maintaining the roads, finance comes from the National Road Fund to which Parliament makes an annual allocation. This is created mainly by car-users—the funds are derived from, among lesser sources, a tax of sixpence per gallon on petrol. This is a very neat exercise in indirect direct-taxation—the one million car-users pay towards the construction and maintenance of the roads their cars use according to the amount of petrol consumed in the process.

Under the old administration the traditional policy was "trade follows the flag". Under self-government it has been: rail-and-road expansion accompanies trade. Transport services being a State monopoly, it has been easy to organise the provision of facilities in correlation with the industrial developments. A typical instance is the new Free State gold-fields; so soon as they passed the blue-print stage, a pair of steel fingers crept across the veld from Johannesburg, 150 miles distant and, before actual mining began, Welkom and Virginia were rail-linked with the rest of the country. Trans-port mirrors industrialism: it is axiomatic that wherever the railway extends, there new industries are being established. Which is another way of saying that the railway service is expanding continuously.

Economic, industrial and financial development are no more the complete answer to the question: what is the recipe of South Africa's recent success? than vulgar fractions are the answer to relativity. In the ultimate it is the people—that ancient institution known as man—that provide the deter-minant in a nation's choice between growth and sterility. A hasty verdict would be that, in terms of social advancement, South African life is distinguished by an aura of provincialism. That would be so hasty that leisure for repentance is required.

With deliberate repetition—because it is all-explaining—I have reported here the significant fact that South Africa, as a unitary self-governing nation, is only fifty years old. This report is, in fact, written within sound of the joyous celebra-tions of Jubilee year when all but a faithful band of Natal churls are rejoicing in the first half-century of national sovereignty. If, in many walks of life, South Africans obtain a minus-mark, that can only be as and when they are unfairly judged by the standards of nations who enjoy the benefits

CURTAIN-UP ON SOUTH AFRICA

of an independent national life that is almost as ancient as the antiquity of the Cheops.

It has been quite a little puzzling to the observer of the South African scene to detect signs of supercilious superiority in references made to the country's social standards by overseas commentators. After trying on a few sneers for size they settle for "ox-wagon-mindedness". This attitude is often found among the more uncultured of immigrants within the country. Keening like something out of a Celtic twilight, they mourn the absence of neon-dazzling shows "back home"; with the clappers of their tongues they toll the tocsin of despair because—in one social class—there are no concert halls and, in another, "there ain't no fish-and-chip shops".

They explain all the gilded delights of "home" which they have sacrificed—in order that South Africa should enjoy the benefit of their presence—with the volubility of an American radio announcer. Exhibiting a positively hypnoidal disregard of the values inherent in the South African way of life, they deplore departed joys like a Walt Disney hen mourning its chick. Such lamentations are not of doubtful virtue—they have no virtue to be doubtful about.

Facts which I have been able to gather all over the country —a somewhat advantageous itinerary by which to obtain them —do not justify this supercilious attitude. I have found a people with a great capacity for enjoying the less sophisticated pleasures of life; with an instinct for making their own enjoyment; with a party-going, party-giving habit; with a social life staged on the family stoep, which might be lacking the veneer of West-Endism but is constructed of the more genuine components of true friendliness and spontaneous hospitality. Social life among South Africans, outside the city-centres, shows that they are a people of well-balanced, well-integrated interests.

Written into the history of every nation—from Greece to Ghana—is this thematic principle: the development of a people cannot be any greater than the carrying power of the majority. Fifty years of South Africa's development expresses the carrying power of the majority. What tempo development will establish over the second half of the first century of South Africa's national independence will be determined by the same factor. Throughout this report it has been necessary, in order to depict the scene in factual terms, repeatedly to refer to that watershed in South Africa's development—the Anglo-Boer war or, as South Africans describe it, the War of Independence: modern South Africa's dateline. Between that wipe-out to the present renaissance, this resurrected nation has emerged miraculously, like Minerva springing from Jupiter's head. Only when the time-limit enclosed between those two dates is fully appreciated can the "carrying capacity" of the people be adequately assessed.

It is the efficiency of a people's thinking apparatus that provides "carrying capacity". Educational levels, not bipedism, form the population test. And when this modern South Africa began, not only education standards but educational facilities were exactly what an Imperialist power considered to be adequate for a colonial, subject people. In respect to educational facilities, South Africa was no different from those of Ireland and India and Ghana when the colonial, subject people achieved independence. South Africa, since unitary self-government, has spent on education in fifty years much more than twenty times as much as was spent by the previous administration in double that time.

Had those figures been reversed, the "carrying capacity" of the people would now be elevating South Africa into the highest-placed group of modern nations. Instead of which, it is clear from my investigations that South Africa, education-wise, has still far to go, despite the fantastic distance it has already journeyed. This can be better understood—blame and praise correctly apportioned—when it is remembered that every adult Afrikaner of thirty years of age or older is the son or daughter of parents on whom the effects of the anti-Afrikaner operations of "the occupation" had been visited, including the extremely limited educational facilities. Ten years ago all the Afrikaners in charge of all aspects of South African life—commercial, industrial, educational, political—were in that category.

Viewed against that background the present educational standard of the people—its "carrying capacity"—ranks as one of the outstanding social achievements of the twentieth century. That, however, is far from sufficient; it is only recorded in order to get a true perspective: to establish the basis of comparison. If, alternatively, the comparison is not to be with pre-independent South Africa but its progress—unfairly, most thoughtful people might say—be measured by an overseas' yardstick, then its "carrying capacity" has a noticeable short-fall. Apart from the exceptions, indigenous South Africans fall below the standards that are normal in such countries as America, Britain, Germany and France, in most of the areas of human activity.

Education in those countries had hundreds of years' start on modern South Africa where, now, educational facilities and educational standards are two different elements: the former compare favourably with those in most overseas countries. An excellent system of primary, secondary and high schools, colleges, technical-training schools and universities network the entire country—except the three British protectorates—but their products are less satisfying.

For some acquired reason a matriculation fetish dominates the family mind as the examination results dominate the pages of the press. To be a matriculant is, to the parents of most youngsters, no different from "putting my son's name down at Eton" was to the British aristocracy. Either the examination standards are low or the matriculants were expert crammer-respondents because, when they get into commercial life, the average practical ability is in most cases below the old British board-school level. It would appear as if the youth of South Africa evaluate education only as the mechanical process of exam-passing and not the essential preliminary to success in life. In fact, their approach to their business future appears less than serious, as though they regarded success merely as the paper helmet of a clown more nimble than his fellows in scrambling for peanuts in the sawdust of some ignoble circus-ring. Even if this is the attitude of this generation all over the world, it is one that a growing country cannot afford.

Nor does it end there. Despite their pride in their educational system—thoroughly well-founded when it is, as it must be, compared with that of fifty years ago—the South Africans who benefit from forms of higher education do not too frequently appear to have done so. Man for man, in job for job, the South African-educated person is, as such, inferior to his overseas counterpart. They certainly are not the cleverest, brightest fellows on God's footstool that they are cracked up to be.

In their unfortunate isolationism, vaccinated with self-satisfaction and constantly taking the temperature of their own self-admiration, most South Africans will resent this statement but their understandable resentment—based on an absence of comparative world-values—will do nothing to amend what is an established fact. It is, also, a demonstrable fact—demonstrated by the overwhelming number of top-echelon

positions which have to be filled with men of overseas qualifications. If all the executive posts in commerce and industry
now filled by men and women qualified by overseas education,
training and experience were compulsorily vacated and filled
with people of exclusively South African qualifications, the
machinery of the entire nation, the entire national economy,
would brake to an abruptly disastrous stop. This, like most of
truth, must be unpalatable to South Africans who, extrovert
though they be, are congenitally introspective and find within
themselves considerable scope for self-satisfaction—an extremely dubious form of egotism because the man who thinks
too much about himself is very often only padding his own cell.

Education being, also, the parent of culture, the tide of South
African cultural life is at low-ebb. There is no theatre apart from
some struggling, often strangled-at-birth amateur repertory or
semi-pro performances, heroically staged in 300–700-seater
halls. These spasmodic specks of light in the dark theatrical
firmament are produced by such valiants as Brian Brooke and
Leon Gluckman whose box-office failures are a credit to them
because a condemnation of South Africa's cultural appreciation.

This was not always the case. The large-scale professional
theatre of a quarter-century back was killed by the late Mr.
I. W. Schlesinger when he astutely saw that the bioscope—
as the cinema is still called—would appeal more profitably
to the South African mind than any cultural enterprise. His
brilliant son, Mr. John Schlesinger, has made many conces-
sions to conscience, in recent years, by bringing out front-rank
overseas companies to stage top-class plays and operas at West
End standards, but the cultural stomach of South Africa could
only digest such intellectual fare every other year. None of
that nonsense for American realism—since the Schlesinger
cinema-chain was bought out by Twentieth Century-Fox the

box-office appeal of the Diana Dors culture has been permitted no stage rival. Both the late "I.W." and Twentieth Century have been right: to cater for the lowest common denominator is financial wisdom when the cultural appreciation of a country is still growling along in first gear.

Significance attaches to the fact that the evidences that now exist of a cultural renaissance come from the Afrikaans-speaking section of the community. This is a direct derivative of the language revival—or, to be absolutely accurate, the language survival. Afrikaans is the baby language of the world. It was not South Africa's original language because Jan van Riebeeck and the earliest settlers spoke High Dutch and that language remained the written-word medium long after Afrikaans began to evolve as the means of speech. Evolved is the right verb; it was never originated, designed, invented or planned. Topsy-like, it jes' grew. In its growth from the feeble innominate it assimilated the languages of a polyglot people—on the Dutch basis, a gradual accretion of Hottentot, German, French, British and Bantu deposited so that a subsoil of those languages repeatedly seeps through the surface of modern Afrikaans.

It was the Anglo-Boer War of Independence which, acting as a spiritual cathartic that purged the people of materialist lusting, gave Afrikaans the irresistible impetus that carried it to the status of an official language. South African history resembles that of Ireland in many ways—including a republican Brotherhood and the Church behind militant nationalism —and this is plainly demonstrated in respect to the national language. Afrikaans and Erse were both given a popular— i.e., of the people—familiarity by the poets who converted words into the living flesh and draped them with the rainbow of tears and sunlight. Patrick Pearse in Ireland and Jan Celliers in South Africa, as of those who weep by the waters of Babylon, sang the dirges of a nation's woe and songs of a nation's vision, in words eloquent with the rich drama of humanity which were the flags of revolt for independence against the language and the suzerainty of the occupying force. Their souls illumined by that ineffable light that bathed the figures of the gods, they took their hanging harps from the willows of past despairs and gloried in the things that concerned their nations' infirmities with a classic disdain for iambic pentameter, dactyls, triolets and other intricacies of mathematic versification in which the humanities of poetry have been so often lost.

During the years of struggle for nationhood, in both countries, the poets inspired national resurgence and, also in both cases, inspired the survival of the national language which the same occupying power had deliberately suppressed. The sequel differed: the Irish, with their great capacity for statesmanship, were more occupied with achieving the end— united republican independence—than making the language an isolationary and insulationary means; Afrikaners are less realistic. Afrikaans has, very unfortunately, acquired a political and divisionary function—in South Africa, unlike Ireland, language is becoming a barrier within the people.

Against that deplorable and excessively damaging defect a supreme benefit can be placed: it is the language of a cultural renaissance. There is now a South African literature, South African poetry, South African drama, all expressed in the Afrikaans idiom. It is producing indigenous artists of eminence. Poets like Van Wyk Louw and Uys Krige have achieved international recognition. Arnold van Wyk and John Joubert have proved that South African composers can make valuable contributions to the world's music. Nadia Nerina, the primaballerina, and John Cranko, the choreographer, have demonstrated that, of all the arts, South Africa excels in the ballet.

Mimi Coertse and Cecelia Wessels are singers of world renown. Moira Lister and Lawrence Harvey have star-spangled the world's screens. The devastating criticism of South African cultural appreciation is that all these artists had to go overseas to acquire their status—a prophet needed a country other than his own for honour.

Music and South Africa are merely on the nodding basis of acquaintance. South African "music-lovers" is a term that describes a sincere handful and a multitude of poseurs. There is an infrequent Opera Season—mainly confined to the Golden City, because there the guilders reside—and plays to crammed audiences, because to be seen (better still, press-photographed) at the Opera is *le dernier cri* among the almighty opulence of the Houghton millionaire area. There was once a fine civic symphony orchestra in Johannesburg but its only salvation from decomposition through sparse audiences was via acquisition by the South African Broadcasting Corporation who, after augmenting it with foreign instrumentalists, use it either for radio programmes or public performances—providing that the Corporation can import foreign conductors and artists to draw the snob public.

It is the Afrikaans-speaking section that is saving South Africa's cultural soul; the English-speaking section is too busy gaining the whole world. It is so busy doing that, in fact, that it has allowed its flag, its anthem and its language to be relegated to second place. While valiantly refusing to be merged with the Afrikaans section, it is being submerged by its own national decadence. Since "the occupation" no world-standard English-speaking poet, writer, artist or composer has been thrown up on the cultural scene; nor, for that matter, on the political scene. The past has been dominated by the British-minded—the future is with the South African-hearted.

267

In that statement of fact resides the secret of South African "carrying capacity" and any attempt to assess possible development—whose magnitude defies specifications—will fail if its full significance is not appreciated. All my investigations, interviews and fact-finding researches point inescapably to one conclusion: the grand and glorious future which awaits South Africa is in the hands of those of its people who are completely and undeviatingly South African in mind and ambition, in service and loyalty. That day can be reckoned cold and dead, when South Africa was dominated by colonial consciousness—the body temporarily in South Africa and the mind permanently at "home"—when loyalty was as divided as the floating iceberg; when South Africa was regarded as "ours" to exploit for personal pleasure or covetous gain; when the immaculate sovereignty of an independent nation was benignly tolerated as adolescent whimsy.

Indirect coercion and envenomed criticism from without, divided loyalties within, can only retard South Africa's progress and limit its potentialities. Attempts to force South Africa to fit an unnatural pattern will stultify South Africa's capacity to perfect its own. Those who have accepted the benefits of South African citizenship and those who, from the be-cushioned security of overseas residence, persist in prodding South Africa into a destructive rapidity must give that country the freedom, must accord it the same intrinsic rights, must recognise its same prerogatives, for self-development in its own elected manner as they have done—to employ one instance but with less justification—to Ghana.

Only the incurably biased can persist in retaining an astigmatic view of the South African scene as it now unrolls itself. Detached viewers will recognise all the salient features of that

268

landscape; of progress as well as reaction. Just as it is impossible to obtain a correct view of any art-gallery exhibit if standing too close to the picture, so the South African scene must be looked at in full perspective: the present superimposed on its past. It is no more possible to interpret the Britain, the America, the Germany, the Russia or any other country of today without the cue-words of their histories. Just so with South Africa and its three-phase history—the first Dutch-Boer period, the British century and the past fifty years of South African self-government.

In fairness to modern South Africa, and in order to get the present picture into true focus, two facts must be recognised before a sound judgment can be made: South Africa has been responsible for its own development only during the past 50 years; it inherited the country when it was terrifyingly devastated and its whole economy shattered by a war that concluded 100 years of British occupation. One hundred years of British administration and half that time of self-government produce the modern South Africa of which these facts are eloquent: at the end of 100 years of British administration the national income was £100,000,000—it is now £2,000,000,000; industrial output was £17,000,000—it is now £1,400,000,000; mining output was £50,000,000—it is now £325,000,000; agricultural production was £32,000,000 —it is now £365,000,000.

One set of figures represents the achievements after 100 years of British administration; the other after 50 years of self-government. Those first 100 years—described by the anglophile Smuts as "the century of wrong"—was an era of maladministration, fumbling and blundering, internal warfare and straightforward imperialist exploitation. British administration was conditioned by Westminster's requirements.

Britain's benefit, not the people's of South Africa, was the determinant. To have encouraged industrial development would have been to close an imperial market for British goods. To have modernised agriculture would have resulted then, as it has now, in South African products competing with British products on the world market. Only in the development of diamond and goldmining did the British administration take positive action—and in those two activities nothing but British capital was invested.

In strict accord with British tradition, South Africa had to be administered for British benefit. That has been the case throughout British imperialist history, as India and Ireland and every other colonial possession testifies. It has never been a principle of British policy under Tory rule to create situations but to exploit them; to extract, even from defeat, victory; from adverse circumstances, benefit. Hence the smooth adaptation of Tory Governments—the architects of imperialism —to the pose of kindly uncle to the new emergent countries of Africa who threw off the British yoke only to find the Whitehall ogre transformed into a phony Santa Claus.

After having repressed the natural instinct for self-expression, self-development and self-government with a war which the conscience of the world denounced and two leading British politicians who were to become Prime Ministers opposed, Britain recognised South Africa's national instincts by handing the country over to self-expression, self-development and self-government. For only half a century South Africa has been expressing, developing and governing itself—the result is what South Africa is today and which can only be accurately assessed by what it was at the hand-over.

It is far from perfect; far, in fact, from what it could and should be. Some critics say that the hand-over was too soon

—"they should have been treated like the defeated nation they were". Much of the evidence I have collected suggests that South Africa did not have sufficient opportunity to develop a sufficiently large corps of statesmen, economists, industrialists, executives and other national élite. There is evidence that South Africa still suffers from a shortage of "presidential timber" in many walks of life. This may be attributable to a depreciated educational standard which is certainly the explanation of many defects in the administration and legislation. Most of the exercises that disfigure Government policy by cruelty and inhumanity are not due so much to police sadism as police stupidity—the ignorance of under-educated men.

Self-government certainly confronted South Africans with a procession of problems. Many of them have been solved; only the "colour problem" remains to any serious magnitude. It is a heritage from the British past. To a great extent it is of British manufacture—the exploitation of Bantu against Boer, the introduction of Pass laws, the establishment of segregation, the deliberate lack of influx-control so as to provide the British-capitalised mines and sugar plantations with cheap labour; those are some of the chickens for which modern South Africa is the roost.

Criticism of South Africa is justified. There is much that merits criticism even if there is ample that deserves praise without receiving it. South Africans themselves are aware of their failures and ashamed of their excesses. They, naturally, resent it when their self-criticism is augmented by the contributions of external critics who destroy the validity and value of their criticism by a complete failure to understand what it is they are criticising. That is worsened when only those aspects of South African life which South Africans know to be defective are criticised and those other aspects, which sparkle with the glory of thermodynamic success, are completely ignored.

Materially, the South Africa of today represents an outstanding achievement in national reconstruction. Spiritually, there is quite a long way to go. In respect to the things of the mind and spirit, it is doubtful whether South Africa shows much advance on pre-self-government days. Many good Afrikaners with whom I have spoken have confessed that, spiritually, South Africa has been static. I endeavoured to soothe their fears by commenting that South Africa is not unique in that respect: it is true of most countries. It is, however, very clear that South Africa's cultural development has not kept abreast of its material advance: one may have been at the expense of the other. If the disparity can be corrected the way to a solution of unsolved problems will be opened.

There rests on South Africa a heavy burden of newly-acquired responsibility and while there are those overseas who can afford to behave like Atlas carrying on his shoulders a soap bubble, South Africa has a more sensitive susceptibility to weight. That burden is not lightened by the dolorous dirges chanted by denunciatory clerics who sound remotely like Gabriel blowing A-flat below middle-C, only more mournful. Nor by the diatribes of peripatetic politicians who excuse their own nation's failures by sneering at South Africa's endeavours. Nor by those experts in sculpting the truth into convenient shape who, serene in their phobias, drop cultured-pearls of advice as contemptuously as ashes flicked off a cigarette. Less still by those who claim to be "well-disposed" to South Africa in its troubles and express the cordiality of a regret they do not feel. South Africa will do much better if spared the avalanche of criticism, well-meant advice and sugar-coated venom. Never has there been such a gushing of verbiage launched on the well-worn grooves of self-righteousness since man took his first tentative steps in the long journey from the dumbness of his prehistoric cave to the inarticulate twitterings of this morning's newspapers.

Unless the non-South African world is to revel in an eluctable orgy of pharasaism, a period of helpful silence is now well overdue. Most of the commentation is as useful as an extra appendix and as empty of original thought as a galaxy of clichés. To produce platitudes with such an amiable air of discovery, as was done on at least one recent occasion, was a talent no listening politician could afford to ignore; but something more constructive than professionalese is surely on the order paper.

No one outside can control or condition South Africa's achieving destiny; no one solve its problems; no one, inexperienced in these problems, advise. There is, no doubt, a percentage of sincerity in such advice but more than sincerity is needed: sagacity is also required; there is an overwhelming urge, among all in South Africa to solve the "colour problem" but desire is not enough: accurate evaluation of the problem, itself, is demanded. There certainly is a "colour problem" but all my observations have convinced me that it is not so much a problem of colour as a problem of economics. As in every country where popular emancipation has been achieved under the banners of "national freedom" and "political equality", the Black nationalist ferment in South Africa is generated by the yeasting of poverty. That is the cause and the core of the "colour problem".

All the present agitation over "the oppression of the Bantu" has no basis in Communism or nationalism or political expressionism. Isms have merely seized upon an original condition and focused it into a pin-pointed form. Poverty has given them their opportunity. Apart from a small

273

minority who have acquired leadership—a minority as intelligent as they are vocal—the vast mass of Bantu are not conscious of a burning desire for political equality, for national independence, for the vote or for "freedom"—apart from the freedom of poverty. Their real politics are the politics of a full stomach. Bread, housing, comfort, economic security now and in old age are the real slogans inscribed on the banners of their inmost aspirations.

Uncountable potentialities indicate South Africa as among the most attractive countries of this concluding century. Nothing proves that more than the worst accusation that this report has been able to make—that, in industry, commerce, agricultural and social amenities South Africa is an under-developed country. It is in its youth. Its optimum is in its future. Only the lid of the Pandora Box has been lifted. It is the country of the beckoning finger. Beneath its surface, in its soil, among its people, are unexplored, unexploited reserves and resources.

Facts are mule-like. They form the record of the past—history, like an overwound watch, cannot be unwound by man, must unwind itself by time. The infuriating facts of the present are eloquent: an enticing land of immeasurable opportunities accompanied by stultifying conditions. The fact of the future is unmistakable: a treasure-chest hasped by injudicious legislation, internal discontent and external hostilities. None of these facts dare be overlooked.

Those in South Africa whose little minnows of souls cannot stand the glory that is South Africa's future, if the price is paid, will remain in their pitiable isolationism and narrow nationalism to enjoy what felicity they can derive from their curiously vicious form of mental solitaire. Themselves not luminous they would be blinded if united with the light.

This report has deliberately side-stepped political issues as such but, being a factual report, it cannot fail to record that South Africa suffers not from a surfeit of politics but from a surfeit of inept politics and politicians. Political ineptitude is not a monopoly or an invention of the present Government; they have imitated, perhaps enlarged, what they inherited. They can well be reminded of the Clausewitz definition of any army because it is applicable to a nation: an army is no better than the functioning of its members multiplied by the quality of its leaders.

Politics in this youthful country manifests all the indiscretions of adolescence. Governments are not wholly to blame—youthfulness is the crime. That can only be remedied by the corrective of age. One of the annoyances of life is that the benefit of experience can only be acquired as the disadvantage of age is acquired—"too old at sixty" means too inexperienced at forty. South Africa is handicapped by the immaturity of youth. Handicap as youthfulness may be, it becomes a great possession as leaves fall off the calendar because there is no more profitable investment than to invest in unfolding youth.

Every yield that South Africa has contributed during its formative years can be multiplied a hundred-fold in the second half of its self-governing century. As this report has shown, the great wealth of South Africa—greater than its gold, its diamonds, its agriculture, its industrial products—is its people, the only real wealth-producers. And its people are as under-developed as South Africa itself. That is not an entry on the debit-side; it is an asset of the immediate future —both the country and the people are richly ripe for development. To strike the balance sheet by concentrating on the liabilities without regard to the development assets would be fatuous accountancy. Most of those liabilities are potential assets—even "the colour problem" can be made to contribute if the "proprietors of the company" are astutely business-like enough to recognise that it is rooted in poverty.

This unknown country has been revealed as far as the facts and information I have gathered during thirteen years of residence are revealing. They show that South Africa's progress, under final analysis, has only two seriously limiting factors—its disabling past and its present "colour problem". One has almost been overcome—a half-century of self-government has enabled a phenomenal recovery to be made. So long as the "colour problem" is an economic problem and is not allowed to degenerate into a racial one, it can, like all forms of social injustice, sustain an economic corrective. If, one day, the home income of the Bantu population was raised to the official minimum living figure, the present "colour problem" would have disappeared by the next.

Courageous statesmanship is South Africa's direst need—statesmanship to recognise the economic solution; courage to enforce it. Failing that, the "colour problem" will pass out of its present economic character and be converted into a Black-versus-White racial issue. "Africa for the Africans"—meaning the Bantu—is already becoming a popular mob-call. "Out with the White people" is being urged. If the "colour problem" is allowed to reach that extreme in the interests of short-term benefits, the point of no return will have been passed. And then Pope's ode will bear a South African application: "On all the line a sudden vengeance waits, and frequent hearses shall besiege your gates."

Johannesburg,
May 1960.